PROTESTANT TEXTUALITY AN[illegible]

PROTESTANT TEXTUALITY AND THE TAMIL MODERN

Political Oratory and the Social Imaginary in South Asia

BERNARD BATE

Edited by E. Annamalai, Francis Cody,
Malarvizhi Jayanth, and Constantine V. Nakassis

STANFORD UNIVERSITY PRESS
Stanford, California

Stanford University Press
Stanford, California

This book has been published with assistance from the Committee on Southern Asian Studies at the University of Chicago.

Suggested citation: Bate, Bernard. *Protestant Textuality and the Tamil Modern: Political Oratory and the Social Imaginary in South Asia.* Stanford, CA: Stanford University Press, 2021. doi: http://doi.org/10.21627/9781503628663.

Printed in the United States of America on acid-free, archival-quality paper

Library of Congress Cataloging-in-Publication Data

Names: Bate, Bernard, author. | Annamalai, E., editor. | Cody, Francis, 1976– editor. | Jayanth, Malarvizhi, editor. | Nakassis, Constantine V., 1979– editor.
Title: Protestant textuality and the Tamil modern : political oratory and the social imaginary in South Asia / Bernard Bate ; edited by E. Annamalai, Francis Cody, Malarvizhi Jayanth and Constantine V. Nakassis.
Other titles: South Asia in motion.
Description: Stanford, California : Stanford University Press, 2021. | Series: South Asia in motion | Includes bibliographical references and index.
Identifiers: LCCN 2020050468 (print) | LCCN 2020050469 (ebook) | ISBN 9781503628656 (paperback) | ISBN 9781503628663 (ebook)
Subjects: LCSH: Tamil language—Political aspects—History—19th and 20th century. | Political oratory—South Asia—History—19th and 20th century. | Rhetoric—Political aspects—South Asia—History—19th and 20th century. | Tamil (Indic people)—Politics and government—19th and 20th century. | Language and culture—South Asia—History—19th and 20th century.
Classification: LCC PL4751 .B38 2021 (print) | LCC PL4751 (ebook) | DDC 494.8/11—dc23
LC record available at https://lccn.loc.gov/2020050468
LC ebook record available at https://lccn.loc.gov/2020050469

Cover photo: Political mobilization through oration in Marina Beach, Chennai. Unknown date. Courtesy of Stephen Hughes.
Cover design: Rob Ehle

For Chalapathy

FIGURE 1. Bernard Bate. Courtesy of Gladys R. Bate.

CONTENTS

EDITORS' PREFACE

Bernard Bate, or Barney as his friends and colleagues called him, passed away in early March 2016 "at the height of his powers," as one of his teachers, John Kelly, put it at a 2016 memorial at the University of Chicago. Barney was on a writing fellowship at the Stanford Humanities Center, working on his second book, this book. This manuscript was very much the prehistory of his masterful 2009 study, *Tamil Oratory and the Dravidian Aesthetic*, a redacted version of his 2000 dissertation in the University of Chicago's Department of Anthropology. Bate finished his dissertation by saying:

> Some definitive statements have emerged [in this dissertation regarding "stage Tamil"]. But I am left with far more questions than firm knowledge. Many of the questions are historical: How did stage speaking begin in Tamil? . . . What was the first "oratorical revolution" like when Tamil was first deployed as oratory (by Christians in Jaffna and Kanyakumari, I think)? How and why were these new models taken up outside the context of the Christian sermon (by a man named Arumuga Navalar in Jaffna, December 1847–September 1848)? . . . In the world of formal political oratory, what were the conditions in which Congressmen and others decided to stop speaking in English and begin speaking in Tamil (c. 1918–1919)? . . . I will pursue these questions further. (2000, 319)

And he did, through archival work in the American Ceylon Mission and Jaffna Diocese of the Church of South India from January to May 2005 and, later, through near seven hundred hours (Bate 2009a) in the Tamil Nadu State Archives from November 2008 to May 2009, along with numerous interviews with journalists, historians, and those with first- and secondhand knowledge and memories of the times he was exploring (including Mayandi Bharati, the late Tho. Paramasivan, Pe. Cu. Mani, A. Sivasubramanian, "Krishi"

Ramakrishnan, Thi. Ka. Sivasankaran, Che. Divan, Nellai Kannan, J. Rajasekaran, V. Arasu, A. R. Venkatachalapathy, and V. Geetha). This intensive research resulted in a series of publications (Bate 2005, 2009a, 2010, 2012a, 2012b, 2013), as well as numerous talks that he gave in the United States, Canada, India, Sri Lanka, and Singapore, all of which were to become part of the book before you.

When we, the editorial team (E. Annamalai, Francis Cody, Malarvizhi Jayanth, and Constantine V. Nakassis), received the manuscript materials, we received something with a definitive shape and plan, though the various documents were both partial and sketchy—filled with bullet-point lists, elliptical placeholders for later elaboration, missing references, notes to self (in particular, in the Introduction)—and abundant and excessive—redundancies across chapters, long descriptions and quotations of primary materials, as well as a panoply of short fragments unconnected to particular chapters. While some of the chapters were almost fully done—for example, Chapters 1–2, versions of which had already been published (as Bate 2010 and Bate 2005, respectively)—others had to be put together from many different drafts (often from talks, in particular, Chapters 3–5) or supplemented with sections from fragments, other chapters, and notes (the Introduction). The final, concluding chapter—the Epilogue—was absent, though implied as to be carved out of existing publications (in particular, from Bate 2013).

We also had to contend with alternative outlines and titles of the book. In a truncated version of a draft of the Introduction, Barney writes in a parenthetical statement that indicates the ambitious Weberian and Durkheimian scope of the project, followed by his instantly recognizable, intimate, oral voice:

> (I'm tempted to call it [the book] Protestant Textuality and the Spirit of Political Modernity, but that might be a step just a little too far. Sort of like people entitling their books with something like "Elementary Forms of the . . ."). Let me give you a sense of the overview of this thing, then: . . .

We have attempted to maintain that intimate voice (indeed, oratorical style) of Barney's, as it moves from the near and familiar to the grand sweep of his sense of history and culture, one well worth, in our opinion, the appellations Weberian and Durkheimian.

A further point to note is that in his many talks on this project, Barney always began with a slightly different, and ever-developing, overview of the project as a whole (Bate 2013 offering a published snapshot of this vision ca. 2012–13). This was a project that was changing over a decade, even if it had its sights set on the questions he identified at the close of his dissertation, defended a decade or so before. We do not pretend that what we put together here is what Barney would have eventually published. It surely would have kept developing and filled out in ways we could not have anticipated or completed ourselves. Instead, we have attempted to provide something true to his vision of the project as it was developing up to and at the time of his premature death. In short, while it is from many chapter drafts, publications, talks, fragments, notes, and outlines that we have put together the book before you—a task that sometimes required filling out prose in what was indicated only fragmentarily and other times redacting or rephrasing redundancies (though we have let many remain as well), as well as inserting transitions, callouts, and the like (these different sources and emendations are indicated through editorial notes in the various chapters; see References for a list of such documents)—it is, irrevocably, Barney's voice and arguments. We hope to have done them justice.

A word on the time line and the editorial process. After receiving the materials in May 2017, the editorial team met to discuss how to tackle the process of editing the book. First, Malarvizhi Jayanth went through the notes, fragments, chapter drafts, talks, outlines, and archival materials, cataloguing them, putting together their time line, and indicating the most definitive or complete versions to work from and supplement. From there, E. Annamalai, Francis Cody, and Constantine Nakassis went over the chapters one by one, editing them in rounds—Frank or Costas taking the first round of a chapter, then followed by the others. We proceeded chapter by chapter from July 2018 to May 2019, followed by a second round of reading, editing, and discussing in May and June 2019. This produced a (relatively) clean near-final copy, which we sent to A. R. Venkatachalapathy and Sudipta Kaviraj to read and write a foreword and afterword, respectively, as well as to two anonymous reviewers at Stanford University Press. All provided helpful feedback and suggested emendations to the text, which we integrated insofar as they explicated and clarified Bate's arguments and points. Reviewer comments that differed from Bate's arguments are mentioned and delineated in editorial notes. With these additions, we present you with Bernard Bate's *Protestant Textuality and the Tamil Modern: Political Oratory and the Social Imaginary in South Asia.*

EDITORS' ACKNOWLEDGMENTS

We would like to acknowledge the help and support of the Bate family, in particular, Noah Bate and Key Jo Lee in helping us access Barney's files and materials for the book; Blake Wentworth for getting the materials to Noah; Whitney Cox for help in the initial stages of discussing how to approach the manuscript; Magda Nakassis for editorial help and advice; Stephen Hughes and Gigi Bate for providing photographs; Era. Chiththaanai, N. Govindarajan, and Indira Peterson for help with bibliographic references; A. R. Venkatachalapathy for corrections on the manuscript and for his foreword; Sudipta Kaviraj for his afterword; Srilata Raman for consultation on aspects of premodern discourse practices; as well as Thomas Blom Hansen and Marcela Cristina Maxfield at Stanford University Press for help with the publication process. The Committee on Southern Asian Studies at the University of Chicago generously helped financially support the editorial process and provided funds for open-access publication.

NOTE ON TRANSLITERATION AND CITATIONS

In the manuscript materials, Bate uses a number of different transliteration schemes and citation styles. Regarding the first: in order to standardize the presentation of Tamil materials, we have opted to use a modified version of the Madras lexicon's transliteration style for Tamil original materials, indicating voiced variants of particular graphemes (e.g., *ṭ* / *ḍ* corresponding to unvoiced and voiced ட், respectively; *p* / *b* for ப்; *s* / *c* for voiceless alveolar sibilant and alveolo-palatal affricative ச், etc.). Tamil materials are italicized. We use, however, conventionalized English spellings and normal font for certain Tamil proper names (e.g., Madurai instead of Maturai, Annadurai instead of Aṇṇāturai, etc.). Regarding the second: we have opted to use in-text reference citations for journal and book publications (mostly, secondary literature) and notes for archival materials. See the Abbreviations listed in the References section for how archival sources are noted.

BERNARD BATE'S ACKNOWLEDGMENTS

Thanks to A. R. Venkatachalapathy (to whom this book is dedicated), Mike McGovern, Doug Rogers, Haun Saussy, Pericles Lewis, and Joseph Errington for reading parts of this manuscript.

Chapter 1 appeared as "The Ethics of Textuality: The Protestant Sermon and the Tamil Public Sphere," in *Ethical Life in South Asia*, ed. Anand Pandian and Daud Ali, 101–15 © 2010 by Indiana University Press. Reprinted with permission of Indiana University Press. Research for this chapter was made possible by a research grant from the American Institute of Sri Lankan Studies (2005) and by generous support from the Department of Anthropology and the MacMillan Center for International and Area Studies, Yale University. Earlier drafts were presented at "Vernacular Public Spheres/South Asia," Yale University (6 April 2007); "Vernacular Social Imaginaries: Public Spheres, Modernities, Nations," CASCA/AES, Toronto, Canada (8–12 May 2007); and "Genealogies of Virtue," University of Vancouver (6–8 September 2007). Thanks to all the members of those presentations for constructive interventions. For very helpful comments on earlier drafts and general encouragement, I thank Anand Pandian and Daud Ali. Thanks also to Rebecca Tolen of Indiana University Press and one outside reader for their helpful suggestions. Very special thanks to M. S. S. Pandian, who originally brought the *Bazaar Book* to my attention in 2003.

Chapter 2 appeared in "Language, Genre, and the Historical Imagination in South India," special issue of the *Indian Economic and Social History Review* 42, no. 4 (2005): 467–82 (used here with permission), translated into Tamil by Cho. Patmanaban, as "Arumukanaavalar: c. 1850 Alavil Caivap Piracanka Marapum, Camaya Nirnayamum," *Panuval* (Jaffna) 3 (2005): 166–87; and into Sinhala by Anuruddhika Kularatne and Harindra Dassanayake, as "Arumuga Navalar, Shaivagamika Anushasana saha Agamehi Seema Nirnaya, 1850

Ashrithawa," in *Shri Lankeya Samajaya saha Sanskrutiuya Patanaya Kireema: Thoragath Nibandha, 2000–2006*, ed. Sasanka Perera and Harindra Dassanayake (Colombo: Institute for the Advanced Study of Society and Culture, 2007). Versions of this chapter were previously presented as "Arumuga Navalar and the Advent of a Prose Orality in Tamil Public Discourse" at the annual conference on South Asia, University of Wisconsin, Madison (16 October 1999); "Arumuga Navalar, Protestant Textual Practice, and the Objectification of Saivism," the annual meeting of the American Anthropological Association, Washington, DC (29 November 2001); as an invited lecture, "Arumuga Navalar and the Materiality of Speech," to the Department of Anthropology, Yale University (19 March 2001); as a paper, "Protestant Textual Practice and the Objectification of Saivism," at the annual conference of the Asian Studies Conference, New York (27–30 March 2003); and as a paper, "Appropriating Rhetoric: Christian and Saivite Sermons in Tamil, c. 1850," delivered at the conference "Language, Genre, and the Historical Imagination in South India," Yale University (20 February 2004).

Chapter 3 was delivered as a paper, "Speaking Swadeshi, Madras 1907," at "City Talk: Language and the Urban Sensorium," Department of Anthropology, Stanford University (28 October 2011). Versions of this chapter or portions of it were also delivered as papers at *Matruveli Uraiyadal* (Alternative Conversations), Bookpoint Auditorium, Chennai (9 February 2009), and as an invited lecture at the French Institute in Pondicherry (25 March 2009). Thanks to V. Arasu, Kannan M., and Rajesh for helpful comments.

Chapter 4 was presented as a paper, "Swadeshi Bharati: Protestant Textuality and the Poetics of Tamil Political Modernity," circulated for "Economy, Reason, Affect: Anti-colonial Sensibility, 1860–1950," Nehru Museum and Library (7–9 January 2014), the Chicago Tamil Forum at the University of Chicago (21 May 2015; thanks to Amanda Weidman for discussant commentary); and the "Workshop on Meaning: Language and Sociocultural Processes," Institute of Social and Economic Research and Policy, Columbia University (23 April 2012). It was also delivered as an invited lecture to the University of California, Berkeley (1 March 2016); the Department of Anthropology, Johns Hopkins University (9 October 2012); CLIC Symposium, "Political Language and the Crises of Democracy," UCLA (8 February 2013); and at the Faculty Seminar, South

Asian Studies Program, National University of Singapore (23 October 2013). Portions of it were presented at the Language, Culture, and History Conference, University of Wyoming, Laramie (2 July 2010); the annual conference on South Asia, University of Wisconsin, Madison (16 October 2010); the South Asia Colloquium, Yale University (10 November 2010); the annual meetings of the American Anthropological Association, New Orleans (17 November 2010); and the annual meeting of the American Anthropological Association, Montreal (16 November 2011, as "The Poetic Structure of the World—an Introductory Fragment to *Speaking the Public Sphere: Protestant Textuality and the Tamil Modern*"). Thanks to participants at these various events for feedback.

Chapter 5 was presented at the annual Tamil conference, University of California, Berkeley (4 May 2013); the annual meeting of the American Anthropological Association, Chicago (22 November 2013); Singapore Anthropology Exchange, National University of Singapore (29 November 2013); Tamil Studies Conference, University of Toronto (17 May 2014); and as an invited lecture for the keynote of the inaugural meeting of the Chicago Tamil Forum at the University of Chicago (29 May 2014). Thanks to Prof. A. Sivasubramanian, who accompanied me on a tour of the port and mill areas of Thoothukudi in January 2009, where we thought about where these events may have taken place. I am very grateful to him for his hospitality, generosity, and guidance.

Parts of the Epilogue appeared in "'To Persuade Them into Speech and Action': Oratory and the Tamil Political, Madras, 1905–1919," *Comparative Studies of Society and History* 55, no. 1 (2013): 142–66 (used here with permission). The research was made possible by senior fellowships from the American Institute for Sri Lankan Studies (2005) and the American Institute of Indian Studies/NEH (2008–9). Time, further financial resources, and support were provided by the Department of Anthropology and the MacMillan Center for International and Area Studies, Yale University. Versions or portions of the Epilogue were presented at American Institute of Indian Studies/Indian International Center, Delhi (18 May 2009); Madras Institute of Development Studies, Chennai (18 June 2009); South Asia Colloquium, University of Pennsylvania (8 October 2009); South Asia Seminar, Harvard University (30 October 2009); South Asia Institute, Columbia University (7 December 2009); and the Departments of Anthropology at Vassar College (30 May 2011), University of North Carolina,

Chapel Hill (2 March 2012), and Bennington College (12 March 2012). Thanks to organizers and participants for their invitations, provocation, and encouragement. Special thanks to Doug Rogers, Mike McGovern, A. R. Venkatachalapathy, and five anonymous reviewers and the editors of *Comparative Studies of Society and History* for their close readings and helpful comments.

Foreword

SPEAKING OF BARNEY BATE

A. R. Venkatachalapathy

Barney, as all his friends will emphatically agree, was an animated conversationalist. But our first meeting was rather quiet. We met at a cinema hall in Madurai, toward the end of 1992, to watch Kamal Haasan's *Thevar Magan* (dir. Bharathan). Barney had apparently been told that I did not like to be distracted when watching a movie, and I had in turn taken him for a serious Chicago academic who did not entertain idle talk. When we soon became thick friends spending long hours chatting—in his adopted hometown of Madurai, in Tirunelveli, in Chicago, and at Yale University—we laughed heartily at this misunderstanding. These memories well up in me as I struggle to write this foreword, made poignant by the knowledge that, of all his friends and interlocutors—and Barney had many—he chose to dedicate this book to me.

Barney's reputation preceded him—as a white man who spoke Tamil like a native and as a scholar fascinated with platform speaking. He was one of the earliest anthropologists whom I knew and from whom learned much about how anthropologists work in the field. His home—on Munichalai Road, a lower-class neighborhood that he chose over posher localities such as Visalakshipuram or Tapal Tanthi Nagar—easily conformed to an anthropologist's home in the field.

I was a fundamentalist Rankean historian then, besotted with sources. Barney was theoretically oriented and prone to discursive analysis. We were, one could say, following Bernard Cohn, inhabiting Historyland and Anthropologyland. Our conversations continued over the years—a committed correspondent, he would pen long letters and, after the advent of email, his

FIGURE 2. Barney Bate and his gurunatar, Professor Tho. Paramasivan. This photograph was posted by Barney on his Facebook page on 27 June 2009 with the caption "Me writing down things that Tho.Pa. says."

responses were unfailingly swift—and gained a new edge when I spent the fall term of 1999 at the University of Chicago. Shortly before he turned in his PhD dissertation, I read its final draft and learned an enormous lot from it. In my comments and conversations, I pushed him into thinking historically. (Another deep influence on Barney's thinking about Tamil culture historically from the ground up was the late, great Tamil scholar Tho. Paramasivan whom he referred to respectfully as *gurunatar*, meaning "mentor" or "preceptor.") I plied him with historical material—excerpts from documents, collections of speeches, Tamil writings on oratory and orators—but Barney was diffident about taking the historical turn.

In March 2003, Barney, along with Rama Sundari Mantena and Lisa Mitchell, put together a panel on "Language, Genre, and Identity in Colonial South India" at the Association of Asian Studies Conference, New York, and the conversations continued next year at Yale as an international roundtable, "Language, Genre, and the Historical Imagination in South India," resulting in a special issue, of the same name, of the *Indian Economic and Social History Review*. It was here that Barney first rehearsed and published his work on Arumuga Navalar.[1] In the first half of 2005 he spent some months in the missionary archives in Jaffna working on Navalar; he was, however, reticent about his time there, and I can only speculate why.

By this time, Barney was deeply taken in by the Swadeshi movement and, on discovering Sumit Sarkar's classic monograph on the Swadeshi movement in Bengal, could never stop speaking about it. However, his archival diffidence continued even when he arrived in Chennai to spend the academic year of 2008–9 to work at the Tamil Nadu Archives, but he soon took to the archives like fish to water. The editors of this book state that he clocked about seven hundred hours there. Like a born-again historian, he spent long days at the archives, often working over weekends. Enjoying the minutiae of archival research, his detailed notes, written in black ink, filled many moleskin notebooks. As historians are wont to do, he even wrote a vignette on a Vellala woman's Swadeshi lecture in Madurai—a piece that *Economic and Political Weekly* unfortunately turned down (but was eventually published, in Tamil).[2] I write this to show how quickly he grasped and mastered the historian's craft.

Like many of us, Barney suffered from writer's block. It was during his work on his second book, I believe, that he fully overcame it, the publication of his first monograph, *Tamil Oratory and the Dravidian Aesthetic: Democratic Practice in South India*, providing the spur.[3] For many years from the middle of the first decade of this century Barney experienced professional anxieties, material worries, and personal travails. But he breathed Swadeshi during these days, and it probably helped him overcome much of them. In the years before his shockingly untimely death he was writing at a furious pace and presenting various versions at seminars and conferences. Barney obsessed over details and could never stop refining his text; he would toss endlessly in bed the night before a presentation. For whatever reason, he conceived this book to a manageable size, stopping at the time of the Non-cooperation movement rather than logically extend it to the rise of Dravidian oratory in the 1940s. But even in its present form *Protestant Textuality and the Tamil Modern: Political Oratory and the Social Imaginary in South Asia* is a patently pathbreaking work. I am not aware of another monograph that treats oratory in any of the South

Asian languages. The editors of this book, apart from paying their tribute to a dear friend, have put the scholarly world in debt by patiently and diligently piecing together this text.

The purpose of this foreword is to fill in some of the gaps and complement this splendid monograph, based on the material I remember sharing with Barney and other sources. Hopefully, younger scholars will pick up the threads and extend the history.

Dissolving in the Wind

Sundara Ramaswamy's evocative obituary of the Communist leader P. Jeevanandam—which not incidentally focuses on his legendary oratorical skills—is titled *Kattril Kalantha Perosai* (The thundering voice that dissolved in the wind).[4] It could not be more apt. Speech vanishes into thin air. Unlike printed material to which historians take first recourse, speech poses an extraordinary challenge to access and reconstruct its history.

For the colonial period, historians need to rely on police reports, contemporary newspaper reports, the speaker's personal files, and testimonies of contemporaries—rare indeed is an autobiography of those times that does not speak of attending public meetings and auditing the speeches. Apart from the fact that much of the intelligence archive remains closed and personal papers of the actors sparse, each source comes with its own problems. As Barney shows in this book, until shorthand for vernacular was invented, there could be no reliable transcripts.[5] What we do have in the colonial archive are English translations and redactions of Tamil speeches. Rarely do we find—at least until much after the time of the Civil Disobedience movement—the original Tamil versions. These translations are surprisingly rather faithful (but awkward), though the original vernacular transcripts, presented in the courts of law, remain to be unearthed by historians.[6] When some of them came up for discussion in the government for prosecution, we get more analysis. When speeches actually went to court, they were discussed threadbare. In the decade after independence, elaborate transcripts of Tamil speeches came to be bound together in government files. Colonial Police Abstracts of Intelligence provide detailed translations purporting to be verbatim.

Early Tamil newspapers—which, until the beginning of the First World

War, virtually meant only *Swadesamitran*—offer some recourse to Tamil originals. But newspaper reports are even more unreliable. Vernacular newspapers did not have trained reporters but only *nirubar*s (literally, correspondents)—who were amateurs if not actually the speakers or organizers of the meeting themselves—to send a report to the newspaper. In this situation, the quality of the reported speech can well be imagined. Here is Thiru. Vi. Kalyanasundaram Mudaliar (Thiru. Vi. Ka.) writing in 1928 (my translation):

> Correspondents of the Tamil press do not take the trouble to learn shorthand. Shorthand is now largely the preserve of the police. I do know of one or two non-policemen who have acquired shorthand skills. As they do not have adequate knowledge of the Tamil language, I see them struggle. If there are indeed persons who both know shorthand and possess Tamil language skills, I am not aware of them. . . .
>
> Tamil speeches are never reproduced faithfully in newspapers. There is no limit to the violence they commit on the speeches. One can only throw up one's hands, exclaiming, "Alas, alas."

Thiru. Vi. Ka. continues his observations under the rubric "The Mischief of Newspapers":

> The correspondent renders the speech in his own words. The views of the speaker thus lose their [original] garb. Sometimes meanings get distorted. Occasionally distortion is deliberate. If I elaborate on the mischief of party newspapers, it will run into pages. In short, one may say that it is rare indeed for talks delivered in the vernacular to be reproduced faithfully in newspapers.
>
> . . . Today I would say something on the platform. In tomorrow's newspapers it would appear in an entirely different version.[7]

Thiru. Vi. Ka. would know. For he was not only Tamil's pioneering orator but also a distinguished political journalist, the hero of Barney's last chapter of this book.

Periyar E. V. Ramasamy provides an excellent example of one such mischief. Referring to a report in *Swadesamitran*, on a meeting regarding birth control, he pointed out that the Tamil newspaper had reported the English speeches in full while adding a plain statement that P. Varadarajulu Naidu had spoken in Tamil. Pointing to such prejudicial reporting, Periyar wondered if this occurred because Tamil was a lowly language or because Varadarajulu Naidu was a non-Brahmin.[8]

However, by and large, Barney did not use newspaper sources. But the future historian, who will need to stand on Barney's shoulders, will need to exploit this source.

In some cases, speakers had a written text. By the 1920s it was common for presidential addresses of major conferences at least to be written up and printed copies distributed at the time of their delivery. For instance, Thiru. Vi. Ka. collected these written texts and published them in book form, and he was by no means exceptional.[9]

When, in 1945, two years after the death of S. Satyamurthy, Chinna Annamalai, the Congress activist and publisher, decided to publish his speeches, Chinna Annamalai sought the help of Satyamurthy's family. On visiting Satyamurthy's home along with his friend S. A. Rahim, Chinna Annamalai was pleasantly surprised when Satyamurthy's widow, Balasundarammal, handed over to him "a cartload of files" containing transcripts of his speeches.[10] Evidently, even a speaker celebrated for his spontaneity prepared notes and texts, if not transcripts, after the speech.

Though the platform was the preeminent forum for public talks, it was by no means the only one. By the mid-1930s All India Radio had come into existence and was a regular forum for talks; some of these have now been retrieved from its archives and are being broadcast occasionally. During the Quit India movement there were clandestine broadcasts, and the Indian National Army aired Netaji Subhas Chandra Bose's inspiring talks. Gramophone records of speeches were not uncommon, but such speeches could only be brief. Radio broadcasts and gramophone records are a different cup of tea altogether and will require separate treatment.

Textual versions of speeches—whether recorded by the police or reported by journalists or written out by the speakers themselves—are but words. But as Barney shows, "vernacular oratory became *the* central communicative frame within which mass politics cohered as a genre of action within . . . democratic politics." Words mobilized people and impelled them to act, and therefore, even if the words themselves dissolved in the wind, the listeners, many of whom went on to become political and cultural actors, recalled and recorded their memories. Barney, for instance, appropriately cites Thiru. Vi. Ka.'s evocative recall of Bipin Chandra Pal's speeches and the British journalist Henry Nevinson's report of a Swadeshi meeting, both delivered in 1907 on Madras Beach.

This draws us to another aspect of what these sources tell us: the context, the numbers, and the effect speeches had on the audience.

Police reports invariably provide specific figures, for the colonial masters were understandably keen to know how many turned up for political speeches. The numbers are likely to have been underestimates—though it is curious, as Barney notes, how tens of hundreds, even as per police underestimates, could hear anything on the beach, even accounting for the lack of noise pollution. The police also applied crude sociological categories identifying the crowd as students, merchants, petty shopkeepers, et cetera, and often on caste lines as well. Crowds were often characterized as mobs, who tended to get irrationally excited. Terms such as "riffraff," "rowdy," and the Anglo-Indianism of *badmash* (scoundrel) were frequently employed. This language has all the elements of "the prose of counter insurgency."[11] The effects on the crowd were also recorded. In contrast to police reports, newspapers tended to be less precise, using terms such as "hundreds" and "thousands" to refer to the crowds, and are better taken as orders of magnitude rather than literally. In the last part of A. Madhaviah's well-known novel *Padmavathi Charithiram*, the protagonist observes: "Newspapers often write outrageous lies. . . . Even in this city of Chennai, after attending a meeting, if we read a report of its proceedings in the papers one begins to wonder if it is a report of the same meeting or it's a dream. Even if only thirty turn up the newspaper exaggerates the numbers as three hundred and three thousand."[12] By the 1930s, we have some photographs, and the occasional, if jumpy, newsreel clips that give us a sense of the crowd.

The public-address system had made its tentative entry by the time of the Civil Disobedience movement. For all its novelty and assumed revolutionary significance, references to its use are limited, and one has to tease them out from the sources. For instance, Kalki states, in 1931, that one Coimbatore Mahalingaiyer, nicknamed *Kodai-idi* (Summer thunderclap), "would not require 'a loud speaker' even when addressing a crowd of a lakh people."[13] Interestingly,

Kalki uses the term "loud speaker" in English and parenthetically describes it in Tamil as *oli perukkum karuvi* (literally, a sound-amplifying device), an indication both of its newness and imminent entrenchment.

Contrary to what technological determinists may believe, the entrenchment of the public-address system was by no means swift or immediate. While the microphone entered the world of South Indian classical music in the 1930s, it was not until the 1940s that it was used for Tamil public speaking.[14] Costs were high and accessibility limited such that it was not uncommon to advertise its use, indicating that it was evidently a novelty that attracted a bigger audience. It also required police permission for use outside a meeting hall, and there were frequent complaints about political partisanship in granting permission. However, it was far from universally welcomed. It was believed that the microphone absorbed—if not the speaker's vital energies, at least—the moisture from his mouth, rendering it dry and hoarse. Speakers, therefore, took recourse to gulping soda water during the speech and after. Soda water bottles—with the pressure-locking colorful glass marbles—were de rigueur in public meetings well into the 1990s.[15]

Even T. M. Deivasigamani Achari, the author of a treatise on public speaking, writing as late as 1949, devoted a chapter to the use of loudspeakers, referring to the speeches of Bipin Chandra Pal in 1907. He remarked that those gifted with a resounding voice had no need for it but grudgingly conceded that "it was helpful to old and infirm [speakers]."[16] (That he devoted a chapter to the need for developing physical vigor and energy on the part of speakers may be read in conjunction with this.) Thiru. Vi. Ka. would have disagreed, for he squarely blamed his ill health on shouting at the top of his voice in the times before sound amplification.

The microphone, for all its revolutionary potential, had one major shortcoming: it tied down the speaker. If the microphone was to pick up the voice, the orator needed to speak into its diaphragm. Earlier, the speaker would pace up and down as he spoke to the audience. (We have the excellent caricatures published in *Janasakthi* where Jeevanandam can be seen in different poses as he thundered to the audience without a microphone to hinder him.) Deivasigamani Achari was particularly uncharitable when he said that the microphone obstructed vision, and the speaker sometimes appeared as a decapitated head to the audience. Deivasigamani Achari's primary criticism was that rather than the speaker training his natural voice and throwing it effectively, he tended to adapt his voice to the needs of the amplifying technology. (Similar complaints were made about vocalists, as the modern Carnatic concert was beginning to be established at the same time.) This precisely was the point. Rather than shout at the top of the voice throughout one's speech, the speaker had ample scope for modulation and pauses through the new technology. C. N. Annadurai's popularity in the 1940s was predicated on this. Anna (Older Brother), as Annadurai was also called, used the new technology to telling effect, conserving energy for long orations, modulating his voice, and punctuating it with pregnant pauses.[17]

Another intriguing device was the megaphone, of which little is known. There is oral evidence to indicate that the megaphone was in use even in the 1940s and the cash-strapped Communists often used it. Megaphones were crude, and it is not entirely clear how it was amenable to voice modulation and the like. P. Jeevanandam was known to have used it, and it is said that he damaged his eardrum by shouting into a megaphone at the top of his voice for long hours.

Orators as Personalities

Barney's promise to "trace the genealogy of twentieth-century vernacular politics and the vernacular politician in South India" would be incomplete if we do not address the period between the 1930s and the 1950s. Though Barney demonstrates in this book "the emergence of vernacular political modernity in the Tamil-speaking lands" by the great satyagraha meeting of April 1919, it was not until the 1940s that the style of public speaking that he so brilliantly ethnographically studied in his first book achieved full form.

Before I attempt to fill this gap, a few words on the transmission of what Barney calls "the communicative infrastructure" that fused Protestant sermonic genres and deeper cultural forms and aesthetics of language that made possible the creation of the vernacular Tamil politician. Arumuga Navalar's ideas and methods found purchase in Tamil Nadu from the late 1860s largely through the polemics between him and his followers, on the one hand, and Ramalinga Swamigal and his disciples, on the other.[18] In the wake of this churning in the Saiva world, from the 1880s a flurry of Saiva *sabhas* (associations) were established, carrying on what has been called the "Protestantization" of the Saiva religion. V. O. Chidambaram Pillai, the key political agent in Chapter 3, states expressly in his verse autobiography (not incidentally while serving a prison sentence for making and abetting seditious speeches) that "I joined the Saiva Siddhanta Sabha [of Tuticorin] and mastered the art of expression." The *sabha* he referred to was one of the earliest modern Saiva organizations (founded in 1883) in the Tamil country and followed by similar *sabhas* in cities far apart as Trichy (1885), Trivandrum (1885), and Palayamkottai (1886). These *sabhas* were coordinated and brought under an apex body called the Saiva Siddhanta Mahasamajam (in 1905), which, apart from performing other functions, provided authorized lists of speakers.[19] Maraimalai Adigal was a key figure in this formation and was regularly invited for public lectures. Many Dravidian orators had close affinities with this Saivite formation.[20]

The transformation of Tamil oratory is illustrated by the emergence of star orators in the two decades or so following the Non-cooperation movement and is best exemplified in the history of Tamil public speaking constructed by two narratives: one by the renowned Tamil writer Kalki R. Krishnamurthy (in 1931) and the other by the Dravidian movement writer Ma. Su. Sambandan (in 1947).[21]

Writing in 1931, at the peak of the Civil Disobedience movement, if Kalki constructed the pantheon of Indian nationalist speakers, Sambandan provides a lineup of Dravidian and Tamil nationalist speakers. Kalki's preamble makes it clear that the political speech had come to stay in the Tamil world. By the time of his writing, humongous political meetings with interminable talks extending from eleven in the morning to nine at night had become the norm. Tongue in cheek, Kalki proposed that the government outlaw all speeches that extended to more than forty-five minutes. Kalki recalled attending political meetings and hearing political speeches from 1918, when he was not yet twenty. His initiation into the national movement, even dropping out of college, he attributed to a talk by the Congress leader T. S. S. Rajan. So, inevitably, the first place in his list went to Rajan. This is followed by his description and detailed analysis of Periyar E. V. Ramasamy, C. Rajagopalachari, Thiru. Vi. Ka., S. Satyamurthy, and Dr. P. Varadarajulu Naidu as speakers. (In a coda, he names a few other speakers as well.) Written in his trademark witty style (with occasional contrived humor), Kalki's sketches are sharp and astute, weighing the speakers' strengths and weaknesses. Kalki's narrative leaves us in no doubt that by the time of the Civil Disobedience movement, public speaking was the primary form of political communication.

By 1947, when Ma. Su. Sambandan (under the pseudonym "Thodarban") penned his *Sirantha Pechalargal*, public speaking was an even more powerful modality of communicative action, but the persona and the field had changed dramatically. Of the ten speakers discussed in Sambandan's book, only two had figured in Kalki's list: Periyar and Thiru. Vi. Ka. The others were new: S. Somasundara Bharati, R. P. Sethu Pillai, Avvai S. Duraiswamy Pillai, K. A. P. Viswanatham, C. N. Annadurai, U. Muthuramalinga Thevar, P. Jeevanandam, and M. P. Sivagnanam—a mix of Dravidian ideologues and Tamil scholars, with the inclusion of a Communist and a communalist demagogue.

The Tamil political sphere had indeed changed in the intervening decade and a half. The Dravidian movement was in full flow, and a major popular struggle, the anti-Hindi agitation (1937–39), had transformed the stage. The technology of the public-address system had also amplified the power of the new speakers.

Though vernacular oratory had come of age during the Non-cooperation movement, English was not entirely displaced by Tamil in the 1930s. Tamil oratory was a phenomenon more of the 1930s and after, with English oratory strictly restricted to an elite class converging in hall meetings. As late as the time of the Non-cooperation movement it had been considered fashionable to say one did not know how to speak in Tamil. Kalki mentions that when Rajaji once began his speech in Tamil, some voices called for him to speak in English. The shift to Tamil in public speech is indexed by the rise of Anna. If Anna's debut in 1935 on the public stage had begun as a translator of A. Ramaswami Mudaliar (who along with "Silver Tongue" V. S. Srinivasa Sastri was a legendary public speaker in English of the times), he had, in a matter of years, emerged as the most popular public speaker, overshadowing all others.

Not only had Tamil displaced English as the primary political language, but the Tamil language itself had changed. Gone was the highly Sanskritized language used by speakers. With the influence of the Pure Tamil movement, pure Tamil words replaced Sanskrit words and the awkward translation/transliteration of English words. If Kalki credited Thiru. Vi. Ka. for inaugurating this process, by the time of Sambandan it had become the norm. Rhetorical devices too had changed; alliteration predominated and drew from what Barney calls in this book "culturally and historically deeper forms and aesthetics of language."[22] The anti-Hindi agitation had brought vernacular politicians and Tamil/Saiva lecturers together in mass meetings that profoundly altered the nature of public speaking. By the 1950s, public speaking was the road to political power.[23]

Codifying Oratory

The entrenchment of Tamil oratory as a dominant communicative practice is indexed by the significant number of narratives produced in the 1940s on the nature and practice of oratory. A key text is Deivasikamani Achari's *Medai Tamil* (Stage Tamil), a pregnant coinage that invokes the many prefixes added to Tamil to describe the language's many facets and attributes.[24] Written in early 1944 (though published only in 1949 with the addition of part 2), this elaborate treatise, running into over four hundred pages (with appendixes, index, glossary, and plates), codifies public speaking with many examples. The book leaves no aspect of public speaking undiscussed: stage fright, preparation, posture, opening gambit, finishing flourish, acknowledgment, memory, physical endurance, rhetorical devices, mellifluousness, and the use of the public-address system. More strikingly, Deivasigamani Achari draws specific examples from contemporary speakers without ignoring any major speaker or prominent style.

As we noted, Sambandan had published his little book two years earlier in which Anna figures prominently. Speakers in the Dravidian tradition were now taking center stage, and a number of other books began to focus on them. By the mid-1940s, Anna's rise was meteoric, especially after his famed public debate with R. P. Sethu Pillai and S. Somasundara Bharati on burning the *Ramayana* and *Periya Puranam*.[25] Youths flocked to his talks—some of them ticketed events—and Tamil associations in various colleges invited him to speak. The political meetings that he addressed were legion. Many of these talks were transcribed by enthusiastic admirers and published as booklets, gaining further circulation. One such transcriber was Anbu Pazhamnee,[26] who went on to coauthor (with K. V. Veeraraghavan, a friend of Anna himself) a booklet on the secret of Anna's success as an orator.[27] These two authors followed this a year later with a book on the art of speaking, *Pecchu Kalai*.[28] The art of speaking was very much the flavor of the times. As could be expected of a primer, this book provided tips and techniques on public speaking. That the book included forewords by, among others, Ilavalagan, a Saivite propagandist, and V. R. Nedunchezhiyan, the Dravida Munnetra Kazhagam (DMK) leader, is indicative of the streams that went into the making of modern Tamil oratory.

Another primer, A. K. Parandamanar's *Pechalaraka*, though published in book form only in 1955, belongs to the same moment. Serialized earlier in Karumuthu Thyagaraja Chettiar's daily, *Tamil Nadu*, it covers the same ground but in a more scholarly manner.[29] A particularly important section is the first chapter, which outlines the history of oratory. While Parandamanar draws from ancient Tamil literature on elocution, verbal skills, and appropriate speech, he was categorical in stating that public speaking was a modern discursive practice. Arguing that earlier practices fell within the domain of courtly speech, religious debate, and textual discourse, he asserted that "only in democratic societies can oratory naturally and truly exist. Public speaking did not and could not have existed in monarchical Tamil Nadu."[30] Tracing its origins to the beginnings of the Indian nationalist movement in the early part of the twentieth century, Parandamanar called Thiru. Vi. Ka. not only the father but also the fostering mother of Tamil public speaking. As an erudite Tamil scholar in the Saiva tradition, Parandamanar could be expected to be familiar with Arumuga Navalar, though he makes no mention of him. And he went on to add that it was the Dravidian movement—the Dravidar Kazhagam (DK) and the DMK—that developed it into a distinct communicative art form.[31]

It is this distinct communicative modality that Barney Bate chose to study and that brought him to Tamil Nadu, the land and the people he loved so much. His two pioneering monographs, richly documented, astutely analyzed, and written with great love and passion will remain standard works for years to come.

PROTESTANT TEXTUALITY AND THE TAMIL MODERN

Introduction

PROTESTANT TEXTUALITY AND THE TAMIL MODERN

> And he said unto them, "Go ye into all the world
> and preach the gospel to every creature."
>
> —Mark 16:15

> Wherever the relevance of speech is at stake, matters become political by definition, for speech is what makes man a political being.
>
> —Hannah Arendt, *The Human Condition*

On 6 April 1919, the first great satyagraha in the Madras Presidency was conducted in Madras City in protest of a new set of restrictions on political activity ushered in under the Rowlatt Act. These laws extended emergency measures instituted during World War I, and thus many viewed them as bitter reward for the loyalty, service, and sacrifice that Indians had demonstrated to King George V and the British Empire during the war. The satyagraha had been billed by Mohandas Gandhi as a "Day of Humiliation and Prayer," and the people were called out to partake in a demonstration against this erosion of their natural rights as citizens of the empire. In response a massive crowd, estimated by organizers and police to exceed one hundred thousand,[1] assembled on Marina Beach before five stages set up for simultaneous oratorical performances, mostly in Tamil and Telugu, some in Urdu. The speeches delivered in English were translated onstage into Tamil.[2]

The stages were aligned one after another, and separate stages were set on either end for members of the newly established Madras Labour Union and Tramway Workers Union. Devotional singing (*bhajan*) groups that had formed in different parts of the city earlier in the day processed via various routes to the Marina, singing and dancing all the way. A police sub-inspector who provided an account of this event derisively noted that the crowds continued to break out into *bhajans* while the orators were speaking. But he also conceded that "the crowd surrounding the speakers was enormous and kept moving from place to place in their vain attempt to hear them."[3] By his own admission, the sub-inspector's report suggests that a large portion of the immense crowd had come to Marina Beach to listen attentively to speeches by the local and national leaders of the day.

By all accounts, the crowd was the largest anyone had ever seen in Madras for a political event, and it shattered the expectations of the organizers. It was probably some four or five times larger than any political meeting in Madras theretofore. The *Madras Times*, an Anglo-Indian paper hostile to the nationalists, wrote on 8 April 1919, "Whatever may be said about the causes which induced the people of Madras to carry out the dictates of the Satyagraha, 'satyagraha Day' (6th April) will be remembered in the annals of the city as [a] unique occasion." Numerous meetings had been held during the month prior to the satyagraha to educate the public and ensure a large turnout. Despite their extensive preparations, the organizers themselves were stunned by the turnout. One of them, a journalist, Tamil scholar, pioneer in public oratory, labor organizer, and politician of profound impact, Thiru. Vi. Kalyanasundaram (Thiru. Vi. Ka.), described the crowd as a "great army, like a surging ocean" moving toward the beach ([1944] 2003, 237).

Even more germane for our purposes, the crowd was quite mixed and not limited to the upper-caste Hindu and Christian boys and men, the students and educated classes that had been the usual participants up to the most recent times. Our sub-inspector wrote, "Muhammadans, though not in proportion to the Hindus, were in much greater numbers than ever at such meetings" and that while "the bulk of those present were middle class persons of the trading, official and student community . . . the poorer classes were also numerous."[4] The *Madras Times* reported on 8 April 1919 that the crowd was composed "mostly of the labouring and trading classes." And the sub-inspector also observed that they were not only men: "There were about 200 women present and they were provided with an enclosure in the 5th platform [one of the labor platforms], but they were all mostly illiterate people of the working classes who had come there merely to see what took place."[5] They had come, rich and poor, Hindu and Muslim, man and woman, to partake of politics.

The birth of modern mass politics in the Madras Presidency has long been dated to this era, and few would question that this period of post–World War I politics represented a phase shift in political action and organization. Many have noted that by 1918–19 virtually all the elements of twentieth-century Tamil politics had converged. The crowd that gathered on the beach that April was a manifestation of a new efflorescence of political action, a new politics that set the stage for the kinds of mass actions that would take place throughout the twentieth century, including the Dravidianism that became the hallmark of politics in later Tamil Nadu (Bate 2009b).

But what had changed from the nineteenth into the twentieth century such that people previously excluded from, or indifferent to, formal political action suddenly appeared in great numbers in the political realm? And how did political oratory, did speech itself, become central to this form of politics?[6]

Protestant Textuality and the Tamil Modern offers a genealogy of this political transformation, of Tamil political oratory, and of the emergence of vernacular political modernity in the Tamil-speaking lands of India and Sri Lanka. It documents how sermonic and homiletic genres introduced by Protestant missionaries in the eighteenth and nineteenth centuries fused with culturally and historically deeper forms and aesthetics of language, providing the communicative infrastructure that eventually enabled a new kind of agent, the vernacular politician, to address and mobilize a modern Tamil people within a distinctive social imaginary. In short, I trace the genealogy of twentieth-century vernacular politics and the vernacular politician in South India, the topic of my first book, *Tamil Oratory and the Dravidian Aesthetic* (Bate 2009b). Doing so, in my view, is to trace the genealogy of the Tamil Political itself.

The Press and the Platform

Scholars have long linked print capitalism—the production, sale, and circulation of vernacular texts (e.g., novels, newspapers) throughout a limited geography—to the constitution of large-scale modern social imaginaries such as the public sphere, the people, or the modern nation-state (Habermas [1962] 1991; Anderson [1983] 2006; M. S. S. Pandian 1996; Geetha and Rajadurai [1998] 2008; Warner 2002; Blackburn 2003; Taylor 2003; Venkatachalapathy 2012). And when speaking of political practice in early twentieth-century South India, scholars frequently link the "press and the platform" in a single phrase. (That is, if we include the platform at all; homiletic oratory, what this study adds to the focus on writing and print, has generally been forgotten in the genealogies of such imaginaries.) Indeed, in much of India, print-mediated discourse of the sort that interests such scholars circulated in synergy with genres of vernacular oratory.

We tend to think of press and platform as similar because of the ways that we read history (or the way we read, period), in particular, because of our penchant for focusing on the denotational elements of the text—that is, what the text says—rather than thinking of these practices as real sensuous activity, as embodied forms of action. It is thus often assumed that such practices—in particular, public oratory—are natural and panhuman rather than part of a new technology (Bate 2014, 544).[7] Yet this is precisely what vernacular, public oratory was in South India at this historical juncture: a new genre and infrastructure of interpellative communication.

Anyone familiar with Tamil Nadu will find this claim bizarre and counterintuitive: twentieth-century Tamil country was an empire of orators. Periyar E. V. Ramaswamy, founder of the first major Tamil nationalist organization, the Dravidar Kazhagam (Dravidian Federation), emerged as a major politician in the 1920s by virtue of his charismatic, if folksy, oratory. "Ariñar" (Scholar) C. N. Annadurai and "Kalaiñar" (Artist) Mu. Karunanidhi likewise recast Dravidianism within a democratic modality with the formation of the electoral political party, the Dravida Munnetra Kazhagam (Dravidian Progress Federation), along with a brand-new refined style of political oratory marked by literary citations, poetic alliteration, and use of language that sounded ancient (Sivathamby 1978; Kailasapathy 1986; M. S. S. Pandian 1996; Ramaswamy 1997; Bate 2009b; Cody 2011a, 2011b). The Dravidian paradigm of political oratory sounded as if the orators were speaking in the voices of ancient Dravidian kings, which was exactly the point: to effect not only a political distinction between the Dravida Munnetra Kazhagam and the Indian National Congress but also a civilizational and epochal distinction between the antiquity and autochthony of the Dravidian Tamils and the otherness of the Northern Aryans. The orator became an avatar of Tamil's purity, antiquity, autochthony, and civilizational right to lead the people. To suggest that there was a time in which such a highly developed and everyday practice did not exist violates the commonsense understanding of the order of things in the Tamil world.[8]

But there was such a time.

The case of Tamil oratory thus presents something unexpected in this otherwise familiar scenario. Tamil contains myriad interpellative practices that stretch back into dim antiquity, including various forms of theatrical and musical performance (e.g., *kūttu*, *villupāṭṭu*; see Blackburn 1988), text-recitation genres (e.g., readings of sacred texts such as the *Tēvāram* or *Kantapurāṇam* in temples; see Peterson 1991), and lower-class and -caste funeral petitions and drums (Clark-Decès 2005). But what is odd in the case of Tamil is that its nearly two-thousand-year literary record demonstrates that there was nothing resembling homiletic oratory[9]—at least embodied by higher-status people addressing anything resembling an undifferentiated mass of lower-status people—until the advent of the Protestant sermon and its uptake in non-Protestant contexts (also see Hudson 1992a, 1992b; Young and Jebanesan 1995).[10] And it was the utilization of that form that, from the middle of the nineteenth century until the first two decades of the twentieth century, eventually became vernacular political oratory in the Tamil-speaking lands.[11]

In terms of sociocultural praxis, the press and the platform are utterly different modes of communicative production that operate through very different political economic modalities and social processes. While the vernacular press developed, famously, through print capitalism, the platform developed in South Asia almost entirely via the passions and values of the orators themselves, whether Protestant Christianity in the Protestant sermon (Chapter 1), Saivite revivalism in the Saivite sermon (Chapter 2), Swadeshism in early vernacular lectures of 1907–8 (Chapters 3–5), or the Home Rule movement in 1915–16 and Labor movement in 1917–20 (Epilogue).[12] In opposition to print—which major theory asserts was spread via capitalist means of production (Anderson [1983] 2006)—modern oratory spread in South Asia (and far more broadly) largely through motivations of the heart, in appeals to the imagination, in promises of salvation and of the reconciliation of God and man and the reconciliation of man and man in the universalization of the concept of natural or human rights. Protestant missionaries, as I discuss later in this chapter and show in more detail in Chapter 1, were agents of such radical Enlightenment discourses, despite their positions within what we might consider rather conservative colonial structures of power. They attacked the caste system along with the priesthood; they fought for the dignity of human beings regardless of sex or status; they educated the population, including young women. Their sermons were not unrelated to these ethical impulses, and through them they spread their universalizing, democratic vision of the Social to new kinds of addressees, inaugurating new kinds of social collectivities such as the "Tamil people."

While both of these communicative modalities—press and platform—were quite consequential in and of themselves, together, or symbiotically, they created something far more powerful than either one alone. To put an even finer point on this argument, I suggest that vernacular oratory qualitatively and quantitatively transformed what politics would be. In oratory, as I discuss in more detail later in this chapter, the elite political class came to interpellate people utterly unlike themselves, calling on them to participate in the political. Eclipsing print by its greater centrality within wider sets of social praxis, then, vernacular oratory became *the* central communicative frame within which mass politics cohered as a genre of action within the Indian Independence movement, Tamil nationalism, and postcolonial democratic politics. By the mid-twentieth century, this process had transformed Tamil Nadu into an empire of orators whose political success depended on mastery of baroque oratorical genres that embodied a vision of Tamil's singular historical, literary, and aesthetic experience (Sivathamby 1978; Bate 2009b). This empire would not have been possible without the oratorical conventions of the Protestant sermon.

The Newness of Oratory

It is an odd thing to say that Tamil oratory is new. It violates the commonsense order of things in the Tamil political—and literary-cultural—in any number of dimensions. In some respects, it is a wildly offensive thing to say. Yet it is true. What was this newness?

Protestant sermons brought along new "epistemizations" of language—that is, new ways of conceptualizing, knowing, and doing with language (what linguistic anthropologists call "language ideology" [Woolard 1998])—reducing the functionality of language to denotation, truth functionality, and reference. This was in contrast to the focus on the sensuous, performative nature of language, as characteristic in Indic concepts of language, textuality, and performance (e.g., in poesy, music, magical incantation, and the like). Under such new epistemizations, above all else the transparency of signs was paramount (Keane 2007). This shift in ideologies promoted vernacular languages that all could understand rather than superposed (ritual) languages such as Latin or Sanskrit, associated with (non-modern) Catholicism or Brahminical Hinduism, that were accessible to only an elite few (on which, more later in this chapter).

Second, during this period new ways of embodying knowledge in textual form came into being, with the production of books, tracts, and sermons. The production of such artifacts involved a completely new sociotechnological machinery, with the emergence of printing houses for newspapers, novels, chapbooks, handbills, and the like; new circuits of distribution and circulation; as well as new concepts and modes of authorship, composition, and textual reanimation (i.e., reading). The production, distribution, and reception of such artifacts were, in novel ways, spatially, temporally, and socially separated from each other (Johns 1998; Warner 2002).[13] What is critical here is that such new text artifacts—and their sociotechnological machinery—stood in contrast to, and partially displaced, older modes of embodying knowledge based on highly restricted modes of recitation and audition of high-value texts (e.g., in caste- and class-marked spaces of the temple, the court, and the like).[14] Indeed, such new texts and ideologies of textuality involved new ideologies and ethics of textual circulation—importantly, the universalization of the text—which is to say, new social relations of textual production and reception.

Most centrally, Protestants mandated that high-value texts be intelligible and available to all regardless of status—an ethic and ideology markedly counter to most Indic modes of textual practice in the eighteenth and early nineteenth centuries (Chapter 1). Literacy was rare, and texts were animated—brought to life in practice—in the social and ritual contexts that were most often purposefully delimited. The call to translate and propagate the vernacular Word of God to everyone regardless of caste, sex, or status entailed the establishment of new institutions and practices: schools, presses, and sermons to preach the Gospel to all people. Only some of those people actually converted to Protestantism, but the universalizing oratorical practices of the Protestant sermon were taken up by non-Christian agents throughout the late nineteenth century and developed in their own educational and religious contexts (Chapter 2). By the first two decades of the twentieth century, as Chapter 3 demonstrates, politicians began to speak in Tamil (rather than English) to larger and larger audiences, first in the Swadeshi movement, India's first modern political mobilization (1905–8), and then later, as I show in the Epilogue, in the establishment of the Labor movement in 1917–20 (Sarkar [1973] 2010; Veeraraghavan 2013).

This turning toward the common man to address him as a political agent was unprecedented and revolutionary in Tamil political speech. With these new oratorical forms, the ideologies of the Swadeshi movement and the Labor movement now crossed outside caste and class boundaries, moving from elite to subaltern spaces, from English to Tamil. As the full-blown mass outrage of the Independence movement was impossible to ignore by 1919, the vernacular became the foundation on which formal politics would be conducted from that point forward. The empire of orators had begun.

The Emergence of Modern Politics

In essence, there could have been no modern vernacular political movements in India without that vernacular turning, and the first two decades of the twentieth century witnessed an eruption of the vernacular within the Indian political at large. This genealogy of the vernacular oratory in South India can be linked to transformed political and communicative practice in a global context, in which political actors deployed a universalizing textuality to address a universal citizen. That is, this vernacularizing process in Tamil Nadu is not linked just to its proximal missionary antecedents but to the global, general emergence of modern politics itself (Weber [1904–5] 1958; Walzer 1965).

Following Max Weber's argument regarding Protestantism and the spirit of capitalism, Michael Walzer (1965) identifies the post-Calvinist saint as the archetype of a new political man, the citizen who held an abstract society at arm's length and evaluated (or epistemized) it as a whole and demanded that all men within it—not only princes, not merely priests—be responsible for its reform. "What Calvinists said of the saint," wrote Walzer, "other men would later say of the citizen: the same sense of civic virtue, of discipline and duty, lies behind the two names" (2). Each man would be equal to another in the eyes of God; no caste or estate would have a privileged role to play in the great work of reform in which all are called to participate. For Walzer, it was the activity of such new men that "played as important a part in the formation of the modern state as did the sovereign power of princes" (2). I argue that the semeiosically stripped-down and universalizing textuality of the Protestant sermon lies at the basis of the communicative production of this new kind of political subjectivity at the heart of modern revolutionary, and more broadly democratic, politics.[15] The political men discussed in this book are direct descendants of these saints.

What I add to Walzer's insight, however, is how communicative genres such as a universalizing oratory and print framed (Goffman 1974) or stipulated (Silverstein 1976, 1993) the social relations, ethics, and ideologies that people would embody in their engagements with the world. That is, the infrastructural process by which their civic vision was effected was communicative. It was poetic (Jakobson 1960; Friedrich 1986). It was rhetorical (Bate 2014). Through a dialogic process (Bakhtin 1981), these new modes of communicative, poetic practice laid down over time new kinds of entities in interaction (e.g., the people, the public, the nation) and ritually instantiated national time and space, the history and geography of a modern people, and a new agency to be mastered by the vernacular politician. The emergence of their oratory—and its associated universalization of the call to the political to everyone—had a material structuring effect on social order.[16]

Yet if what we broadly call the *poetic* was central to the formation of modern social imaginaries, this was in two ways, corresponding to two senses of the term. The world, the Tamil world—the world that could be named Tamil in the modern sense of a people, a polity, a transhistorical ethnolinguistic community inhabiting a place called Tamilagam—was structured, in key respects, by the first aspect of the poetic. And that structure was given life, palpability, and power by the second. The first was a foreign import, brought over by missionaries, that restructured the social relations of textual production; the second was born of Tamil soil wherein songs have come from far away, to be sure, but have a singularity of rhythm and melody and image and feeling peculiar to the Tamil lands. The first is what Roman Jakobson called the poetic function of language; the second is poesy itself.

Jakobson's (1960) poetic function of language—what he also later called "poeticity" (1987, 368)[17]—is that aspect of every utterance that calls attention to the form of the message, the parallelisms (in rhyme, meter, image) that define poetry as a special form of language. The formal elements of poetic texts point to the fact that such texts are "poetry," or at least they are special kinds of language that stand apart from what we think of as "ordinary language" (though, to be sure, the difference between them is hardly hard and fast). It is this difference that adds a kind of fundamental frame around an utterance that stipulates a particular meaning, not denotationally but in terms of what kind of communicative form the utterance is. So just as it is the poetic function of language that tells us that a poem is a poem, it is that same poetic function that stipulates that an oration, for instance, is an oration.[18]

The second use of the poetic is closer to more conventional notions of the term, what I here call "poesy": the relationship language draws between sound, myth, emotion, and the imagination, what we might broadly call the aesthetics of language. Jakobson called this the "palpability of language," "when the word is felt as a word and not a mere representation of the object being named" (1987, 378). Needless to say, poesy has long occupied a central concern in philosophies of language going back to Aristotle. However, anthropologies of language (Friedrich 1979, 1986, 1991, 2006; Fernandez 1986, 1991; see also Tyler 1978; Strecker and Tyler 2009) posit a much more powerful role for poesy, those elements of language that structure the mind and move the heart, draw connections between disparate domains of life, link macro- and microcosms in ritual or politics, and ultimately massively affect the individual imagination and move individuals to action. In this way, too, the poetic is world building (Chapter 4).[19]

One of the big arguments of this book, then, is that rhetoric and oratory—as embodied in real, dialogic, sensuous textual practice (i.e., in its poetics and its poesy)—have infrastructural effects on the unfolding of history and the structuring of social order (Vološinov 1977; Bakhtin 1981). By demonstrating the emergence of political modernity through a genealogy of Tamil political oratory, this book shows how this vernacularizing process was both aesthetically singular to the Tamil world—for all its newness, vernacular oratory tied language to older and deeper cultural aesthetics, poetics, and lifeways (Kaviraj 1992, 2005a; Chatterjee 1993, 2004; Ramaswamy 1997)—and exemplary of the global emergence of new geographies and histories of political belonging of modern peoples, nations, and publics. Indeed, modern nationalist oratory all over the world—for example, in the Philippines (Rosaldo 1984), Madagascar (Jackson 2006, 2008, 2009, 2013), Papua New Guinea (Kulick 1993, 1998; Robbins 2001), Nigeria (Larkin 2008), Indonesia (Keane 2007), and West Africa (Irvine 1989; Yankah 1995; also see Makihara and Schieffelin 2007)—appears to have had, at its roots, Protestant forms of textuality (Chapter 1).[20] It may not be universal, but it is certainly a broad pattern across the world: new modes of address that interpellate these strange new modern social imaginaries are strongly marked by Protestant forms of textuality, often carried forth by poet-figures, oratorical artists such as Subramania Bharati, arguably the greatest Tamil poet of the twentieth century and the national poet of the Tamil people, a figure that I discuss in Chapter 4 who embodied and effectuated these transformations.[21]

Protestant Textuality, Tamil Modern

As its title suggests, this book is divided into two halves. Chapters 1–2 deal with what I call "Protestant textuality" in missionary, religious, and literary discourse that emerged in what we might call the long nineteenth century (though I focus on the second half of the nineteenth century). Chapters 3–5 deal with what I call the "Tamil Modern," the co-emergence of political oratory and the modern political field in the first decade of the twentieth century. In the rest of the Introduction, I sketch out this history, aspects of which individual chapters take up in more detail.

Protestant Textuality

Part I of this book considers the proposition that Protestantism brought with it the basis of communicative modernity in the Tamil country of India and

Sri Lanka and that Protestant forms of textuality mediated the production of such modern social imaginaries as the public sphere, the nation, and the people (Taylor 2003).

By *textuality*, I refer to ideologies, ethics, and aesthetics of discursive semiosis, to cultural and historical concepts of what semiotic, communicative activity is and should be, can and should do. As I show in Chapters 1 and 2, new textualities tracked the production of new kinds of communicative institutions and practices central to the political transformations that concern this book. Many of these practices and institutions were built squarely on semiotic ideologies of the Protestant Bible brought with the first Protestant missionaries in the early eighteenth century—the Halle Mission at Tranquebar—and developed by subsequent missionaries of the Wesleyan Methodist Missionary Society, London Missionary Society of Tirunelveli, and the Americans of Jaffna, Madurai, Madras, and Arcot (Frykenberg 1999). In particular, the necessity of translating and propagating the vernacular Bible to everyone regardless of sex or status—a peculiarity of Protestant textuality—entailed the establishment of three kinds of institutions and institutionalized practices: schools to teach the Gospel; presses to produce Bibles, tracts, and newspapers; and (often forgotten but immensely important) sermons to preach the Gospel to the people. This attitude toward the Bible is well-known, but it shared semiotic ideologies with other new rationalizations of semiotic functionality in Isaac Newton and Gottfried Wilhelm Leibniz's calculus, Francis Bacon's science, and John Locke's semiotic (Bauman and Briggs 2003), among other foundational works of what Sudipta Kaviraj (2005b), following Weber, called "cognitive modernity."

Arguably, the essence of this modern semiotic ideology is that signs must be carriers of fixed and stable meanings: a sign must have a single referent, must have a single sense; it must be clear (or transparent); and it must carry the same meaning regardless of who speaks to whom or in which context. My use of the term "must" is pointed, for this ideology was an ethical as much as a semiotic imperative, as we shall see (Bauman and Briggs 2003; Keane 2007, 13–16). It is no accident that just such semiotic ideologies (of fixed referentiality, transparency, and universality) were deployed along with the teaching of the Bible and science in Protestant schools in nineteenth-century South India (cf. Peterson 1999, 2002).[22]

Equally essential was the Protestants' ethical imperative to broadcast the Word of God to the world at large: "And he said unto them, 'Go ye into all the world and preach the gospel to every creature'" (Mark 16:15). Such an imperative has long linked Protestant forms of universal interpellation to the formation of modern social imaginaries in what has been called "informational revolutions" (Bayly 1993, 1996; Frykenberg 1999). In India, this entailed the transformation of processes of information transmission and reproduction from kin- and caste-based systems to systems that basically universalized texts by interpellating generalized "publics" (as it were).[23] Missionaries encountered literate elites of Indic religiosities, including Indian Catholics, whose textualities, from their Protestant perspective at least, emphasized states of being over states of knowing, memorization of the sheer aesthetic experience of linguistic sound (*nāta*) over the denotationality of the word (*logos*), poetic over prose forms, onticity over episteme, and in Valentine Daniel's (1996) terms, mood over mind.

They also encountered a world in which the social relations of the text were often purposefully highly restricted in terms of person, space, and time. High-valued texts had been animated in highly restricted contexts, usually among those men whose caste and training qualified them to animate—or enjoy the benefits of animation—in times and places set aside for their recital. Many such higher-status literary people such as poets, teachers, and scholars had very different understandings of textual authority: rather than interpellating an audience, much of their authority resulted from the rote memorization of texts and their recitation in highly restricted contexts.[24] The texts, as Kamil Zvelebil (1992) and others (e.g., Kersenboom 1995) have argued, were performative and tended to forefront the quality of *nāta*, the power of sound itself (Yelle 2003), over *logos*, the word in its denotational functionality (Kaviraj 1992, 27). The reciter (*ōtuvar*) of text was, in essence, the text embodied (a relation taken up later by Dravidianist politicians as a form of political legitimacy; see Bate 2009b), a stark contrast to the ideological model of modern oratory, where the object was to effect some kind of change, to transform the world and the hearers from one state in a linear chain of becoming to the next.[25]

Protestants confronted such Indic textualities with righteous vigor, and their efforts were not in vain. By the mid-nineteenth century, schools, presses, and sermonizing had been widely taken up by non-Christian agents such as Arumuga Navalar and others (Chapter 2; also see Hudson 1992a, 1992b, 1994; Grafe 1999; M. S. S. Pandian 2007; Young and Jebanesan 1995) in the epistemization of entirely new modes of religiosity that we call "Religion" (Asad 1993; King 1999; Daniel 2002) and, some decades later, into new modes of agency and political subjectivity that we call "Politics" (see Chapters 3–5)—that is, what Paul Ricoeur (1965, cited in Marchart 2007, 35–60) called *la politique*, that realm of action expressly epistemized, set apart, and named as such, in contrast to *le politique*, "the political," that set of practices that involves any number and kinds of calculations and weighings of instrumental action (also see Arendt 1958; Bate 2014, 147–48).[26]

While I discuss such transformations in ideologies of textuality in Chapters 1 and 2, I here consider two linked elements of textuality that were transformed by Protestant missionaries.[27] The first is the social relations of the text. The second is the reduction of textual functionality to the referential or denotational function. The example comes from the first half of the nineteenth century, surrounding events reported by missionaries of the American Ceylon Mission (ACM) between 1827 and 1855 in what was then considered a comparative backwater, Jaffna.

In Jaffna of that time, the *Kantapurāṇam* (known in English as *Skanda* or *Scanda Purana*) was among the highest-valued texts associated with the ruling Vellala caste on the peninsula. The missionaries took it, along with the Vedas, to be a textual other par excellence. The American H. M. Scudder, writing in the first Tamil homiletic, *Kiraṇamālikai* (*The Bazaar Book, or, Vernacular Preacher's Companion*, 1865), cites the *Kantapurāṇam* extensively to illustrate Hindu falsehoods and errors of "Sastras," especially in regard to geographical or astronomical knowledge that could be compared against scientific forms of the Europeans (1865, 20–21). The false information contained in the shastra, however, was merely a superficial problem compared to its social relations of textuality and lack of referential transparency.

In a sermon titled "The Sastra" (in this case referring to the four Vedas), Scudder inveighs against the fact that the Vedas pertain only to Brahmins and others invested with the "sacred cord" and excludes women and Sudras who "are in no case to read or even hear them read," an unthinkable act if it is God, indeed, that gave the Vedas to man (1865, 19). Scudder further notes that the Vedas' language, Sanskrit, is "utterly unknown and unintelligible to ordinary people," as well as "abstruse and obscure" in its style, and thus "useless to the world of mankind" (19). As Scudder concludes, the Vedas must not have God as their author but the "fraudulent and tricky Bramins [*sic*]" (19). In contrast to this is the Christian Veda, "the true Sastra," a text whose language and expression is plain and intelligible and thus through which truths are easily understood (25) and salvation able to be discovered. For Scudder, textual transparency is linked in an intimate fashion with the social relations of textual animation. And these two elements not only lie at the basis of a rationalized mode of scientific inquiry leading to truth in the mundane world but to the truth of the Gospels as well.

For the Saivites, however, the point was that texts such as the *Kantapurāṇam* (and all other sacred texts, including those that dealt with natural history) were not only about the transmission of denotational textuality but, more important, the embodiment of the text in its recitation by a person qualified to do so, both by social standing and training. Texts were to be memorized and sung in highly restricted times and spaces, such as in temples on auspicious dates and times by and to people qualified to hear it (most often, upper-caste men). Recitation operated on the logic of what we might call "textual emblematization," where the animator iconically and indexically embodies the text, effecting, as it were, consubstantiality between text and person. In terms of the aesthetics of hearing the text, it was probably closer to hearing music: the denotationality of the text (*logos*) was less important than its sheer sound and musicality (*nāta*), which itself would have beneficial consequences for the hearers as well as for the world at large, a world in which the text had been sung.

The differences between the two forms of textuality came to a head when the American missionaries at Vattukottai attempted to teach the *Kantapurāṇam* in their schools. "It had often been remarked," wrote the principal, "'that if you were acquainted with the contents of the Scanda Purana, you would not think it necessary to make known to us the Christian Scriptures.' The use of this book in the Seminary produced no small degree of excitement among the people around, some of whom exerted themselves to hinder the students from reading it" (ACM TR 1830, 4).[28]

Focusing on the denotational aspects of the text, the missionaries had the instructor transform the text by "rendering" it "from the Poetic dialect into plain Tamul prose" and read it out loud to the students in a general assembly:

> At the first meeting for this purpose, there was a very unexpected disclosure of feeling; some of the Students were evidently afraid of the consequences, some much ashamed, and others were pleased that the hidden mysteries of the Scanda Purana were about to be brought into the light. These proceedings immediately excited the attention of many in the vicinity. Sad predictions were uttered, by the Brahmins and others, against all who were in any way concerned in this profanation of their sacred writings, and many considerations were suggested, for the purpose of dissuading the members of the Seminary from risking the consequences of entering on forbidden ground. As it was left optional with all whether to attend the meetings for reading, or not, the number of attendants gradually diminished, and consequently the exercise was discontinued. Enough, however, was read to convince all who would reflect, that the book is filled with the most extravagant fictions, many of which are in an immoral tendency "for all the people will walk every one in the name of God." (ACM TR 1830, 23–24)

It is impossible to know exactly what happened, whether the sad predictions were found fulfilled and the students refused to return to the readings out of concern for the blasphemous reading of the text out of its ordained spaces and times or, as the missionaries felt, that the readings proved the inconsequentiality of the text. From the missionaries' point of view, of course, the failure of the exercise was only a confirmation of the virtue and superiority of their faith and of the system of textuality in which that faith was transmitted. It is ironic that the passions that moved missionaries to travel across the world would be passionately embodied in systems of semeiosic rationality. And that rationality would be fateful.

The Tamil Modern and the Communicative Revolution

The career of the ACM was impressive from a social transformative point of view, if not from an evangelical one. From the missionaries' landing in 1816 to 1855, they had produced a network of elite English and vernacular Tamil schools—for both boys and girls—that resulted in the education of some 30,000 students in a population estimated to be approximately 120,000. They had established a major press, Ceylon's first Tamil newspaper, the *Morning Star* (*Uthayatharakai* in Tamil), and began producing a new colonial elite among upper-class Jaffna Tamils. A comparative hinterland in the world, a dry peninsula far from any major city, Jaffna may have been among the most literate places on earth.

Yet during a period of evangelical efflorescence and conservative reaction in the United States, the American Board of Commissioners for Foreign Missions (ABCFM), the governing board of foreign missions, decided that the ACM had basically failed, that it had spent a great deal of money and energy educating all of these people for forty years with only four hundred or so members in the church.[29] Furthermore, the main seminary in Vattukottai had since shut down, as it had become a center of anti-Christian and pro-Saivite activism among the student body. A successful (formal) testament to the ACM's (substantive) failure, these well-educated young men bypassed the Protestant message and took up the political principles of the Enlightenment as new kinds of free political agents. In essence, the mission had failed to do what the missionaries had hoped it would do: they wanted Jaffna to be a burned-over district, a land where the fire of the Gospel burned away all error and sin, where the population would be evangelized and fervent in their faith. It was not to be.

But while Protestantism had failed, Protestant textuality emerged as dominant. The communicative revolution of Arumuga Navalar—about whom we will have more to consider in Chapter 2—serves to illustrate the point. A Saivite educated by the Wesleyan Methodists (who followed the Americans), Navalar produced Saivite institutions that were, in essence, organized according to Protestant textuality. He was involved in the first productions of prose Tamil in Saivite and educational literature; the establishment of Saivite schools; and a vast expansion of Tamil printing through his presses in Lanka and Madras. And, significantly for our purposes, he is credited with being the first non-Christian to give a sermon along the lines of Protestant homiletic, on 31 December 1847, inside the high-walled grounds of a Siva temple outside Jaffna Town. His role as printer, builder of educational institutions, "reformer" (better, rationalizer) of Saivism as a "religion" per se, and his oratorical and literary impulses suggest that Navalar was producing Tamil as a language that could be used to address some wider imagined community, a Tamil that could be used to address something resembling a public.

Arumuga Navalar's communicative revolution was not all that revolutionary from a Protestant point of view, and it was loudly decried as such at the time. But outside a Christian context it was profoundly revolutionary. It began a process that utterly transformed Jaffna society on the basis of new forms of textuality that established entirely novel types of social action, not least of which was the agency of the orator. It was that communicative restructuring of textual practice, that new interpellation, that spoke into being the Tamil public sphere. Here, language came under a peculiar kind of scrutiny, reepistemized as a new way of knowing and being that could be used to imagine a population that had a commonality in, and solidarity based on, language (Trautmann 2006; Mitchell 2009).

Previously, people who spoke Tamil were not Tamil as such; rather, they could be characterized with any number of identities based more on local community, caste, lineage, hereditary office, religious sect, and so on (Frykenberg 1999, 6–7). But after this communicative revolution, to speak Tamil was to *be* Tamil, and a new kind of political subjectivity was born that could enable the imaginary of a homogeneous sociality ("Society"), a flat social order of "zero-degree individuals" (Kaviraj 1997, 90) to accompany a new flat spatiotemporality (i.e., homogeneous empty time). And, indeed, those categories that were politicized at the same time, in particular, the Brahmin (see M. S. S. Pandian 2007), became problematic categories that were to be resisted in every conceivable way. And therein lies the heart of twentieth-century Tamil politics, that is, that dual process of modernization that involves a radical and simultaneous individuation and totalization, the formation of new specific social categories within a total social order.

But while the Protestants made history, to be sure, they did not do so as they pleased. There were other textualities still operating that were the ground, so to speak, upon which the Tamil public sphere would be experienced. An ancient vernacular aesthetic of textual production appears to have remained immanent, perhaps we can say *inhered*, within the transformations of Protestant textuality that yielded a qualitative difference in the nature of the formation of the public. The poetic and rhetorical textual forms were carried over from the ancient into the production of the modern. And it was those poetics and rhetorics that made the experience of a Tamil public sphere utterly different from the experience of the public sphere in other times and places. The bodily apperception of the sheer sound of language, the music of language (*nāta*), remained a key element of the entire project and would come to have fateful political impacts later on in the Dravidianist uptake of such poesy as an index of their Tamil cultural authenticity and their antiquity in the new democratic order of mid-twentieth-century Tamil Nadu (Bate 2009b), even as the poetic form of such sonorous poesy was the modern, Protestant homiletic sermon.[30]

The Newness of Vernacular Political Speeches

Politics (*la politique*) in royal courts in India, certainly in the Tamil-speaking lands of South India, were polyglot affairs. A wonderful index of this polyglossia is the library of the eighteenth- and nineteenth-century Marathi-speaking court of Thanjavur. A brief tour of the public exhibits of their vast palm-leaf manuscript collection features Sanskrit texts written in Tamil, Telugu, Bengali, Modi, and Nāgarī scripts. At that time, specific scripts for specific languages had not been rationalized as such, in contrast to today, when each language is written in a script of its own. Indira Peterson (2011) has unearthed a vast trove of plays staged for the court whose characters spoke in Marathi, Telugu, Tamil, and Brajbhasha (Hindustani), each language indexing different stock characters, kinds of persons, qualities of personhood, ethics, and humors. The world of the early modern political in India was heteroglossic, from top to bottom.

In general, despite monoglot (sub)nationalist histories of Tamil and Telugu in South India, languages had yet to become fixed, parallel codes mapped onto a territory for the purposes of state or education. Literate people would find themselves using a wide variety of codes to do a variety of different tasks. Scholars such as Bernard Cohn (1996) for North India and Lisa Mitchell (2009) for South India have shown how different spaces of dealing with the state involved different registers of speaking and writing. The British, wrote Cohn, encountered a profoundly heteroglossic situation with languages they did not understand—not only denotationally but as they were used in different contexts by different peoples for different purposes. Specialists in language abounded: *akhunds*, or "Muhammadan school teachers," in Bengal were specialists in composing and interpreting letters in Persian; *dubashis* (literally, two languages) were official interpreters; *vakils* (lawyers) were specialists in the appropriate modes of court procedures. In early nineteenth-century Madras, one might write a letter home in Tamil, compose poetry and lyrics in Telugu, petition the government in Persian, trade with coastal merchants in Portuguese and inland merchants in Moors (Hindustani), and present wares to another market in English (Mitchell 2009; also see Bhavani Raman 2012 for a discussion of "cutcherry Tamil").

In short, the situation the British encountered in India was among the most profoundly institutionalized heteroglossias in the world. Languages were not parallel codes (Sakai 1997), each one appropriate for all tasks. What linguists might call languages, mutually unintelligible codes, functioned more as registers for different purposes, social contexts, and projects. Cosmopolitan actors used a wide range of such codes to index their erudition and sophistication in a wide range of institutional settings. For Tamil to become the naturalized language of the Tamil people (*tamiḻarkaḷ*) in Tamil lands (*tamiḻagam*), for Telugu to become its counterpart in Andhra, there had to be a massive transformation of what languages were and how they were practiced.

This is the import of the eruption of the vernacular in the first decade of the twentieth century. For it was around 1905 that Tamil and Telugu emerged nearly simultaneously as political languages in the transformation of a previous regime of linguistic practices associated with statecraft to what we can call a vernacular, monoglot imperative that characterized twentieth-century political praxis.

Vernacular political oratory exploded across British India as the political modus vivendi of the Swadeshi movement, 1905–8, what some have called India's first modern political mobilization (Chapter 3). Such oratory became the defining feature of a new kind of political practice associated with Swadeshi that emerged across British India in 1905 following the partition of Bengal. This was the first time that political actors systematically took to vernacular oratory. This is not to say that Tamil oratory itself was created at this moment.

But the Swadeshi movement saw the first *systematic* use of vernacular political oratory delivered to far-flung "common" or "illiterate" people well beyond anything that had gone on before. In other words, the meetings of the Swadeshi movement were the forerunners of the new kinds of practices that dominated twentieth-century politics in Tamil Nadu.[31]

We know that there was, of course, a prehistory to this eruption. The great Congressman and pioneer newspaper publisher G. Subramania Iyer had taken a speaking tour in July–August 1882 throughout the Tamil-speaking parts of the Madras Presidency (Suntharalingam 1974, 181–82).[32] G. Subramania Iyer was a giant in the Madras Presidency, one of the founders of *The Hindu* and the founding editor of the Tamil daily *Swadesamitran*. He was also one of a core group of young men to form the Madras Mahajana Sabha (Madras Gentlemen's Society) and the Indian National Congress (INC) itself in the early 1880s (Suntharalingam 1974). G. Subramania Iyer undertook his 1882 tour—and another in 1888—with the aim of propagating new ideas surrounding the formation of the INC. In conjunction with these tours, a series of "Congress Catechisms" (*Kāṅgiras Vinā Viḍai*) was developed to answer questions about self-rule and elite political organizations such as Madras Mahajana Sabha and the INC.[33] Written in a clear and simple Tamil, the question-answer catechetical style was borrowed directly from missionary practice to bring the Gospel to the widest possible audience (Chapter 1). A *Swadesamitran* editorial of 24 December 1887 used the Christian metaphor of "irrigation" or "drawing water" (*iraittal*) in its announcement that "little books of easily understood catechism had been printed and Congress Committeemen were coming to irrigate every nook and corner of every village and town about the Congress and independence" (Mani 2005, 22).

But it is not clear that these were Tamil-only speaking tours; it is more likely that most of the speeches were in English, as G. Subramania Iyer was famous as an accomplished English speaker well into the Swadeshi period.[34] The historian R. Suntharalingam writes that "his visit to the mofussil towns excited interest among local leaders who were anxious to know his views on important public questions" (1974, 182), suggesting to me that these were meetings of English-speaking elites, not the *pāmara makkaḷ* (common people), as they would have been called in the language of the time.

In any event, the 1880s tours appeared to be one-off events, and the Congress did not engage in any systematic vernacular oratory addressed to subaltern publics for another twenty-some years. It was only with the eruption of the vernacular in the Swadeshi movement (Chapter 3) and, later, the Home Rule movement and Labor movement of 1917–20 (Epilogue) that such tours were undertaken in earnest and with transformative effect.

Something within the political changed dramatically during the two decades between 1900 and 1920 insofar as elites began quite pointedly to direct their utterances toward people they never bothered with before as political agents. The difference is the universalization of Ricoeur's politics (*la politique*). And this was well understood at the time. B. P. Wadia, a Theosophist and elite labor organizer, wrote the following in an open letter published in *New India* in June 1918:

> We want to bring the masses into line with the educated classes. Much lecturing work has been done already and what seems now necessary is to combine them in . . . Agricultural societies, Trade and Labour Unions, Ryot Combines, Craft Guilds. . . . The masses do possess political outlook; they have lost the art of making themselves heard, and our task should be to persuade them into speech and action. (1921, xvi)

In this passage, Wadia links the political, the masses, speech, and action in a way that is perhaps entirely unprecedented in Indian history—and he ties it together with a particular form of action, "lecturing work." This, we might say, marks the transformation from the political (*le politique*) to politics (*la politique*), from a generalized set of actions into what Hannah Arendt (1958) called Action itself. And when elites made the conscious move to turn toward, to face (*nōkku*) and begin addressing the common man, when the everyman was called to join into the political, a new agency—the orator (Chapter 4) and the people (Chapters 3, 5)—was formed along with a new definition of what politics would look like.[35]

A Pause in Lieu of a Conclusion

The themes of the Swadeshi speeches of 1905–8 were the boycott of *paradeshi* (foreign) clothes, support and patronage of *swadeshi* (national) industry, a call for a "return" to Indian ways of doing things, Indian gods, Indian spirituality, Indian epic literature, and Indian brotherhood. The Swadeshi movement, in the largest sense, pioneered and established the basic idioms of the Indian Independence movement, forms and themes that Mohandas Gandhi would appropriate in his satyagraha over the next forty years. But perhaps the most basic innovation of Swadeshi was the attention to new forms of language, especially as the leadership sought to bring the light of freedom to the darkness of the uneducated masses in places such as the Andhra deltas. They did so in whatever language was appropriate to the region within a single ideological paradigm, a single nationalism. It was a polyglot nationalism, to be sure, articulated through the means of each vernacular language: Tamil, Telugu, Marathi, Bengali.

And so perhaps one of the great ironies of that pragmatic ideology was the formation of new geographies of monoglot politics, new spaces within which those very languages would become not merely expedient but necessary codes of political and ethnic belonging. By the late 1940s and early 1950s, it was the southern language areas, first the Telugu-speaking Andhras followed very quickly by the Tamil-speaking southern districts of the Madras Presidency, that would be the first of all Indian polities to demand recognition for their languages (Trautmann 2006; Mitchell 2009; Bate 2009b); to demand a monopoly for those languages within the newly established postcolonial states of Andhra Pradesh and Tamil Nadu; to even die for their languages. What changed to enable such a transformation was nothing less than the redefinition of language itself.

PART I THE PROTESTANT MODERN

Chapter 1

THE ETHICS OF TEXTUALITY

Eighteenth- and nineteenth-century Protestant missionaries to the Tamil lands of southern India and Ceylon were appalled by Indian textuality. They encountered a world in which the social relations of the text were highly restricted in terms of person, space, and time, and a world in which the meaningfulness of the text appeared to reside somewhere beyond the word. High-value texts were largely animated—brought to life in practice—in places and times set aside by persons qualified (by gender, caste, and training) for people qualified to hear them. Literate elites among the Saivites of Jaffna, for instance, deployed Sanskrit Vedas or texts such as the *Kantapurāṇam* written in an archaic Tamil; for the wielders of such texts did not necessarily consider the denotational function of the word, or *logos*, as more important than the aesthetic and spiritual power of *nāta*, the "originary form of sound," the source of language, music, and the universe itself (Kaviraj 1992, 27–28; cf. Yelle 2003). Indic textuality appeared to emphasize the sheer aesthetic experience of linguistic sound over the denotationality of the word, states of being over states of knowing, poetic over prose forms, mood over mind (Daniel 1996).[1] For the Protestants, on the other hand, *logos* was critically important within the highest-value text, the Bible, for the salvation of people's souls depended on it

Originally published in Pandian, Anand, and Daud Ali, eds. *Ethical Life in South Asia*, pp. 101–115

(Kulendran 1967). They therefore translated the Bible, built schools with the aim of producing literate populations, propagated passages and interpretations of the Bible in tracts to be widely distributed, and—crucially—went out among as many people as they could to preach the vernacular Gospel in the marketplaces, *mandapams* (outdoor halls), and bazaars of villages and towns all over the country.

Textuality itself, then, including the social relations of textual animation, was a major site of ethical evaluation for the missionaries, and they waged a campaign against what they judged to be wicked textual ethics that would deny the masses access to the Word of God. It was not only what the sermons said that was important in this struggle but also the ethics of the social—or textual—practices themselves. This Protestant turning toward a stranger-audience in tracts and sermons marked a radical departure from existing Indic forms of text, at least among men of higher status.[2] In many ways, the Protestants prevailed. Though they converted only a small fraction of the population to Christianity, the wider society was, textually, Protestantized. For by the mid-nineteenth century, schools, presses, and sermonizing had been widely taken up by non-Christian agents (Hudson 1994, 95, 123; Young and Sebanesan 1995; Grafe 1999, 69–93) in the formation of entirely new modes of religiosity that we call "religion" (Daniel 2002; King 1999) and, some decades later, into new modes of agency and political subjectivity that we call "politics" (*la politique*, in Paul Ricoeur's terms). That turning toward everyone, a turning to and calling to all, embodied a new ethic that had a great deal to do with the production of the ethical universe of strangers that we call the modern public sphere (Anderson [1983] 2006; Warner 2002; Taylor 2003, 2007; see also Chapter 5).

To illustrate this suggestion, I rely on a set of Tamil tracts on Christian preaching in common public places titled *The Bazaar Book, or, Vernacular Preacher's Companion* (in Tamil, *Kiraṇamālikai*, 1865), one of the very earliest treatises on Tamil homiletic (which we briefly discussed in the Introduction). Written by H. M. Scudder (1822–95), a Tamil-literate American missionary born to a prominent family of missionaries to the Tamil lands, the text offers a vision of the vernacular preacher delivering a sermon in that space of stranger mixing, the marketplace or "bazaar," deploying his Tamil Bible along with native texts. "Each address," Scudder writes in the English introduction, "contains, woven into its texture, a few poetical quotations, selected with great care from Hindu works" (1865, vi). Prominent among these texts was the *Nālaḍiyār* (*Nālaḍi Nānūṟu*), one of Tamil's most famous treatises on ethical being in the world.[3] The *Nālaḍiyār* is especially prominent in discussions on language and the conditions surrounding public sermonizing. The vernacular sermon here involves a conjuncture of European and Tamil notions of text and textual animation along with a conjuncture of moral and political dimensions of being in the world. So, despite the sermon emerging as an alien textual practice in India, something was Indian about these sermons, too, for the texts that were animated in them had ancient lineages in the Tamil world. Although the artifactual (e.g., "books") and interactional (e.g., "sermons") forms of the text were transformed by Protestant textualities, a quintessentially Indic rhetorical framing of being in the world (i.e., the doctrine of *trivarga*) and the poetics of the expression of that being inhered within the new texts, including sermons.[4] We find these poetics inhering also within a whole series of practices, from worship to lullabies and dirges, riddles, proverbs, folk songs, games, and—as Anand Pandian (2009) has discussed—in the myriad, quotidian, and bodily engagements of the cultivator with the soil. In other words, that which appeals to the largest and oldest ideologies and aesthetics of being in the world as structured via mythopoeic and rhetorical forms provided an embodied ground on which Protestant textual forms would work to transform the world. Indexes of these rhetorics and poetics are the two texts most commonly deployed, even sometimes eclipsing the Bible, in the tracts of the times in mid-century Tamilagam: the sixth- or seventh-century CE Jain masterpieces of being in the world, the *Tirukkuṟaḷ*, and its companion, the *Nālaḍiyār*, texts that are named for the very poetic forms they take: the couplet (*kuṟaḷ*) and the quatrain (*nālaḍi*). The Christians who wanted to capture souls for Jesus knew that their own texts must first have Tamil souls.

Nālaḍiyār and the Bazaar

The *Bazaar Book* is among the very first texts to provide an outline of Tamil homiletic and models of Tamil sermons (although individual tracts dating back to the 1840s were similarly structured in theme and tone). With the exception of a brief English introduction, the *Bazaar Book* is composed of thirteen "addresses" to a "heathen audience" on topics such as "Guru," "Sin," "God," "Man," "Expiation," "Fate," "Transmigration," "Idolatry Sinful," "Idolatry Ruinous," "Caste," "Brahmanism," and, most important for our purposes,

"Shastra" (text, textual precept) and "Mantra" (auspicious and efficacious sound, word, or phrase). The *Bazaar Book* appears to have included a number of tracts that Scudder had been preparing when he took sick leave to return to America, but the tone of the addresses is very much in line with the rather aggressive and offensive style of tract publishing and preaching that characterized the Protestant missionary engagement with South India and Sri Lanka from at least the beginning of the nineteenth century (Grafe [1982] 1992, 140–41).[5]

The tracts that were joined together in the *Bazaar Book* were clearly meant to be read aloud to a group of people, perhaps memorized and delivered by native assistants or catechists. The addresses are written in an extremely simple Tamil, somewhat more Sanskritic than today's standard in Tamil Nadu, but the sentence structure is quite easy to grasp, with quick syntactic punches perfect for oral delivery. Other features of the orality of the text include directly addressing the audience as *piriyamānavarkaḷē* (Dearly beloved) or simply *janaṅkaḷē!* (O people!). They include a great deal of rhetorical questions designed to engage listeners in situ, and the language is shot through with very simple proverbs, similes, and other appeals to oral literature:

> *Piriyamānavarkaḷē, "nīr mēl kumiḻ pōl nilaiyilā kayam" enkiṟa paḻamoḻiyai nīṅkaḷellām kēṭṭiruppīrkaḷ.* (Scudder 1865, 5)
>
> Dearly beloved, you all will have heard the well-known proverb that the "body is as ephemeral as the bubble on the surface of the water."

For complex reasons, the *Nālaḍiyār* was highlighted in the *Bazaar Book* at moments involving the animation of the text, the bringing of text to life in the sermonic encounter of missionary or catechist with the stranger-audience in the bazaar itself. Though less prominent today than the *Tirukkuṟaḷ,* its far more famous companion and model, *Nālaḍiyār,* was the second Tamil text that we know of to have been printed outside a Christian context by Tamils for Tamils, in Madras in 1812 (Zvelebil 1992, 219; Blackburn 2003, 82). Its priority in the thinking of Tamil literati (at least) is indexed by its primacy in the order of publication, like the Gutenberg Bible, an index of the *doxa* of textual importance for Tamil people. The nineteenth-century Tamil philologist G. U. Pope writes that the "peculiar terseness and vigor of its style and the fidelity with which it reflects the thoughts and ideas of the great mass of the Tamil people, and indeed of the yeomanry of India," leads it to be called the *Veḷḷāḷar-Vētam*, "the Bible of the Cultivators" (1893, viii). Its import is attested by the fact that U. Ve. Swaminathaiyar (1855–1942), one of the great universalizers of ancient Tamil literature, took it up as his very first lesson after his appointment to Government College in Kumbakonam in 1880 (Zvelebil 1992, 189). And by 1893, in G. U. Pope's famous critical edition and translation, the author asserts that it was "taught in every vernacular school in the Tamil country" (1893, viii). It was also used among Christians from a very early date and was included in the formal syllabus of the Americans in Jaffna, for instance, from the foundation of their seminary there in 1816 (ACM TR 1830). Like the *Tirukkuṟaḷ*, the *Nālaḍiyār* in its simple moral counsel was—and remains—immensely attractive to Christians (and everyone else, for that matter). Even Pope, who worked zealously to purge the church of a great deal of indigenous aesthetics in the mid-century (Peterson 2004, 49–51), endorsed the texts wholeheartedly and wrote that the two together throw "a flood of light upon the whole ethical and social philosophy of the Tamil people" (Pope 1893, vii).

The *Nālaḍiyār* contains extraordinarily beautiful verses embodying a timeless ethic with universal appeal. Some of Pope's translations give a taste of their poesy and power.[6] On wealth, *Nālaḍiyār* 28:10 is profound:

> Gathering it together is trouble, and even so the guarding of resplendent wealth is severe trouble. If the guarded heap diminish, it is trouble. If it perish, it is trouble. Wealth is trouble's very dwelling place!

Nālaḍiyār 20:5 would not be out of place in contemporary humanist critiques of caste:

> When men speak of "good caste" and "bad caste" it is a mere form of speech, and has no real meaning. Not even by possessions, made splendid by ancient glories, but by self-denial, learning, and energy is caste determined.

Or who could remain unmoved by the striking observation in *Nālaḍiyār* 3:4 of a funeral procession by some sixth-century poet who transcended his time and place to capture a chilling truth of the human condition?

> They march and then strike once! A little while they wait, then strike the

> drum a second time. Behold, how fine! The third stroke sounds. They veil it, take the fire, and go forth—the dying bear the dead.

Although today the *Nālaḍiyār* is not nearly as well-known as the *Tirukkuṟaḷ*, its structure is noteworthy for its artifice—and therefore for what might have been important to Tamil speakers for a very, very long time. The origin of the text itself is unknown, though most think it started with the Jains and many felt it to be among the earliest texts of Tamil literature. Traditional scholarly lore has it that prior to the twelfth century, the four hundred quatrains were organized in no particular order. It was reorganized by Pathumanar in the twelfth century according to the well-known structure of Indic didactic texts, namely, the three aims of life (*trivarga*): *dharma* in Sanskrit (*aṟam* in Tamil), right conduct; *artha* (*poruḷ*), material gain and rule; and *kama* (*kāmām*), romantic or sexual love. To place the *Nālaḍiyār* at the forefront of sermonic practice, then, is to see it not only as the new use of a native text but one that is organized according to a much earlier and deeper pan-Indic aesthetic of human life. It embodies a vernacularization of even earlier metastructural concerns in the lives of Indian people, concerns that are quite old, indeed, formulated as a paradigm perhaps two thousand years ago. It provides, then, a perfect icon of the ways that preexisting phenomenologies of human action and textualities are taken up in the new newnesses of modern textual forms.

Perhaps the *Nālaḍiyār* was at the forefront of the *Bazaar Book* because it lent itself more easily to the Christian (and, peculiarly, the Tamil modern) exclusion of *kāmām* (romantic love) from the public world. Visible genres of Indic performance would, in previous ages, emphasize *kāmām* as an element of life in both oral and scriptural practice—for example, the *Kamasutra*—in both the home and the visible world of kingly procession (Bannerjee 1990, 127–79; Narayana Rao, Shulman, and Subrahmanyam 1992). Entire genres of *pirabantam* (medieval verse poetry), for instance, were devoted to outlining the love life of the king (*ulā pirabantam*) (Ali 2004; Wentworth 2009), and erotic stories and songs rang out among clutches of women in marriage ceremonies all across the land (to the shock and outrage of the missionaries, of course) (Raheja and Gold 1994). Contemporary Tamil public life, however, tends to shunt such expressions either to the most stigmatized forms of theater and street performance (e.g., *karakāṭṭam*, or "pot dancing") or to the realm of whisper and gossip regarding the multiple partners or nonstandard sexual practices of the political class. Whereas the *Tirukkuṟaḷ*, for instance, gives almost equal time to *kāmām* (330 of 1,330 verses), the *Nālaḍiyār* devotes only 10 of 400 quatrains to the subject of bodily desire. Thus, the *Nālaḍiyār*, even more than the *Tirukkuṟaḷ*, appears to embody a new kind of sexless publicity that becomes, eventually, the standard for nineteenth- and twentieth-century public discourse.

In taking up the *trivarga* structure, the *Nālaḍiyār* as a textual source for a Protestant ethical sermon emblematizes the overall conjuncture of Indic and European modes of textuality, as it is a Tamil text that will now be cited and discoursed on just as a Bible verse would be. This predominance of the denotational (as opposed to, say, poetic) functions of the text was a key element of the newness in Protestant textuality. At the same time, the denotational elements of these texts enabled the deployment of ancient Indic ethics that were timeless, pure, true, and almost all but absent from what the missionaries felt was a wicked and degenerate Hinduism then being practiced. Here was an Indian ethic that the missionaries could wield as Indian—a rhetorical sleight of mind caught as it was within a new ethics of textuality generally.

Protestant Textualities and Their Others

That Scudder cites the use of the *Nālaḍiyār* in the bazaar also provokes rather fruitful conjunctures and contradictions. We imagine that Scudder had in mind a public place where he felt he could address some generalized humanity, some group of "zero-degree individuals" (as Sudipta Kaviraj [1997, 90] has put it), all equal in the sight of God and all deserving of God's good news and salvation. The bazaar may certainly have looked like such a place of stranger mixing, a site of commerce between people who would normally not interact with one another at all in buying and selling—a place, in other words, of common aims. To be sure, the bazaars of the Tamil lands became the first sites of public meetings and political oratory in the coming decades and the following century (Chapter 3, Epilogue). But a bazaar is not a public place in a commonsense understanding of the term for several distinct reasons. Most striking, perhaps, is that it is not opposed to some private realm. Rather, it is the very paradigm of what we have come to understand as one pole of a quintessentially Indic opposition between a ritually enclosed—and therefore semiotically coherent interior—space and an exterior essentially defined as a negative space, a non-interior. Rabindranath Tagore's famous opposition, "home and the world" (*ghare/baire*), for instance, is not strictly an opposition between the "home" and the "world"; more precisely, it is an opposition between "inside the house" and "the outside," between a space positively defined by coherent social order and an incoherent negative space defined by its value contrast in opposition to the interior (Kaviraj 1997, 93). The exterior, for which Dipesh Chakrabarty used the bazaar as a paradigm, "has a deeply ambiguous character":

> It is exposed and therefore malevolent. It is not subject to a single set of (enclosing) rules and ritual defining a community. It is where miscegenation occurs. All that do not belong to the "inside" (family/community) lie there, cheek by jowl, in unassorted collection, violating rules of mixing: from feces to prostitutes. (1991, 25)

Again, this is where the *Nālaḍiyār* is most prominently deployed in the *Bazaar Book* and provides a sense of just how non-interior, non-ordered these spaces were from the preacher's point of view. Just over half (nine of sixteen) of the *nālaḍi*s (quatrains) cited in the *Bazaar Book* are found in a final section titled "Various Topics," all but two of which are deployed in the subsection titled "Street Opponents, Unfair Disputants, and Cavillers." Reading through the quatrains in this subsection gives us a sense of the general tone that may have greeted these sermons in the altogether non-polis-like atmosphere of the bazaar. Here the vernacular preacher offered *Nālaḍiyār* 26:6 to the "Noisy Disputant":

> No sound comes from the green leaves of the Palmyra tree, but its dry leaves rustle noisily evermore. So learned and wise men, fearing lest they be betrayed into faulty expressions, keep silence; but ignorant men are always jabbering.

To the "Abusive Disputant," Scudder suggested the use of three quatrains:

> Senseless as a ladle, which knows not the sweetness of the gruel, empty-headed fools ridicule the words of loving men, who discourse graciously

> on virtue. The wise, however, accept those words as full of substance. (*Nālaḍiyār* 33:1)
>
> Words Spoken by an unguarded tongue always scorch the speakers themselves. Hence, men of mature wisdom and intelligence will never hastily give utterance to harsh and angry expressions. (*Nālaḍiyār* 7:3)
>
> It is the duty of great men not only to forgive abuse cast upon themselves; but also to grieve, because their vilifiers must, as a consequence of their wicked conduct, fall into a fiery hell. (*Nālaḍiyār* 6:8)

And to the "Disputant Who Scorns and Rejects Truth," the vernacular preacher might deploy *Nālaḍiyār* 26:9, which states:

> Base and contemptible souls are like the fly, which, passing by the honey distilled in perfume-breathing flowers, greedily seeks everything that is foul and disgusting. Of what profit to such persons are the clear and sweet words, which drop, nectar-like, from the lips of the great and the wise?

Finally, I think the following suggests, perhaps, the most non-interior-like qualities of the bazaar by offering to the "Obscene Disputant" a universally understood insult:

> When fools, who have failed to profit by instruction, speak detestable words, wise and excellent men feel ashamed, and greatly pity the mother who gave birth to those fools. (*Nālaḍiyār* 32:6)

But the *Nālaḍiyār* and the *Tirukkuṟaḷ* are also cited positively as elements of an ethical universe to which the missionary is bound as much as he is to the Bible. The most famous of all *nālaḍis* (14:135) offers the following against the use of Indic shastras:[7]

> Countless is the number of Sastras [*sic*], but few are the days of those who study them, exposed to a thousand fatalities. Therefore like the Swan, which separating the milk from the water with which it is mingled drinks only the former; let the wise carefully discriminating reject worthless Sastras and study only those which are valuable. (Scudder 1865, 17)

This translation, by H. M. Scudder's brother, Dr. J. W. Scudder, contains a minor but highly motivated slippage in its translation of the term *kalvi*, "learning," as "shastra," a textual form. Pope's 1893 translation gives a better sense of the lovely and famous Tamil line, *kalvi kar̲aiyila karpavar nāḷsila*:

> Learning hath no bounds, the learner's days are few. If you think calmly diseases many wait around! With clear discrimination learn what is meet for you, like the swan that leaving the water drinks the milk. (Pope 1893, 62)

Sleight of hand or not, the *Bazaar Book* spent considerable time focusing on what the missionaries felt were evils of textual practice associated with *sāstiram* (shastras) and *mantiram* (mantras, auspicious poetic formulas). Among the most heinous elements of Indic textual practice from the Protestant point of view was the restricted social relations of the text. Scudder complains that the "Sastras" pertain only to Brahmins and others invested with the "sacred cord" but exclude women and Sudras who

> are in no case to read or even hear them read. How is this? Can we suppose that God, in giving a Veda, would deny it to Sudras and bestow it only upon those who wear a cord? Is it to these alone that he gives his rain, his wind, and his sun-shine? (1869, 19)

Continuing a long-standing theme that Protestants applied equally to Catholic priests and their Latin Bible, they criticized both the restrictions of the texts and their semiotic opacity:

> These four Vedas are written in Sanscrit, a language utterly unknown and unintelligible to ordinary people. They are rendered still more difficult by numberless transmutation, augmentation, and elisions. They have been purposely made abstruse and obscure. Not one in a thousand, even among Brahmins, can read and explain them. Such Vedas are utterly useless to the world of mankind. Hence we cannot allow for a moment that these four Vedas have God for their author. Far from being divinely revealed, they are evidently the productions of fraudulent and tricky Brahmins. (19)

In contrast, the missionaries claimed that the Christian Veda, "the true Sastra, is perfectly plain and intelligible. Anyone can read it, anyone can understand it, anyone can meditate on it. Even those, who are not readers, may by the ear easily apprehend its truths, and discover the good way of salvation" (25).

More broadly, the American missionaries understood that they were dealing with minds that processed information darkly. In 1839, one missionary wrote:

> No one who has not had some experience on this point, can understand what is meant by the expression, the darkness of a heathen's mind, or know how difficult it is to communicate any correct notions of the Gospel to an uneducated heathen. In order to become intelligent hearers of the Gospel, they must be taught the first principles of Christianity in childhood. (ACM TR 1839, 24)

But it was not merely a matter of teaching the principles of the Gospel in childhood; more important was to transform their minds based on rationalized semiotics. Another American missionary with twenty years of experience in Jaffna wrote, in 1837:

> Their own false systems blind their understanding. For instance, I call fifty men and women of middle age to hear the following sermon:—
>
> Friends, we are all sinners. We need a Saviour. God has provided a Saviour, Jesus Christ, who will save us from hell and take us to heaven. Repent, therefore, and believe on Jesus Christ!
>
> This sermon if preached to a purely heathen congregation, means either nothing at all, or else these attentive hearers have applied the whole to the most absurd notions of heathenism. *Sinners* means those who are shut up to poverty and suffering through the influence of fate; *God* means Siva; *Jesus Christ* is some unknown deity; *Heaven* means Kailaiyam; *Hell* is the suffering of many transmigrations; and *Repentence* is some dictionary word which they cannot understand. (ACM TR 1839, 25–36)

They complained systematically in just this fashion that terms lost their referential grounding, that their denotationality was floating and unstable, that heathens could make words mean precisely what they wanted them to mean. So, in addition to referential fixity, the Protestants were focused on semiotic transparency and the ability to deploy signs in socially universal contexts—just like, or so they imagined, the bazaar.

Thus, the Protestants encountered an entirely different phenomenology of textual production and embodiment of textual knowledge where texts were to be memorized and sung at highly restricted times and only in certain spaces such as a temple, on auspicious dates and times, and by and to people qualified to hear it (mostly upper-caste men). Recitation operated on, what I called in the Introduction, the logic of textual emblematization, where the animator embodied, became an avatar of, the text. Socially, that was the point. Ethically, Protestant textuality found an Other and a mode of seeing or epistemizing itself: to cultivate the kinds of minds that would be ready to learn the Gospel required a transformation of signs, their textual carriers, and their functionality itself. The Protestant missionaries accomplished this through schooling, publishing, and distributing tracts and Bibles, as well as sermonizing. As mentioned at the outset, though only a fraction of the population was converted to Protestantism, the entire society would, over the course of just a few decades, become Protestantized. By the time the *Bazaar Book* was published in 1865, Tamil Saivites had already begun to establish and staff European-style schools, sermonizing broadly and printing new, clear editions of sacred texts that would be simple for all to understand.

The ethics of Protestant textuality lay at the heart of the project to produce a universalizing system of signs. The missionaries recoiled at the restrictions on the animation of the text and sought new institutional means and performative spaces such as schools and bazaars to bring the text to all the people. The ability to universalize texts so that everyone could understand them—to produce vernacular texts written in the language of everyday life—was asserted as ethically superior to the Indian forms of texts that, in the missionaries' view, were ethically unconscionable, for only a qualified few could understand them and comprehend their meaning or, in fact, were even licensed to hear them.

Moreover, in terms of producing the kind of large-scale social imaginary that is the Tamil world today, the Protestant ethic of textuality was also at the center of many of the transformations that we have come to understand as "public" in the most generic—indeed, European—sense of that term. Language came under a peculiar kind of ethical scrutiny, was recognized as a new way of knowing and being that came to be used, eventually, to imagine a population that shared a commonality in, and solidarity based on, language. This new understanding enabled language to be used in new ways, to be circulated in new textual forms, particularly in forms designed to interpellate a generalized people, a public—that is, universalized print and universalizing sermons (and, later, political oratory; see Chapters 3, 5). It was that communicative restructuring of textual practice, that new interpellation, that would eventually speak into being the Tamil people and the Tamil public sphere.

The ethical underpinning of Protestant textuality brought with it transformations in the materiality and ideology of textual artifacts and in the praxis of textual production. These transformations resulted in textual shifts from the poetic to the prosaic, from an aesthetic of the power of sound (*nāta*) to an ethic of denotational rationality (*logos*), from a sonocentric to a logocentric universe. In combination with the profound shift from restricted to universalized social relations of textuality, new Protestant forms of textuality utterly transformed the entire project of what one was to do with words and, indeed, the kinds of persons that would be licensed to do those things in new spaces and temporalities. A new kind of agency was born, that of the sermonizer, who would be licensed to speak to and transform the world according to any number of different ethical systems but on a new, mass scale. By the first few decades of the twentieth century, that same agency would come to be applied to various projects such as the human rights of lower castes, women's rights, the Labor movement (Epilogue), and eventually independence.

It is worthwhile to recognize, however, as noted in the Introduction, that although the Protestants made history, they did not do so just as they pleased. Other textualities were still operating that would be the basis on which the Tamil public sphere would be experienced. An ancient vernacular aesthetic of textual production—the poetic and rhetorical textual forms carried over from the ancient into the production of the modern—appears to have remained immanent within the transformations of Protestant textuality that yielded a qualitative difference in the nature of the formation of the public. Moreover, it was those poetics and rhetorics that made the experience and disposition of a Tamil public sphere utterly different from the experience of, say, a French one. For texts such as these—and even the ancient ethics of Indian textuality—continued to be deployed by the new agents in their transformative projects of the coming decades and century.

Even in 1893, in his edition of the *Nālaḍiyār*, Pope provided a thorough discussion of the poetic meters of the text so that readers could appreciate its poesy. In both his editions of the *Tirukkuṟaḷ* and the *Nālaḍiyār*, Pope expended a great deal of energy ensuring that readers would be sufficiently familiar with the lovely meter called *Veṇbā* (from the root *veḷ*, meaning "white, bright, clear," and *pā*, meaning "verse"). In essence, readers would be lost—unable to parse the morphemes—were they unable to scan the poem prior to understanding it (Pope 1893, xxviii, xxix).

More than that, however, readers would be lost aesthetically. Sound itself (*nāta*) was important, the sheer sound of words and music as they worked on the hearts of the hearers. Even the missionaries, in their use of Tamil texts such as *Nālaḍiyār*, knew that their sermons—however rational and denotationally explicit—would fail to move the souls of their auditors without a poesy alien to their own ethic. Consider the sense of the sound symbolism between the beating of a funeral drum and the assertion of a callow young man who claims that life is characterized by the bliss of wedded life (*Nālaḍiyār* 3:5):

> *kaṇam koṇḍu cuṟṟattār kallenṟu alaṟa*
> *piṇam koṇḍu kāṭṭu uyppārk kaṇḍum—maṇam koṇḍu, īṇḍu*
> *uṇḍu, uṇḍu, uṇḍu ennum uṇarvinān cārrumē,*
> *ḍoṇ ḍoṇ ḍoṇ ennum paṟai.*

> To him, who, although he sees them bear the corpse to the burning ground, while friends in troops loudly lament, boldly asserts that wedded life is bliss on earth, the funeral drum speaks out, and mocks his vain utterance. (Pope 1893, 18)

Between the reduplicated echo of the two lines (lines 3 and 4), *uṇḍu, uṇḍu, uṇḍu* (It is, it is, it is) in the third line, and the onomatopoeic drum beat, *ḍoṇ ḍoṇ ḍoṇ* in the fourth line, is caught a sense of mocking irony for which the

English translation—even at its best in Pope—requires an extra phrase, "and mocks his vain utterance."

The bodily apperception of the sheer sound of language (*nāta*), the music of language, and the poetic form remained a key element of the entire project and would come to have fateful political impacts later on in the Tamil nationalist Dravidianist uptake of just such poesy as an index of their own antiquity, of the nationalists' Tamil cultural authenticity, in the new democratic order of mid-twentieth-century Tamilagam. Examples of this sort are copious in any of the major Dravidianist speakers, such as Kalaiñar Mu. Karunanidhi or Ariñar C. N. Annadurai.[8] This uptake was mediated, as we see in the next chapter, through Saivite reformers such as Arumuga Navalar.

Even the embodiment of knowledge through the memorization and recitation of text was resurrected by the Dravidianist politicians who combined the precolonial textual emblematization—indexing and iconically instantiating a consubstantiality of person and text—with the sermonic form in oratorical discourse. To cite the ancient text was to embody it, to become an avatar of the text itself and all its properties: grammatical refinement, antiquity, and civilizational authenticity. This kind of emblematization became a key element of the very character of the interpellation of the Tamil public sphere, of its leaders and its people.

This is a strikingly clear example—among many we could enumerate—of how deep vernacular aesthetics track the manner in which the new newnesses of modernity would be laid down in South Asia (and elsewhere). In this case, it was these ancient, broad, and deep Indic rhetorical and mythopoeic structures that provided an embodied ground for the infrastructural transformation of the Tamil public sphere—one based on the ethical prescriptions of textuality and textual practice associated with the Protestant Reformation and the European Enlightenment.

Chapter 2

ARUMUGA NAVALAR AND THE PROTESTANT MODERN

> Sivaist preachers and stewards appeared and formed and worked a circuit somewhat on the Methodist model.
>
> —E. J. Robinson, *Hindu Pastors*

On 31 December 1847, Arumugam Pillai, some months later given the title "Navalar" ("The Able-Tongued" or "The Learned"), delivered a sermon (*pirasaṅgam*) in the Vannarpannai Siva Temple near Jaffna (Robinson 1867, 121–29; Young and Jebanesan 1995, 121–22.).[1] In doing so, he is said to have inaugurated what has since been called *mēḍaittamiḻ*, "Tamil stage speech" or "oratory" (Sivathamby 1979; Kailasapathy 1986; Bate 2000, 2009b), a practice that came to define political communicative behavior in twentieth-century Tamilagam. We know that other Tamil speakers, both South Asian and European, had delivered Tamil orations for many years before that in the form of Protestant sermons (see Chapters 1, 3). But when Arumugam spoke that night, he began a process of transforming the nature of Saivite temple practice and hence inaugurated a transformation of Saivism itself into a religion per se, on the model of Christian worship practice.

In this chapter, I consider the production of the Tamil sermon in Christian and Saivite practices, circa 1850, and suggest the fateful entailments of oratory to far larger realms of practice and understandings of the social, historical, and political order. Whatever else it may be, that which we call the political (*la politique* in Paul Ricoeur's terms) is largely composed of communicative practices. Oratory, like print capitalism, is associated with the development of large-scale political entities such as publics and nations (Habermas [1962] 1991; Anderson [1983] 2006).[2] Both print capitalism and oratory share certain dominant analyses: both have been viewed as centrally productive of particular forms of social and political consciousness, and both have been seen as communicative modes of the production of certain sociological formations. While significant attention has been paid to the role of print in producing the public sphere or the contemporary nation-state, the role of the orator has been largely hidden in this history (see Introduction for more discussion). It is of course far easier—though not easy—to trace the development of print culture because it left a material record in the form of text artifacts. Nineteenth-century Tamil oratory, however, has left only palimpsests of its production, impressions on the minds of those who heard it and thought to describe it. There are no tape recordings or detailed linguistic transcriptions of these texts, though we can occasionally find notes by the speakers themselves or members of their audiences. We can also find texts (e.g., tracts, catechisms, or homiletics) that offer tantalizing suggestions about how their authors felt a sermon, for instance, *should* be delivered.[3] However, in comparison to American and European oratorical traditions, there is scant evidence of the material form of these events or of the texts themselves.

This is a problem. I suggest here that oratory embodies a quotidian model of social order, a ritual instantiation of the way that people understand the kinds of persons and agencies that exist within their social worlds. Any oratorical address involves peculiar notions of agency, temporality, and social being. The orator attempts to transform something or someone, to change the order of things as they stand at that moment, and to do so within a linear temporal order that can be changed (rather than merely experienced, as in a cyclical temporal order of some kind). Further, the orator (say, a Protestant missionary, a Saivite sermonizer, or their descendant, the political speaker) embodies the center of a social order that he is thought capable—entitled, authorized—of changing. He is an icon of that order and embodies it ritually as he speaks. Like the literate consumer of print, the subject par excellence of Benedict Anderson's nation-state, the orator enacts and imagines a social world that includes him and the interpellated audience as indispensable elements of that world. The case of Arumuga Navalar, his interlocutors, colleagues, and opponents provides a privileged insight not only into the social world of the time but also into the production of whole new discrete domains of practice such as "religion" and, related to that, formal mass "politics."

Language and the Delimitation of Religion

The notion that "religion" is a somewhat recent demarcation of a wide range of practices has been argued since at least the 1950s and 1960s, specifically in the work of Cantwell Smith (1962). It has been taken up by a wide range of scholars more recently, such as Talal Asad (1993), S. N. Balagangadhara (1994), Richard King (1999), and Valentine Daniel (2002), among many others. The basic argument, with which I am in agreement, asserts that religion is not a panhuman category but rather (1) an irreducibly Christian concept; (2) a function of colonial power relations, especially in the nineteenth century; and (3) a phenomenological-cum-practical process of the demarcation or definition of a set of practices as a discrete realm of action and belief that are different from other realms of belief and practice. This last part of the problem, an element of what we might call the "blessed rage for order" that characterizes Western modernity, I argue, can be seen as a demarcation of communicative practices of one sort or another as well. Consider, again, the idea that Protestantism was defined precisely as that form of Christianity that would have a direct, unmediated, and *semantically coherent* relationship with the Word of God. A new kind of *Knowing*, to borrow Daniel's (2002) distinction, was to supplant an earlier, Roman Catholic, and (from the Protestant point of view) erroneous way of *Being*. And this Knowing was based on the idea that the Bible was the Word of God and that we could, with care, understand it even through various translations. And given that we could know it, it became imperative that we do so—hence, literacy and its institutional mode of production, schools, flourished in Protestant societies. It was, ultimately, a social movement based irreducibly on a theory of signs.

Contemporary Theravada Buddhism, too, developed as a new understanding of a great many earlier communicative practices. For Theravada Buddhism, the "game of religion" was played out through a series of public debates beginning in the 1840s and reaching their apogee in the late 1860s and early 1870s (Daniel 2002, 46–50). It was also played out in the transformation of the Sinhala *dharmadesana*, these days translated as "sermon." But prior to a reformation of sorts inaugurated by Anagarika Dharmapala (1864–1933) in the late nineteenth century, it was basically a highly systematized and ritually elaborate recitation of Pali texts. As H. L. Seniveratne describes it, most listeners prior to Dharmapala's time would not have been concerned with the actual denotationality (or semantic coherence) of the texts but rather in the evocational experience of the sheer sound of the text, an aesthetic experience that in itself was generative of merit (2000, 74–76, cited in Daniel 2002, 49; see Chapter 1). It was only later in the "reforming" movements of Dharmapala and others that the term *dharmadesana* began to resemble the didactic and denotationally coherent sermon: it was reduced in length from approximately twelve hours to one hour, stripped of elaborate ritual and dramatic elements, and focused on the "meaning" of the ancient Pali text to be explicated. H. L. Seneviratne writes:

> Above all [the new *dharmadesana*] focused on a theme, a feature structurally integrated to the sermon in the form of a Pali verse that the preacher chanted explicitly recognizing it as the theme (*matrka*). While there are some precedents for this in the mediaeval Sinhala literary works which were essentially dharmadesana in written form, the new dharmadesana in its succinctness and unity resembled more the sermon that emanated from the Christian pulpit, like the ones which the young Dharmapala heard over and over again. (2000, 80–81, cited in Daniel 2002, 49–50)

As this chapter demonstrates, the transformation of the Sinhala *dharmadesana* toward the end of the nineteenth century was foreshadowed by a parallel transformation of the Saivite *pirasaṅgam* in the 1840s and 1850s by Arumuga Navalar and his colleagues. I suggest here that the focus on communicative practice by Navalar was the central activity in the production of Saivism as a religion per se. This, of course, is not to claim that Saivism did not exist as a coherent body of practices, including textual practices. I claim, however, that the Saivism we know today, the *religion*, found its first condensation *as* religion through the focus on communicative practices that Navalar began. I also want to suggest that it was on the bases of these new kinds of communicative practices that new kinds of political agency and new social imaginaries would later be founded. In particular, the public Tamil that was first produced in Christian sermons and borrowed by Saivism was delivered within the first ritual instantiations of what would later become a Tamil public.

This chapter, then, is an attempt to recover the figure of the orator as a major player in the objectification of Saivism and a singularly Tamil public sphere through the production and transformation of communicative genres, that is, named models of discursive interaction. I later discuss the speaking events of 1847–48 and consider them in terms of their antecedents in Christian sermons and, taken together, their fateful quality as an originary moment in the production of Tamil oratory. The discussion begins with an account of Arumuga Navalar and his times, provides some rather detailed descriptions of the events in question, and closes with what I think is the significance of shifts in speech genres with transformations of larger-scale political organization. Basically, I make the claim that political transformation is intimately associated with transformations in the material form of communicative practice and in the apperception of those practices.

Arumuga Navalar, "The Able-Tongued"

Many Tamil scholars say that the sermons (*pirasaṅgam*) that Arumugam delivered in late 1847 and 1848 in and around Jaffna were the beginning of Tamil oratory. They were not the beginning of Tamil oratory. They were just the beginning of Tamil oratory outside a Protestant context, which, as it turns out, was momentous. I would call it the first Tamil oratorical revolution, and it had some rather profound historical effects.

Navalar is a giant in modern Tamil history. He has held the attentions of serious Tamil scholars since his death in 1879. His prominence in Tamil letters seems only to grow with time, the mark of what Marshall Sahlins (2004) would call "systemic agency," the mark of agency that was licensed to truly transform things—like Napoleon, for instance. He has been deified in Saivite hagiographies, considered the father of Tamil Eelam, made into an agent of working-/middle-class resistance to imperial rule, and given the title "The Champion Reformer of the Hindus."[4] I suggest here that his importance is due precisely to his role in the transformation of the materiality of Tamil communicative practices.

In addition to his oratorical prowess, he is known for his role in the first productions of prose Tamil in Saivite and educational literature, the establishment of Saivite schools, and a vast expansion of Tamil printing through his presses in Lanka and Madras. His role as printer, builder of educational institutions, "reformer" (better, rationalizer) of Saivism as a religion per se, and his oratorical and literary impulses suggest that Navalar was producing Tamil as a language that could be used to address some wider imagined community. Indeed, I believe he was producing a Tamil that could be used to address something resembling a "public."

Navalar was born Arumuga Pillai in 1821. His father was a poet and Tamil scholar, well versed in the Saivite canon and trained in the recitation of these texts—also called *pirasaṅgam*, the same term that Christians used for "sermon."

After receiving a traditional Tamil education by his father up to 1834, Arumugam became the favorite student of the Reverend Peter Percival, who that very year became head of the Wesleyan Mission School and principal of Jaffna Central College. There, he quickly mastered English, was made a Tamil tutor when he was fourteen years old, and was appointed teacher of Tamil and English at the school in 1841, when he was nineteen years old. Percival, in his role as head of the Jaffna Auxiliary of the Bible Society, also employed Arumugam as his assistant translator for what was to become a new Bible translation. By the end of 1847, when Arumugam began conducting his anti-Christian/pro-Saivite sermons, he had finished his work as translator and was preparing to accompany Percival to Madras to present their Bible to the Bible Society administrators, which they did in March 1848.[5]

Arumugam and Percival's Bible project met little success in Madras (though elements of it would be incorporated into a new version about twenty-five years later). In July, when he and Percival returned to Ceylon from their failed mission to the Bible Translation Society in Madras, Arumugam continued to give sermons in the temples until September 1848, when he and Percival broke their formal ties. Curiously, Arumugam engaged in these anti-Christian activities before, during, and after his trip to Madras to pitch his Bible. And his activities were common knowledge—indeed, some source of controversy. But Percival kept Arumugam on at the school for nine months, and by all accounts their parting was cordial. The two men, it is said, remained high in each other's esteem for the rest of their lives (which speaks well of them both in my mind).

From that point on, Arumugam became the leading activist in Saivism and in the creation of non-Christian educational and printing institutions until his death in 1879.

The Sermons

Let us examine more carefully the events of 1847 and 1848, the sermons in question, and the first cause of Arumugam's celebrity.

The Reverend Edward Jewitt Robinson, a missionary of the Wesleyan Methodists in Ceylon, provides the first detailed description of these events in his 1867 memoir, *Hindu Pastors*. This account becomes foundational to almost all subsequent writings about what happened. Reverend Robinson begins by relating the development of an organized opposition to Christianity in Jaffna that was of some concern to the Wesleyans:

> Sivaist preachers and stewards appeared and formed and worked a circuit somewhat on the Methodist model. In connection with the reading and recitation of passages from their sacred books, a lecture or sermon was delivered every Friday evening, in a spacious shed on the holy ground within the high wall round the temple of Siva at Wannarponne [Vannarpannai]; and appointments, though not of such frequent occurrence, were also kept [in temples of the surrounding villages] and at the important villages of Chunnagam and Manepy. Before the delivery of the 1st lecture, December 31, 1847, the officiating priest of the temple broke a cocoa-nut, in honour of Pillaiyar and the undertaking; and at the close of the meeting he solemnly rose and said, that the omens for the association were very auspicious. In the first place, the cocoa-nut had broken evenly into two equal parts; and secondly, at the commencement of the address, he had heard the sound of a bell within the temple. The principal orators, both of whom had been day-pupils in our Jaffna school, were Arumugavar, the first and most frequent, and the presiding genius through all the movement, and a friend of his named Cattigasayar [Karthigesaiyar]. The former, of the Vellala or agriculturalist caste, good looking, intelligent, studious, reserved, of grave demeanor and blameless life, not better acquainted with the Hindu shastras than with the Christian Scriptures, had been for a long period, day after day, the worthy companion and valued assistant of the gifted and plodding

> Mr. Percival in preparing and editing treatises and hymns in Tamil, and translating the Prayer-Book and the Holy Bible. Cattigasayar, a round, oily Brahmin, physically inferior to his colleague, and naturally less austere and resolute, but equally learned in Hindu lore, and quite as patriotic, would not alone have originated such an enterprise. He was the writer's [Robinson's] respected and faithful moonshee; and when bantered in the study, admitted without hesitation, and in the best temper, that he did not himself believe much of what he thought it necessary to relate to the people as unquestioned history. Poor men! (1867, 122–23)[6]

These sermons (*pirasaṅgam*) caused something of a stir. Though the Christian authorities and others were interested in receiving published accounts of them, Arumugam was loath to provide any details of the meetings; Robinson even reports that Arumugam refused a "public offer" of twenty dollars by the American editor of an important Tamil and English daily newspaper, *Uthayatharakai-Morning Star*, for authorized accounts of the sermons (123). Robinson, however, managed to receive reports of the meetings from a "zealous" young Tamil catechist named Richard Watson. Watson, armed with "the wisdom of the serpent" (124), probably bribed or otherwise cajoled a "Sivaist" participant who made notes of the meetings in Tamil on palm leaves (*ōlai*), which he translated and gave to Robinson, who writes:

> I possess in his handwriting copious outlines of twenty-nine of the addresses given at Wannarponne from February 18th to November 17, 1848. Incoherent and nonsensical to the Christian mind, yet they were not more earnestly delivered and attentively heard than for their object carefully and suitably prepared. They were constructed in imitation of such sermons as the zealous Catechist himself [Watson] was wont to deliver; a text being selected from some reputedly sacred book, and discussed under so many heads. The subjects of the discourses supplied were the following: Initiatory prayer; the holy necklace; the love of Siva; the sacred writings taking away the life of animals, two lectures; festivals; the public worship of Siva; the mortality of the body; the leading doctrines of Sivaism; the duties of women; impartial judgment; earthly and heavenly treasures; adultery; charity; sacrilege, two; drunkenness, three; gratitude; almsgiving; educa-

> tion; unity of God; the veneration due to cows, two; imitating the wise and the good; the vanity of earthly pleasures; and credulity. (124–25)

Despite Robinson's obvious and understandable prejudices, he provides a reasonably accurate account of the events that concern me here. Other accounts confirm that Arumugam began his sermons at the Vannarpannai Siva Temple on 31 December 1847 (Kailasapillai [1918] 1955, 25–26; Young and Jebanesan 1995, 121). The fullest account (thus far) published of one of these meetings, which took place at the Manippay Skanda (or Murugan) Temple, was made by an assistant to Benjamin Meigs, an American missionary in Jaffna. Again, the details here are important. Meigs writes:

> On the evening of 18 March [1848] there was a meeting at the Temple of Skanda at which about 100 people were present. The service was commenced by singing verses of Tiruvasakam [one of the central texts of the Saivite canon] by Tamber, one of the officiating Brahmins of the temple. He then showed us how to appear before the holy places of Siva. First we must wash ourselves. Secondly we must rub ashes in the form of Tripoondaram. Thirdly we must wear on the head garlands of Rutteratsham. Fourthly, the head must be bare, not covered with a turban or handkerchief. Fifthly, when we approach the temple, we must prostrate ourselves so that the eight and the five parts of the body [male and female, respectively] may touch the ground. All who will not perform these ceremonies in the prescribed form must suffer the pains of hell, where they will be obliged to sit and walk and step on pointed needles. . . .
>
> After this [Arumugam] approaching the bench professed as the subject of his discourse, to prove that there is but one God. . . . [Materialists] say that the four elements, earth, air, fire, and water are God. . . . These however are not God. Again, if we inquire if [the Jain Mahavira] is God, in my estimation he is not, but the meanest of all the gods. Neither is Budhu god [referring to Buddha], because he was procreated. But the Christian religion is the meanest of all. The God whom the Christians worship cannot therefore be the true God. Justice and mercy are prominent attributes of the true God. The God whom the Sivas worship possesses these attributes. He permits the transmigration of souls, through several births. Thus men

> atone of their sins by the sufferings which they endure. After these successive births, he receives them to heaven. In this he displays both his justice and mercy. But the God of the Christians is not so. Though a man be ever so moral and conduct himself with the greatest propriety, yet if he does not outwardly repent and be baptized, he cannot get to heaven. Therefore, the God whom the Christians worship is not just and merciful. The God of the Sivas is therefore the true God. Thus saying he finished by singing a Tiruvasakam. He also gave notice to his audience that on several succeeding weeks, he would preach upon the attributes of Siva, and show that the God of the Christians does not possess these attributes. (American Board of Commissioners for Foreign Missions, 6/115, 11/04/48, Houghton Library, Harvard University, cited in Young and Jebanesan 1995, 121–22)

Analysis

There are a number of striking aspects about these accounts. His years among the Christians, his thorough familiarity with the Bible and with Protestant liturgical practices, gave Arumugam an insider's view not only of Wesleyan Methodism but perforce with how a religion per se operates: something phenomenologically demarcated from other realms of life, bounded off, and ideologically rationalized (in the Weberian sense of the term). As Robinson observes, his lectures "were constructed in imitation of such sermons as the zealous Catechist himself was wont to deliver"; his and his colleagues' travels from temple to temple are described as working "a circuit somewhat on the Methodist model."

The very form of the meetings was quite novel (from the point of view of Saivite worship practices, if not from Protestant ones): Arumugam chose some textual swatch from one of the principal texts of Saivism and proceeded to offer an exegesis and discussion in the form of a sermon that was "mellifluous to the ears and easily understood" (Muttucumaraswamy 1965, 20). One account also claims that he was able to extemporaneously deliver an address when his colleague, Karthigesaiyar, had to suddenly miss his appointed turn (Kailasapillai [1918] 1955, 26–28; Muttucumaraswamy 1965, 18–19). Based on these feats of oratorical prowess, as well as his organizational and educational activities, Arumugam "earned a reputation as the best Methodist the Jaffna

Wesleyans ever produced" (S. Sivathamby, pers. comm., cited in Young and Jebanesan 1995, 123).

Such practices would have embodied a radical contrast to the types of discursive activities theretofore practiced in the temples. Again, consider the word *pirasaṅgam*, which we have translated as both "temple recitations" of the Saivite canon and as Protestant "sermon." The *pirasaṅgam* of old involved the recitation of texts written eight hundred to one thousand years earlier, in language that, in the mid-nineteenth century, was quite archaic. Most listeners would have known the stories already, but they probably would not have followed every word that was being spoken. Rather, like the experience of nineteenth-century Sinhala speakers listening to Pali *dharmadesana*, most medieval listeners of church Latin, contemporary people listening to *fus'ha* recitations of the Qur'an, or the Sanskrit heard in temples all over India, language was not so much denotational—referential and predicational—as evocational.[7] In Valentine Daniel's terminology, it appealed more to mood than to mind (1996, 104–34; see Chapter 1). In striking similarity to Seneviratne's account of Dharmapala's transformation of the Pali *dharmadesana* some three decades later, Richard F. Young and S. Jebanesan explicitly remark on the difference between the Saivite recitational *pirasaṅgam* and Navalar's sermon:

> The performance of *piracaṅgam* was intended to evoke scenes and moods that lifted listeners out of the present into the realm of myth. Although myth subsequently provided thematic material that Āṟumukam discussed in lecture format, the content at this stage was dominated by apologetics solemnized by the exposition of texts and structured around liturgical formulas adapted from Māṇikkavācakar's Tiruvācakam and (later) the Tēvāram hymns. (1995, 122–23)

What might this oratory have sounded like? It is safe to say that it was like nothing heard in a temple before. But this does not provide us with any sense of what meanings people would have attributed to its form. While this is one of the main questions further research on this matter should attempt to address, for the moment we might begin with descriptions of his prose and some of his prescriptions for the recitation of the sacred texts. Again, his speaking was described as "mellifluous" and "easy to understand." This suggests that he was using a contemporary lexicon, one based on the ordinary conversational Tamil heard on the streets (and on the pulpit)—but not like the archaic lexicon of the major Saivite texts. But at the same time, it was also described as *sentamiḻ*, "beautiful," "fine," or "refined" Tamil, the Tamil associated with the written word, with prosody, literature, and grammar. *Sentamiḻ* is also, perforce, defined in opposition to *koccaittamiḻ*, "vulgar" Tamil, or *koḍuntamiḻ*, the "bent" Tamil of the illiterate speaker.

In light of this distinction, then, consider the description of Navalar's prose offered by one of the senior Tamil scholars of the twentieth century, T. P. Meenakshisundaran. "On the one hand," he writes,

> there was prose known as High Senthamil, and on the other hand Kochchaithamil—an ascent and a descent—(a crest and a trough). Navalar leveled these, applied plaster to it; he made it a shining white wall. Yes! In this levelling process, many beautiful paintings on the peaks have disappeared. . . . But Arumuga Navalar did yeoman service, by ploughing and levelling a rugged old terrain that never saw the plough, and he had to sow the seeds and clear the weeds. . . . Therefore, Arumuga Navalar was the father of modern Tamil prose, and laid its foundations firm and secure. (T. P. Meenakshisundaran, "Ceylon Tamil Poets," quoted in Muttucumaraswamy 1965, 28–29)[8]

It is appropriate at this point to parenthetically note that Navalar vastly expanded the use of punctuation in Tamil and broke words up on the printed page according to word boundaries. His published texts of the classics of the Saivite canon included in their titles and introductions the phrase "easy to understand." Such practices were associated with the emergence of silent reading—a quite new model of textuality at the time—all over Tamil lands (Venkatachalapathy 1994). Clearly, Navalar was very concerned with the denotational aspects of text, reference, and predication. He was concerned, in other words, that masses of people actually understand what they were reading.

This, it seems, is the genius of his prose, and probably, too, of his Christian sermon-like oratory: the ability to combine aspects of written and spoken forms of Tamil into a new kind of oral performance in the Saivite context that would be "mellifluous," like the prosody of the sacred texts, and as "easily understood" as the Tamil of everyday interaction (insofar as "everyday" discursive interaction is actually easily understood). That Navalar believed that Saivite discursive interaction *should* be easily understood as referential and predicational text—rather than some other form of the aural experience of sacred verse—is suggested in his prescription written in a famous and highly influential "manifesto" (*Vikkiyāpanam*) of 1860 that the "readers" (*ōtuvār*) to be appointed to recite the sacred works in Siva temples throughout Tamil lands "recite in a clear fashion" (*suttaṅgamāka ōtavum*) (Kailasapillai [1918] 1955, 49). That he should make a point of prescribing proper enunciation indicates that *pirasaṅgam* was probably not, at the time, recited in a clear fashion. And, I think, denotational clarity was not even the point (see Chapter 1).

When Navalar took these aesthetics of language along with the model of the Protestant sermon outside the church and into new arenas, he thereby re-created the arenas themselves as something brand-new. An index of this transformation is the word *pirasaṅgam* itself. One of Navalar's grandnephews, an accomplished Tamil scholar in his own right, T. Kailasapillai, made the following observation:

> *Pirasaṅgam* is a Sanskrit term. We have yet to devise its Tamil equivalent. Even in Tamil texts it is used in many different senses. Of these, the sense of one man (*oruvar*) skillfully speaking on a topic only appears in (Navalar's) time. In times before, there were many excellent *vidhvans* who wrote textual commentaries; but I have not heard that they rose up in their assemblies, took up each topic one by one and taught the people. It must have been by (Navalar) himself that *pirasaṅgam* gained this meaning in Tamil. ([1918] 1955, 25)

That a scholar of Kailasapillai's experience could not think of a single instance in all of Tamil literature wherein an individual stands up to address an audience is not surprising: in two thousand years of continuous literary production in Tamil, no single high-status rhetor addresses a multitude until the 1891 publication of a play, *Manonmaniyam* (Tho. Paramasivan, pers. comm.).[9] Solitary rhetors did not address multitudes; it was the multitudes (of poets, usually) who addressed apical figures (such as gods or kings). Where gods or kings (or other high-status beings) do speak in the Tamil record, they do so in dialogic, not monologic, modalities. When Navalar delivered a sermon, a monologic form of discursive interaction, as an element of Saivite temple *pirasaṅgam*, he instantiated a semeiosocial revolution that utterly transformed the representation of status in discursive interaction and the possible inhabitable roles higher-status persons in Tamil can embody.

The Materiality of Oratory and the Objectification of Saivism

The year following his first sermons and his break from Percival found Arumugam again in the Tamil soil of the Indian mainland. The highlight of the trip, and another turning point of his life, was an event at a Saivite center of higher learning (an *ātīnam*, or "math" or "mutt") in Thanjavur District. It was here that Arumuga Pillai became Arumuga Navalar. One of his hagiographies describes what happened:

> While in India, Navalar visited several sacred shrines and delivered religious lectures everywhere. When he was at Kumbakonam, the head of the Thiruvavaduturai Adhinam invited him to his Math for the purpose of honoring him. The head of this Math had all along been regarded as the spiritual head of the Saiva world. He received Navalar with great regard and love. At his request Navalar delivered a lecture, and the head of the Math, in order to honour him, or rather to honour it, gave him the title of Navalar. He stayed there a few days spending his time in reading rare Agamic works, not available anywhere else. Though he accepted the title, he would not accept anything tangible.[10]

The title Navalar—*nā* (tongue) + *valam* (skill)—is now almost universally translated as "orator," but it had previously been given to poets and those who recited the texts of the Saivite canon in *pirasaṅgam*. But when it was given to Arumugam in 1848, the award was based on an entirely new aesthetic of an entirely new practice, that is, the "lecture" or "sermon." From that moment on, Navalar was a sensation, a man using a model of discursive interaction that had theretofore been associated exclusively with Protestants—the very people who were at that moment waging a spirited attack against Saivism and all other forms of what we now call Hinduism. Among his admirers were wealthy men who backed Navalar financially and made it possible for him to begin a series of new activities on behalf of Saivism, including the establishment of his school and the purchase of printing presses in Ceylon and Madras—a skillful tongue, indeed. The next few decades in Madras are called the "Navalar" or "Jaffna Period" for the revolution in communicative practices he inaugurated and later institutionalized.

Those communicative practices were, in essence, Christian or, more precisely, Protestant. The Christianity that faced Navalar as a hegemonic Other in the mid-nineteenth century was instantiated in Jaffna as a set of discursive practices defined by explicitly metapragmatic stipulation of some distinct sphere of knowledge and action that we today understand as "religion": such things as catechism; the theological training of Methodists, Anglicans, and the Congregationalists in terms of certain discursive procedures; homiletic; the "circuit rider"; and of course, the Sunday sermon. The Saivism of the time, on the other hand, involved various experiences and emotional states that were also produced in real-time discursive interaction. But there was no institutionalized realm of the metapragmatic stipulation of that action, no sets of procedures ideologically itemized, rationalized, and made available for objective uptake and distribution among those who might be called Saivites. In the Saivism of the day, being and feeling were privileged over knowing; the aesthetic over the ideological; Firstness, in Peircean terms, over Thirdness, or in Daniel's terms, mood over mind.

Arumugam's sermons, and his related liturgical rationalization, began a process in which Saivism became a religion per se, a mode of institutionally regulated/regularized action that could be stipulated in a set of discursive practices that themselves involved the institutionalized stipulation of their own production (cf. Meigs's notes on the meeting at the Vannarpannai Siva Temple on 31 December 1847: first, wash yourself; second, rub ashes; third, wear garlands of Rutteratsham; fourth, head must be bare; fifth, proper prostration, etc.)

The semeiosic stipulation of a set of beliefs and practices as a discrete realm of action is precisely what distinguishes a religion from the vast range of practices and ideas people have had regarding deities, spirits, the afterlife, cosmogony, et cetera. As Émile Durkheim so famously put it, a "religion" is a system of beliefs and practices relative to the sacred that unites all adherents into a church—a church, note, that can be distinguished from any other church ([1912] 1995, 44). But we should point out that not all such ideas and practices relative to the sacred were, in fact, "religions" in the way we currently understand that term (as it is used, for instance, in departments of religious studies). Prior to the missionization of Jaffna by Protestants (and perhaps, Catholics), it is unlikely that most of the people who worshipped the various deities associated with Siva called themselves "Saivites." They certainly did not call themselves "Hindus," as they do today. But if one were to ask any worshipper if he "believed" that the image he worshipped in the temple was God, he most likely would have found the question nonsensical. From his point of view, the image was in fact God (or a/the God) whether one believed it so or not. The existence of the deity—and one's identity as a worshipper of it—was irrelevant to any theory of its existence.

This, of course, is not the case in Christianity, which, as Daniel discusses, is the first true religion insofar as it demands of its practitioners the total acceptance of what amounts to a theory of God (2002, 36). One cannot be a Christian in the Protestant sense of the term without professing a belief that Jesus was the Son of God/Man, that he died on the cross, that he rose up on the third day, et cetera. While Islam is most certainly a religion in this respect, most of the beliefs and practices relative to the sacred in the majority of South Asia were most certainly not. What made such things as Buddhism and Saivism religions, in the way we understand them today, was grounded in elite responses to the colonial project of Christianization and the transformation of older practices (such as *pirasaṅgam* and *dharmadesana*) into ones that were modeled explicitly on Christian ones.

As discussed at the outset of this chapter, such an observation regarding the relative "newness" of the Hindu and Buddhist "religions" is nothing new. But what I hope to have emphasized here is that the modality of transformation from some pre-religious phenomenology of the sacred to an expressly religious one is communicative and metacommunicative. Arumuga Navalar's activities in the "reforming" of Saivism were almost entirely in the transformation of communicative practices and their primary institutions. In today's Jaffna, we can speak of Saivism as a discrete phenomenological realm of action and belief that is defined precisely as Arumuga Navalar defined it in his educational institutions, in regularizing the Tamil language to facilitate printing and in sermonizing that would be "easily understood" and "mellifluous to the ears." The transformation and objectification of Saivism as a religion was undertaken precisely on the basis of a Protestant theory of signs and their uptake in material institutional practice.

It is this ideological and aesthetic objectification of discrete realms and phenomenological entities in communicative practice that is the object of this chapter. But it also represents the beginning of a longer inquiry into the transformation of far wider realms of sociocultural and political-economic production. When Navalar inaugurated his communicative revolution that transformed Saivism into a religion, he also took the first step in the production of the material form of discursive interaction that would come to define the "public" spaces of Tamil lands—from the first public speeches in Tamil associated with the freedom struggle in what became Tamil Nadu, beginning sometime around 1904 (Chapters 3–5). And the full impact of Navalar's revolution can be appreciated in consideration of the fact that, by the second decade of the twentieth century, some seventy years after he first offered a sermon extolling the compassionate nature of God in a Siva temple near Jaffna, the Tamil lands of India and Ceylon had become an empire of orators, lands in which anyone who engaged in the sphere of formal political action was, by very definition, a *nāvalar*.

PART II THE TAMIL MODERN

Chapter 3

SPEAKING SWADESHI, MADRAS 1907

> The name of Surendranath Banerjee first fell on my ear in the year 1902 when I was studying in the Fourth Form. Ananda Charlu, G. Subramania Ayer, Doctor Nair, Vi. Krishnasami Ayer and others would speak now and then about the Congress. Sometimes, my friends and I would go to those meetings; we would enjoy the honey of their speech and debate as to whose English was better as we walked home.
>
> —Thiru. Vi. Kalyanasundaram, *Vāḻkkai Kuṟippukaḷ*

> He spoke in his childhood's Tamil, and when he had finished speaking he went upon his way, while the meeting dispersed, and dying shouts of "Bande Mataram!" mingled with the roaring of the surf.
>
> —Henry W. Nevinson, "On the Beach"

Madurai Mayandi Bharati, freedom fighter, Communist activist, journalist, and lifelong political man, was born in 1917. Sitting on his bed in February 2009, half blind, very old, fully bright, he channeled for us the sounds preceding a public meeting of the late 1920s and 1930s in the temple town of Madurai. There were two men in particular who regularly advertised events in that town—*taṇḍōrā pōḍutal*, it was called (playing a small drum hung from the shoulder)—the brothers Arunachala Rao and Renganatha Rao. Mayandi Bharati sang the words, more or less, emphasizing the nasals and the long vowels, especially the long *ā* (ஆ), as he held and rattled an imaginary *tappaṭṭai* between his hands, the two-sided drum beaten with a curved stick: *takka takka takka takka takka takka.*

Innnnnṟu māāāālaiyil
Toddddday eeeevening

immmmmmmmaturai māāānagaram
in this greaaaat Mmmmmmmmadurai town

Kāṅgiras Kamiṭṭi cāāārpil
on behaaalf of the Congress Committee

Innnnr̲u māāāālaiyil
Toddddday eeeevening

āāāāār̲u maṇikki
at siiiiiiiiiiiix o'clock

Tilakar maitāāāāānattil
at the Tilakar Maidaaaaan

potuk kūṭṭam naṭaiper̲um.
a public meeting will take place.

Maturai makāāāāāā janaṅkaḷ
Madurai's geeeeeentlemen

anaivarum varuka!
all are welcome!

Madurai of that day was a small city, maybe seventy-five thousand people, mostly single-story houses, maybe a few at two stories. Certainly nothing that would rival the massive *gopurams* (towers) of the Meenakshi Sundareswarar Temple, which would have been visible in the distance to pilgrims for at least a day or so before they arrived. No loudspeakers, of course. The brothers' *taṇḍōrā* drumming would have been heard from one end of the city to the other.

The meetings themselves would begin with someone calling out "*vantēēēē mātaram*!," a phrase introduced during the Swadeshi period.[1] They would then begin singing songs, often those penned by the poet Subramania Bharati (Chapter 4) more than a decade earlier during the Swadeshi movement itself, songs such as "Vantē mātaram" (Mother, I bow to thee), "Enr̲u taṇiyum inta sutantira tākam" (When will this thirst for freedom be quenched?), "Accamillai accamillai" (Fear not), or "Pōḻutellam" (All of time [I said this]).

The meetings were small. If two to three hundred people showed up, it was a very big meeting. No stage. The people sat in front of the speaker, some to the side. Some benches were brought from nearby stores, and on either side were Petromax lanterns, sometimes kerosene. The speakers' voices varied according to style, but they tended to speak deliberately and slowly. Mayandi Bharati used the term *gambīram* to describe almost all of them—a term applied to a king or great man, a kind of manly profundity, majesty. Their voices were marked mostly by their poetic abilities, their training and affinity to literature, or their eschewal of that for the vox populi, the common man.

Meetings lasted only about a half hour or so. They often ended with a procession and more singing. If it were a great man's birthday, such as that of Bal Gangadhar Tilak, participants in the meetings took photographs of him around the city along the Masi streets, those used by the goddess Meenakshi on her *dik vijya* (victory march) or in her wedding procession.

I had come to ask Mayandi Bharati what these meetings would have sounded like, what they looked like, how people without "mic sets" (microphones and speakers) organized themselves, and how many people could hear when they got together. I was looking for the beginnings of these things, what they looked like before they came to dominate political life in the twentieth century. He was able to channel his memories as a bright ten- to twelve-year-old boy who, inspired by these meetings, already knew what his life's work would be. And what was striking to me here is that a paradigm first set out in the Swadeshi movement was fully formed by the late 1920s—and looked very similar to what we see described in 1907 and 1908.

Among the most prominent aspects of the sensorium in twentieth-century Indian cities has been the sound of oratory broadcast from loudspeakers. During the weeks and months leading up to elections, the voice of the politician would ride the winds along with cinema and devotional tunes. It has struck many, in fact, that one of the chief indexes of "public space" in India has been the sound of the loudspeaker—though voice amplification would not be widespread until the 1950s and later. Such a thought is pleasing, that the voice would index a public, for it was the voice that first spoke into being the community of strangers that understood itself to be related in a queer way (Warner 2002).

In the Madras Presidency, orators and poets first articulated this new, queer social imaginary in a way that we understand it today, as a modern social imaginary. At least, the orators and poets were the ones who articulated and ritually instantiated that imaginary in moments of an odd collective effervescence that became known as public meetings.

There were other voices before them, of course: voices chanting the Vedas (in Sanskrit), voices singing *Tēvāram* or *Tivyapirabantam* (in Tamil), theatrical voices from *Harikathā* drama (in Marathi), the voice singing theatrical news in genres of public singing known as *noṇḍi cintu*. We might also mention the *bhajan*, a simple, folksy, devotional song sung "publicly," not necessarily from a temple but from a home or "public" *mandapam*. Many of Subramania Bharati's nationalist songs were written as *bhajans*, songs designed for the people. But it seems that the *bhajan* in Tamil Nadu (at least in the form we see it now) was a fairly new thing, about as new as oratory.

As shown in Part I, vernacular homiletic oratory is a relatively newer communicative-cum-ritual form, whose systematic use dates to the Swadeshi movement of the early twentieth century. Such oratory became the defining feature of a new kind of political practice associated with Swadeshi that emerged across British India in 1905 following the partition of Bengal (Sarkar 1970), and the British government had passed the Prevention of Seditious Meetings Act, 1907 by the end of that year. The act was written to counter these political practices, and its passing indexes the newness of these practices. I believe that this was the first time that political actors systematically took to vernacular oratory.[2] In the Madras Presidency, then, vernacular political oratory was a direct response to the events in Bengal and inspired, in particular, by visits to Madras by leaders such as Bipin Chandra Pal in 1907.[3]

Responses to the partition were split among the several factions of the Indian National Congress. The Moderates advocated continued Anglophone meetings as well as memorials petitioning the English government and, via the British press, the people—that is, the people in England. The Extremist or Nationalist approaches advocated a faster path to *swaraj* (literally, self-rule) via the promotion of Swadeshism (that is, national independence), boycott of foreign goods, and universal literacy through the establishment of national (*swadeshi*) education and such things as reading rooms devoted to nationalist literature and training. For the first time in India, this latter—and younger—group of political actors was systematically taking to public spaces and speaking to larger and larger crowds in vernacular languages such as Bengali, Marathi, Telugu, and Tamil.

The ideological differences between the so-called Moderates and the Extremists were articulated through entirely different communicative forms—staid hall meetings of elites, on the one hand, whose "public" was actually the rulers and common people of England, half a world away. On the other hand, the Extremists gathered in meetings of "the people" numbering in the thousands in the squares, bazaars, and other open spaces of Calcutta, Bombay, and Madras. And because they knew that there were other people besides those in the cities, a few provincial Congress committees and other groups organized speaking tours of "preachers" to villages and towns of the mofussil, taking the gospel of *swaraj* to the ordinary Indian.

But to say that this was the first time that political actors systematically took to vernacular oratory is not to say that Tamil oratory itself was created at this moment. To be sure, the oratory of this period seems very well worked out—indeed, with people able to deploy already extant oratorical forms that had been developed in Tamil, Telugu, Kannada, and other vernacular languages as modes of preaching in Christian (churches), and later Saivite, contexts (*Saiva sabaikaḷ*, starting in the 1880s), as discussed in Chapters 1 and 2, respectively. These forms were probably also borrowed from court- and mutt-based literary commentary practices among scholars; and they were, no doubt, also deployed by teachers and scholars using oratory to address classrooms and audiences in some colleges (e.g., Sanskrit College in Madras). It seems, too, that vernacular oratory was heard in some political meetings and tours in the 1880s, in particular, G. Subramania Iyer's speaking tours of 1882 (about which, more later in this chapter); the Madras Merchants Association meetings in Egmore of which Iyothee Thass writes; and within caste associations, for instance, by Irattaimalai Srinivasan of the Adi Dravida Mahajana Sabha in the 1890s.[4] But if not totally new, the Swadeshi movement saw the first *systematic* use of vernacular political oratory delivered to far-flung "common" or "illiterate" people (*pāmara makkaḷ*) well beyond anything that had gone on before. These were the forerunners of kinds of practices that dominated twentieth-century Tamil Nadu politics (Bate 2009b) and through that came to be a major feature of the urban sensorium in Tamil towns: the spoken voice riding the city winds.

Imagine, for a moment, what Tamil politics would have looked like if it had remained an English-only affair. If it had remained an affair of elites and not the ever-widening expansion of political participation that marked the twentieth century, would democracy itself be possible? It is certainly possible to have a democracy with the "cosmopolitan" language of rulers. But I do not think it could have been the *deep* democracy that we see in India. While Indian citizens and political observers may criticize the Indian democratic system, it cannot be denied that Indian democracy has drawn greater and greater numbers—and categories—of people into the political system. And could there have been the creation of a (or even the) "Tamil People" without the addressing—the interpellation—of the people themselves?

Crores of people spoke Tamil, but one hundred years ago, there really was not anything called the "Tamil People" outside the imaginations of a tiny group of elites, who were very well aware that they were not reaching the people whom they wanted to reach. The people who spoke Tamil were broken into thousands of named *jātis* (castes), occupations, hereditary positions, and named geographical areas. But when Swadeshi activists spoke to the Tamil people in Tamil, a new kind of imaginary was born that would only grow stronger and stronger over the next half century.

This is the importance of what happened in the Swadeshi movement, and far more powerfully, in the Home Rule movement and Labor movement a decade later: the necessary interpellation—or the calling into being—of the common person in the Tamil (and Telugu and other) lands, an interpellation that instantiated "the people" as a category of a new modern social imaginary. Indeed, vernacular political oratory provided an *interpellative infrastructure* that enabled brand-new kinds of actors and social entities—in particular, the vernacular politician and the people, both of whom came to recognize themselves as wielding new kinds of political agency. These are not superstructural matters, mere rhetoric, or some kind of epiphenomenon to some other more real material practice. Rather, these new practices represent an infrastructure that allowed an entirely new set of practices to flourish and a new imaginary of social and political order: the Tamil people and the Tamil public sphere.

Speaking Tours

Let me go back to the newness of vernacular political speeches. As noted in the Introduction, G. Subramania Iyer had taken a speaking tour, perhaps the first of its kind, in July–August 1882 throughout the Tamil-speaking parts of the Madras Presidency (Suntharalingam 1974, 181–82). G. Subramania Iyer was a giant in the Madras Presidency, one of the founders of *The Hindu*, the founding editor of the Tamil daily *Swadesamitran*, and one of a core group of young men to form the Madras Mahajana Sabha and the Indian National Congress itself in the early 1880s (Suntharalingam 1974). He went on his 1882 tour—and another in 1888—to propagate new ideas about the formation of the Congress. With these tours, a series of "Congress Catechisms" (*Kāṅgiras Vinā Viḍai*) were developed to answer questions about self-rule and elite political organizations such as Madras Mahajana Sabha and the Congress. This question-answer catechetical style was written in a clear, simple Tamil for the widest possible audience, borrowed directly from the missionary practice discussed in Chapter 1. As a *Swadesamitran* editorial of 24 December 1887 announced, using the Christian metaphor of "irrigation" or "drawing water (from a well)" (*iṟaittal*), "little books of easily understood catechism had been printed and Congress Committeemen were coming to irrigate every nook and corner of every village and town about the Congress and independence" (Mani 2005, 22).

It is not clear that these were Tamil-only speaking tours. More likely was that most of the speeches were in English, as G. Subramania Iyer was famous as an accomplished English speaker well into the Swadeshi period.[5] R. Suntharalingam writes that "his visit to the mofussil towns excited interest among local leaders who were anxious to know his views on important public questions" (1974, 182), suggesting to me that these were meetings of English-speaking elites, not *pāmara makkaḷ* (common people), to deploy the language of the time.

These tours, numerous articles, and essays by members of the elite indicated that they knew that they were not reaching "the masses," the common man in the towns and villages, and that "public opinion" was composed of a tiny group of men who spoke to each other only in English. Unlike Jürgen Habermas ([1962] 1991), whose early writings on the bourgeois public sphere were class-blind as to just how limited and privileged such a space was, these men were quite well aware that they were speaking only to themselves.

Consider two examples from one year, 1902, that illustrate elite understandings of their own political and rhetorical impotence. The first example is another childhood memory of someone who would become a major political figure, Thiru. Vi. Kalyanasundaram (better known as Thiru. Vi. Ka.):

> The name of Surendranath Banerjee first fell on my ear in the year 1902 when I was studying in the Fourth Form. Ananda Charlu, G. Subramania Ayer, Doctor Nair, Vi. Krishnasami Ayer and others would speak now and then about the Congress. Sometimes, my friends and I would go to those meetings; we would enjoy the honey of their speech and debate as to whose English was better as we walked home. ([1944] 2003, 194)

In 1902, just prior to the Swadeshi movement, critically thinking youngsters such as Thiru. Vi. Ka. (born in 1883) were evaluating political actors based on their English oratory. The idea that there might be Tamil political oration was not even considered.

The second example is Hindu activist K. Sundarama Iyer's discussion on "Religious Education in Indian Schools," published in the *Indian Review* in 1902. His is merely one of many laments during this period regarding the need to begin interpellating the vast majority of people beyond the Anglophone classes. He writes:

> Some highly educated men . . . seek out a hundred opportunities for making a stir in the minds of the few who are akin to them in tastes, pursuits and aims. *The leaders as well as the rank and file of this cultured minority of Indian society create but very little impression on the immense population around them on whose behalf they work and for whom they speak.* As people concern themselves but little with their view or activities in regard to public needs and wishes and as in most cases their views and feelings find expression in a language unknown to the millions, they produce little or no effect on the practical life of society at large, or any section of it. Hence there is little real vitality in the movements set on foot for the formation and expression of public opinion or for the achievement of social progress and unity. (Sundarama Iyer 1902, 174; emphasis added)

This passage is striking: for in 1902 the author could make this claim about elites engaging in political agitation (in this case, Hindu elites demanding that Hinduism be taught in the schools to counter Christian biases and conversions), yet they could get no purchase on "the people." Events would not cohere as such, and they could only dream of a time when "the people" would join them. Yet by 1920 the entire field had shifted so that the political would be a far more encompassing game: in Tamil (or Telugu); to the masses (who in this passage, note, are not a part of the "public" of "public opinion"). I do not believe that this situation changed until some very brash young men began concerted efforts to speak in the vernaculars during the Swadeshi movement.

Political Meetings in the Madras Presidency

In the Madras Presidency, political meetings seemed to be taking place in three main locations under circumstances very different from each other: (1) the deltas of the Krishna and Godavari Rivers in Kistna (or Krishna), Godavari, and Guntur Districts in modern-day Andhra Pradesh; (2) Thoothukudi and Tirunelveli, in modern-day Tamil Nadu, in association with V. O. Chidambaram Pillai (V. O. C.; 1872–1936), Subramania Siva (1884–1925), and a convergence of Swadeshi capitalism and the Labor movement; and (3) Madras City, in several distinct spaces.

First, the Guntur-Kistna District Association made provisions for a number of young men to go on what appeared to be itinerating tours of small villages and towns throughout the delta regions of the Krishna and Godavari Rivers, some of the richest paddy production areas in the Madras Presidency. Again, the model appeared borrowed from missionary activities, a likeness not lost on authorities who referred to them as "preachers." Among these were three men who would become quite prominent in coming decades, especially once formal vernacular politics was firmly established by 1918: G. Harisarvathama Rao, Bodi Narayana Rao, and A. Narayana Rao. They were, almost to a man, rusticated students from the *vantē mātaram* incidents at Rajamundry College in 1907, where many students were suspended for wearing "Vande Mataram" badges and for crying out "*vantē mātaram*" during the half-yearly examinations. Their activity was so startling to the officials at Fort St. George that the Criminal Investigation Department (CID) sent out at least two special sub-inspectors on spying tours of the deltas to assess the impact of these young men. Their

FIGURE 3. V. O. Chidambaram Pillai (V. O. C.)

reports provide a fascinating quasi-ethnographic account of the villages and towns in the deltas.

Second, for a period of approximately forty days in February and March 1908, two men—V. O. Chidambaram Pillai and a mysterious itinerant preacher and *sanyasi*, Subramania Siva—set the town of Thoothukudi in southern Tamil Nadu alight in oratorical incandescence, ending with their arrest, riots, the burning of the magistrate's office in Tirunelveli, and four dead by police shootings. This was a very strange story, especially when we think how short a time it was and how spectacular the results. Consider that their lectures drew several thousand men, mostly laborers in local mills, to almost daily meetings at the south beach, in crowds that police estimated between one thousand and five thousand people. These lectures resulted in the first systematic labor movement in Tamil Nadu (Sivasubramanian 1986). But what I find truly stunning about these meetings is that in less than forty days, from almost no movement whatsoever, the two men, via sheer oratorical charisma, managed to move the workers—the *pāmara makkaḷ*—of Thoothukudi into a genuine mass political force that even involved the Madras Presidency's first major work stoppage at the Coral Mills. This movement to tie a freedom struggle to the rights and welfare of working men, women, and children foreshadows the successful production of a stable vernacular political scene in Tamil Nadu in 1917–18 with the labor activism of P. Varadarajulu Naidu and Thiru. Vi. Kalyanasundaram.

Third, in Madras City the meetings took place mostly in three places: the south beach of the Marina, opposite Presidency College in Triplicane; the Esplanade, in a *maidan* just opposite Pachaiyappa's College in Georgetown; and the Moore Market, just behind Central Station.

The Marina Beach meetings, headed by the young nationalist poet and newspaperman C. Subramania Bharati, mostly involved students and *vakil*s (lawyers), the educated classes of Indians to which the British had become accustomed as their most articulate challengers. Crowds of similar, though somewhat more complex, composition gathered in a *maidan* opposite Pachaiyappa's College in Georgetown. It is, of course, no accident that these spaces were opposite colleges and set amid two of the most densely populated—really urban—areas of Madras (most of which was fairly suburban). The Marina meetings established a space on the south beach that would become the most significant site of mass meetings throughout the Madras Presidency, in both the Indian Independence and Dravidian movements.[6]

The Moore Market meetings, however, featured Telugu speeches by an enigmatic young man named Ethiraj Surendranath Arya, who addressed not only students but what police reports described as "coolies and labourers," an entirely different class of political actor to which the British authorities were accustomed. We know that Ethiraj delivered some fifty speeches from April 1907, when the police first noticed him, to July 1908, when he was arrested. It is significant that the police first noticed him speaking in Perambur, an area with a great many cotton mills, factories, and an important railway workshop, where ten years later the Labor movement in Madras would take root and flourish. Unlike the Marina Beach meetings of more forward, or elite (caste) communities, the Moore Market has been largely forgotten as a major political space. It was demolished after a fire in 1985 and became the site for a commuter rail station terminus next to Central Station.

These meetings across Madras were not those of the Mylapore or Egmore cliques, the established groups of lawyers, government officials, and other professionals who for several generations made up the leadership of the Madras Presidency Congressmen in the well-established Madras Mahajana Sabha. These were a new generation of leaders who came to call themselves, in telling contrast, the Chennai Jana Sangam (Chennai People's Society) (Kesavan 1991, 75–96).

And the meetings were huge—both police and newspaper reports regularly estimate crowds in the thousands (more on these meetings, and their acoustics, discussed later). The British journalist Henry W. Nevinson, for example, writes in a famous passage in *The New Spirit in India* about the "four or five thousand" gathered around a lit stage on the beach (1908, 125), probably describing the February meetings of 1907, perhaps February 27, in which Bharati first sang "Vantē mātaram." Similarly, police estimates of these crowds concur that they ranged as high as eight thousand people for one of the Bipin Chandra Pal meetings and regularly into the low thousands.[7]

There were some other speakers, here and there—notably Krishnaswami Sarma (also known as Krishna Aiyar), a Tamil Swadeshi lecturer paid by the National Fund (a Swadeshi organization). He is the only speaker I can find who was a paid Swadeshi preacher on the model of the delta speakers in Andhra. There was also some systematic preaching going on in the Cauvery delta of Thanjavur District, though very little in Madurai. (There is, however, a wonderful fragment from a CID report that indicates that "a Vellala woman, aged about 40, gave a swadeshi lecture in front of the new mandabam";[8] see Bate [2009b]. This was at least nine years prior to the tentative beginnings of women's participation in formal politics and the first time that the official record indicates that a woman—any woman—gave a lecture in a political meeting.[9] We know nothing else about her, though.[10])

But the movement itself was very short, perhaps about eighteen months to two years. These young men were an upstart presence in the Madras Presidency and—at least from the points of view of both the officers in Fort St. George and the vernacular newspapers—dominated common discourse and imaginations in 1907 and 1908 until they were all either arrested or fled into exile.

After the riots, V. O. Chidambaram Pillai and Subramania Siva, the Thoothukudi speakers, were sentenced to rigorous imprisonment (i.e., hard labor)—at first for life, though later commuted to six years. Subramania Bharati fled into exile in Pondicherry, where he would remain for more than a decade. Many were hauled in front of magistrates and humiliated into signing apologies. To the shock of the Presidency, even G. Subramania Iyer was arrested briefly. By the end of 1908, British prosecution of the Swadeshi speakers was so total that by April 1909, J. T. W. Filson, author of the CID's "History Sheet" on Ethiraj Surendranath Arya, could boast that "since his conviction, public speaking in Madras has ceased, and the Chennai Jana Sangam has ceased to show any outward signs of activity."[11]

In contrast to Bengal, where the movement was far larger, far more broad based, and far more willing to take matters to another level in revolutionary terrorism, the movement in the Madras Presidency came to a standstill very quickly with only less than a dozen prosecutions. Despite its opposition to Moderate and established elite politics, however, Swadeshism across the Madras Presidency was almost exclusively an upper-caste Hindu movement (predominated by Brahmins), with some Christian, and virtually no Muslim, participation. It is not an accident, for instance, that it was most prominently marked in the deltas, in wet-rice agricultural areas with disproportionate Brahmin landownership. The oratory that bloomed in this period would not be heard again at the same volume for nearly a decade, until 1917, during the Home Rule movement, the formation of the Madras Presidency Association, and the linking of the formally "political" concerns of the educated elite to the concerns of ordinary people—mostly in the Labor movement—in the vernacular speeches of P. Varadarajulu Naidu, Thiru. Vi. Kalyanasundaram, and the return of Subramania Siva and V. O. Chidambaram Pillai, Harisarvathama Rao, Krishnaswami Sarma, and other luminaries of the Swadeshi movement. But in 1908, it was over, probably because they had not managed to link their politics to the people they thought to mobilize through their oratory. The nation, at this time perhaps, was too abstract.

Uncontrollability of the Vernacular

What provoked the British was something brand-new in the world, something they could not control or, perhaps more important, comprehend. And they knew it. Up until that time, most of those who had engaged in formal politics (*arasiyal enkiṟa kaḷam*) had been members of the educated elite (mostly Brahmin—Iyengar and Iyar), hailing from families boasting generations of service to, and critical engagement with, the British government. "Politics" (*la politique*, in Paul Ricoeur's terms) had been conducted in English from the first glimmers of respectable political engagement in the Madras Native Association in the 1850s to the forerunner of the Congress itself, the Madras Mahajana Sabha in the 1880s.

English oratory, thus, was largely controllable because the social fields in which it was delivered were fairly small and circumscribed. The educated elite who orated did so in hall meetings, largely at Pachaiyappa's Hall or Victoria Public Hall in Madras, or places such as Victoria Edward Hall in Madurai, and the social groups were also limited to the elites themselves. They also had a lot to lose—many of them had government jobs, or at least standing among the ruling British, which would be jeopardized by open antagonism toward the authorities.

More than this, though, for some thirty years, formally since at least 1874 but actually from a little earlier, the authorities could monitor "native public opinion"—even vernacular public opinion—via the agency of the Native Newspaper Reports. Newspapers, once printed, stayed put. They were knowable by and vulnerable to authority. They could be stilled, translated, examined. Texts could be extracted and their authors confronted. Presses could be threatened with forfeiture of monetary security, the withdrawal of license, or even seizure of the press itself should their proprietors exceed the bounds of propriety set up by the British authorities, crossing the line beyond "reasonable" comment and criticism into the realm of sedition. And, of course, the proprietors had not only money to lose but also their ability to engage in the sociopolitical world of the ruling race, a privilege they might jeopardize with too harsh criticism in print.

By contrast, the new oratory was very, very difficult to monitor, and it took some time before colonial authorities were aware of it happening (Bate 2012b). Printed material did not appear to provoke the authorities' concern nearly as much as speaking did, primarily due to its fleeting nature, its impermanence, its in situ vernacularity. Public speeches, unlike newspapers, were ephemeral and difficult to pin down.[12]

A letter of 25 June 1907 from Sir Harold Stuart, secretary to the Government of India, to his provincial counterparts gives a sense of the newness of these practices, at least from the point of view of the government:

> I am directed to draw your attention to the efforts which are being made to extend political agitation to the masses by means of lectures and speeches and the danger that this method of disseminating seditious sentiments among illiterate villagers will be largely developed in the near future. The Government of India find that there is an initial difficulty in the way of local Governments in dealing with this phase of the agitators campaign due to the fact that, although the itinerant politician not infrequently preaches open sedition, it is often impossible, in the absence of any report made at the time, to prove to the satisfaction of a court of law the exact words used, and he can not, therefore, be prosecuted with a reasonable prospect of success.[13]

As far as I can tell, it was as late as mid-1907 that officers were coming to understand that these new meetings were occurring, and they began to scramble to figure out new modes of surveillance and recording, as well as new standards of evidence, by which prosecutions might be instituted against any violators of law. A great deal of correspondence begins just before Bipin Chandra Pal's famous set of speeches on the south beach in Madras in the first two weeks of May 1907. The first police report of Ethiraj Surendranath Arya's Telugu speeches, for instance, was in Perambur on 14 April 1907;[14] his first Moore Market speech was recorded only on 26 August (but he may have been speaking there earlier prior to notice). We see speeches on Marina Beach reported in newspapers as early as February 1907 (Viswanathan 1998, vol. 2), but very few earlier than that. The exceptions are V. O. Chidambaram Pillai's subscription speeches in Shiyali and Madurai shortly after the formation of the Swadeshi Steam Navigation Company in April 1906, but we are not sure if those were in English or Tamil. V. O. Chidambaram Pillai is noted as "speaking in Tamil" in meetings on the beach in Madras in March 1907.[15] And no doubt he spoke in Tamil in his subscription drives in Madurai in 1906 when he spoke at the Jhansi Rani *pūṅgā* (park) or the *anti kaḍai poṭṭal*, today's Meenakshi Park, just between the Puthu Mandapam and the Central Market (probably the same place where the Vellala woman spoke).

But the unknowable of these speeches, I believe, was a key reason why the police came down so hard on the speakers. Consider an example from Kistna from 1907. One district sub-inspector of the Special Branch (for intelligence), F. B. M. Cardozo, wrote on 25 June about reports of oratory and the menace of schoolchildren shouting "*vantē mātaram*" in the deltas. Cardozo's frustration is very close to the surface in this letter:

> I am sorry I could not trace those school boys. There is no doubt that some organization exists for every school town or village has the cry vande mataram. I believe that the school masters are all in league: or at all events connive at the teaching of the cry. What can one do in the matter? If only Govt. would issue some definite order in plain language and say that students found stumping the country would be expelled from all Government schools—anything definite like that—we could do something, but at present the boys have evidently been taught that we can do nothing to them; they are as cheeky as they possibly can be.[16]

The frustrated tone moves into paranoia in Cardozo's next fragment: "Some inspectors do not report properly and leave me in the dark as to what is going on around me."[17]

The extreme violence that this movement was met with from the police was based on the epistemological darkness that is clearly at the heart of this note. The uncertainty not only forced the speakers into jail or into exile in Pondicherry. It also spurred new modes of knowing and new kinds of police procedures, such as the strange ethnography in the deltas and police openly taking notes in public meetings. Perhaps the most fateful of these was the development of Tamil (and Telugu) shorthand (see Bate 2012b). The letter from the secretary to the Government of India quoted earlier provoked officials in Fort St. George to call for shorthand reporters, only to find that there was virtually no systematic vernacular shorthand of Indian languages available, with the exception of two recent attempts by missionaries for the purpose of transcribing vernacular sermons—one using a method devised for French, the other for German. Reports reproduced in both government offices indicate further that there were simply no experts in the field at all in the Madras Presidency for either Tamil or Telugu. Given indigenous textual practices, it had never been necessary to develop.

The notion of how the technical problems of shorthand and Swadeshi politics come together is writ large in a letter by Registrar of Books V. Krishnamachari, who developed and proposed a new system to the government. In August 1907 he writes that while he was preparing his "principles of phonography," as "a loyal son of His Majesty the King Emperor," he realized that shorthand would be necessary to the police:

> In my humble opinion some such system of shorthand is of very great importance in the conditions now obtaining in India. I have purposely not published this system in a book form and before doing so I think it my bounded duty to inform Government of this, so that in case they see fit, they may utilize the art for their purposes. With this object I am keeping the matter strictly confidential.[18]

Shorthand here is tied in with "loyalty," "the conditions now obtaining in India," "bounded duty" to His Majesty, and secrecy. The development of shorthand, like fingerprints and other modern techniques of knowing, was very much a part of the penetration of an epistemological space that went hand in hand with the colonization of the land and people themselves.

In the process, both oratory and shorthand shared a similar idea of how language works: both techniques stripped language down to its denotational function, the relationship between words and concepts, the signifier and signified, and stripped individuals down to their words as threatening or benign, loyal or seditious. Oddly enough, however, officials also appeared to have an intuition of how codes themselves, rather than their denotationality, were critical in their political meaningfulness. Thus, a vernacular newspaper article was not only easier to monitor, but it also presupposed and entailed a very different kind of interaction—and political import—than a vernacular public meeting, whose denotations and politics were far murkier and potentially far more dangerous.[19]

Politics in the Bazaar

But apart from official darkness and uncertainty, from the point of view of Tamil practices, even more profound was the transgression of the "proper" places and social bounds in which politics otherwise operated in Madras. Though the new orators hailed from prominent—or at least educated—families in the mofussil, they were not a part of established Madras society. They transgressed the linguistic-cum-sociocultural boundaries of respectable politics by speaking to lower-class, illiterate, and status-less audiences in open-air meetings and in the vernacular. Neither the orators, their audiences, nor the media were of the requisite status to engage in "politics" (*la politique*).

The meetings were met by contempt by the authorities and Madras Mahajana Sabha alike.[20] Indeed, the low status of activist lecturers in the Swadeshi movement was a frequent target of derision. Often, the activists were students or student-aged: no titles, no honors, no record of engagement with the government or Congress.[21] They were upstarts who, from the perspective of both official India and established Indian society, did not understand how politics was conducted, whom one needed to know, to whom one needed to speak. And the audiences of the meetings that they conducted were composed of very young people: students in the case of Subramania Bharati's meetings on Marina Beach; or "coolies, farmers, and labourers" in the case of meetings in the bazaars of provincial towns such as Madurai or in the villages of the Andhra deltas, which were stumped by young "Swadeshi preachers" paid by the Krishna District Association.

The places they spoke, too, beaches and bazaars, were indexes of their lack of status. In contrast to proper gentlemen of cities and towns, who spoke a highly cultivated English in named halls, the Swadeshi speakers spoke in bazaars to illiterate petty vegetable retailers, "coolies and labourers." In the case of Madurai, they spoke at a place called the *anti kaḍai poṭṭal*. This is what they meant by "in front of the temple," on the east side, just between the Puthu Mandapam and the Central Market (which was, up to 1906, the town's jail). According to a 1948 report in *Maturai Jillā Tiyākikaḷ Malar*, this was the space where V. O. Chidambaram Pillai came to collect subscriptions for the Swadeshi Steam Navigation Company in 1906.[22]

A hall was a controlled space, socially, where people of a certain class could gather and discuss, in English, the important matters of the day. A bazaar, by contrast, was the ultimate space of mixing, of discourse and commerce between people who were very, very different from each other (Chakrabarty 1991; Kaviraj 1992). The bazaars and beaches were probably the closest thing to a public space in colonial India, public in the sense of "free and open to all without prejudice" (although some, such as Dalits, were excluded, no doubt). And such places were the first sites of vernacular public oratory, first in Protestant sermons, later in political oratory. And that "publicness" was a part of its vulgarity, another index of the low status of those who would speak there.[23]

As the letter penned by the secretary to the Government of India discussed earlier indicated, what was particularly unprecedented and highly unnerving was how such speeches crossed lines of caste and class and, thus, how new ideas and attitudes toward government previously contained within the upper, educated classes (via newspapers and English-medium public meetings) might possibly move into the general population of farmers, laborers, and "coolies," that is, into the masses. *Vantē mātaram* had also appeared to cross social categories and ages. As an unnamed officer reported,

> The intention to annoy Europeans has permeated into the lower classes everywhere. The other day riding on the beach some two miles south of Adyar river in the early morning half a dozen little naked fisher boys aged five or six shouted Bande Mataram at us as we trotted past them on the sand.[24]

Though motivated by other interests than the preservation of the Raj, our correspondents from Krishna District, Ramaswamy and Krishneyya, perhaps put it most succinctly:

> Not satisfied with the agitation carried on in the town these Politicions [*sic*] of the New School—whose chief end and aim is to set up Swaraj on the grave of British Government—have commenced overtaking the Rural parts with the flood of seditious eloquence with a view to infusing a rebellious spirit into the minds of the illiterate and ignorant rustics, by holding so-called Swadeshi meetings in almost all big villages. . . . It is absolutely unimaginable the effects and consequences that would result to the coun-

> try, if these ignorant ryots numbering several thousands should take into their heads to revolt against authority and assert to establish "Swaraj."[25]

What they termed "the demon of Bande Mataram" and the unknowable of this "flood of seditious eloquence" were linked, and they served as the primary motivation for the police to come down hard on the speakers (see Chapter 5 for more discussion). "Demon" is a fine and telling index of their anxiety—a supernatural being, a spirit that can be glimpsed only from the corner of one's eye and never controlled. Both "*vantē mātaram*" shouted at a passing carriage by a nameless schoolboy from a crowd and the vernacular orator whose words are fleeting, unknowable, and dangerous shared this same demonic spectrality.

The authorities were provoked into new modes of knowing to fill an epistemological gap. Light had to be thrown on the darkness of an impenetrable mob, of crowds of *ryot*s (farmers) hearing the speeches of Swadeshi preachers somewhere in the interior, or even the frustration aroused by a naked little boy.[26]

In these contexts, it was the English language that was the unmarked form of political communicative action. The use of the vernacular, Tamil and Telugu, in open spaces in Madras constituted an entirely new public that would only expand to become the Tamil people themselves. This would be a demos constituted by increasingly inclusive categories of people, men and women, Brahmin and non-Brahmin, non-Brahmin elites and what we call today Other Backward Classes (or OBCs), and most recently, Dalits and others within the most subaltern groups. It is only when people standing in marked categories begin to move into and co-constitute the "public" (women, subaltern classes of one sort or another) that one can see the markedness of the previously unmarked categories of people.[27] And it is in these meetings—though still largely composed of educated people, audiences and speakers alike—that some of the most significant moves toward the interpellation of a generalized public, well beyond elite or even literate classes of people, begin.

Sensorium of "Sedition"

I want to end my discussion where I began, with the feel of these events, the sensorium. There is very little secondary writing on them from either the police (who focused on the denotation of the speeches in order to provide "texts" that could be extracted to prove sedition) or in memoirs by people who saw them. In fact, there are only a handful of the latter, Thiru. Vi. Ka's ([1944] 2003) *Vāḻkkai Kuṟippukaḷ* being the best known.[28] His descriptions of events are far more fulsome for the politics that begins in 1917–18, however, as he was still a young man during the Swadeshi movement. But he did attend some meetings, in particular, those of Bipin Chandra Pal in 1907. As he put it, "an ocean of water on one side, an ocean of humanity on the other (*nērkaḍal oru pakkam; janakkaḍal innoru pakkam*; 195).

Another exception to this is a vivid description offered by Henry W. Nevinson, a British journalist and traveler who published an account of the Swadeshi movement from Bengal to Madras and Bombay, quoted earlier in the chapter on the size of the meetings (1908, 125–33). Nevinson offers an account of a Swadeshi meeting on the Madras Marina, 23 November 1907, in celebration of the release of Ajit Singh and Lajpat Rai from custody. He mentions that the meeting began in the evening—"the sky was full of the deep and ominous colours of an Indian sunset in the rains" (125)—and ended a few hours later with "the late moon" risen high "in the clouds and stars" (132). Earlier, he writes that

> on the broad, dry sand, between the esplanade and the surf, a vast circle of people was gathered round a little platform and chair. They were seated by hundreds on the sand—between four and five thousand of them altogether—and round the outer edge of the seated circle hundreds more were standing upright, like the rim of a flat plate. (125)

I find this description remarkable, if also somewhat difficult to imagine how a crowd of five thousand people, no matter how they were organized, could hear what was said in as an acoustically challenged space as an open beach. I have seen small circles of fishermen—perhaps as many as fifty—listening to sermons and political orations just to the south of the space where these meetings took place. But a crowd of five thousand is another matter.

In this as in many other speeches described, the cadence was said to be slow and steady. Nevinson describes "a little boy with head half shaven and a long tuft of black hair at the back" standing on the platform, singing "Vantē mātaram" "amid complete silence . . . in his native Tamil": "in this boy's singing the words were fairly distinct, and the repeated cadence gave a certain solemnity" (1908, 127).

Clearly, though speaking—the core ritual act—was what drew people to the beach, there were other elements of the meeting drawn from other ritual and phenomenological realms. In particular, the use of song and procession was central to all of the events described by police and diarists. Nevinson's account included such a description:

> Through the middle of the crowd came a line of white-robed students carrying a yellow banner with a strange device. "Bande Mataram! Bande Mataram! Hail to the Motherland! We bow before our mother!" rose the familiar cry from the thousands seated there. But there was no wild gesticulation, no frantic excess, such as we might imagine in a fanatical East. A Trafalgar Square crowd is more demonstrative and unrestrained. Nor was a single soldier or policeman visible, though the occasion had been publicly announced as a meeting of the Extremists. In the audience I was the only European present. (1908, 126–27)

Of the half-shaven little boy's "Vantē mātaram," Nevinson described the music as "that queer Eastern kind, nasal, quavering, full of turns and twists, such as one may hear from the Adriatic to Burma, and very likely beyond" (127). This made it seem to him to be somehow unfitting for a political anthem:

> It is obviously too tender for a stirring "Marseillaise." There is not enough march and thunder either in words or tune to enflame the soul of trampling hosts. The thunder comes in the cry of "Bande Mataram!" But the tenderness, the devoted love of country, and the adoration of motherhood are all characteristic of the Indian mind. (128–29)

Nevinson then turns to describing "the chairman" (perhaps G. Subramania Iyer?) who rose to speak (in English). Nevinson's description is also singular and rare insofar as he makes another key description of the appearance of the speakers, the stage, and some of the crowd's actions.

> The Chairman rose, and the darkening air glimmered with the petals of flowers thrown in handfuls, as the custom is. Round his neck heavy garlands were hung, pink and white, to match the lesser garlands which surrounded the photographs of the two national heroes on the table. He spoke in English, like all the subsequent speakers till the last. One felt at

> once how great a contribution to Indian unity the English rule makes in the gift of a common language which all educated men can understand, while even in Madras alone four distinct native languages are spoken. He summarized the history of the last year of suspicion, repression, deportation, imprisonment, flogging of boys and students for political causes, and the Seditious Meetings Act. It was all done without passion or exaggeration, and he ended with a simple resolution calling on the Government to repeal the deportation statute as contrary to the rights which England had secured for herself under the *Habeas Corpus*. (130–31)

This resolution was supported by the next four speakers. Nevinson describes again their "quiet reasonableness" and lack of passion in the speeches, the way that the crowd held onto every word,

> and all spoke with the same quiet reasonableness, so different from our conception of the Oriental mind. But for clapping of hands and occasional shouts of "Bande Mataram!" or "Jai!" . . . , the immense crowd remained equally calm. There was no frenzy, no disorder, no excitement, beyond intense interest and desire to leave no word unheard. If a speaker was just a shade too emotional the crowd laughed a little scornfully, just as an English crowd does. . . . The speaking was average straight-forward stuff, free from flowers, and even free from quotations, which are the besetting tendency of many Indian minds. Indeed, I remember only one quotation—just a hint at a parody on Mark Antony's speech, with John Morley and the Liberal Government as the honourable men. (131–32)

"Only Anglo-Indians," Nevinson concludes, "could have called the speeches seditious," for "though this was avowedly a meeting of Extremists, the claim in the speeches was for the simple human rights that other people enjoy—the right to a voice in their own affairs, and in the spending of their own money" (132).

Conclusion: Interpellative Infrastructure and the Return of the Event

Vernacular politics begins in earnest around 1918–19. It was during these years that all the elements of twentieth-century Tamil politics came together for the first time: human rights, women's rights, labor rights, even caste reservations. The only thing missing was Communism per se, which only begins to be articulated outside the idiom of "Bolshevism" by M. Singaravelu in 1923. Major historians (e.g., Washbrook and Baker 1975) have already noted that the explosion of politics in 1919 was based on the formation of elite factions with horizontal roots in the mofussil that were able to respond to a series of events (e.g., Jallianwalla Bagh, the fall of the Khalifat post–World War I, and the Non-cooperation movement of Mohandas Gandhi).

But I argue that it was not merely events and factions. The "events" had to occur within some kind of sociocultural context in which they could cohere as recognizably relevant events to large groups of people who would then mobilize as such (see Sahlins 1991). More pointedly, the events emerged at a moment in which mass politics was possible due to the infrastructure of new communicative forms. There could have been no mass politics without the presence of such interpellative networks, without the interpellative infrastructure of the mass meeting and the "public" oration—that is, a practical basis of action within which certain kinds of agency could affect certain kinds of effects, a practical basis of action in which a very specific set of agents and entities was possible, a practical basis of action in which a speaker could interpellate an audience. Without the interpellative infrastructure of the public address, the forms of politics we see emerging in 1918–19 could not have occurred.

But they would not emerge just as they pleased—the new social political forms would be modern, but they would also be Indic—and increasingly, the more time passed, as twentieth-century politics would become Tamil politics itself, the more Indian those forms became.

Let me conclude this chapter and lead to the next with one last image: in February 1907, Subramania Bharati was described as leading a procession from Triplicane to a vast meeting on the beach following the singing of *bhajan*s at the Parthasarathi Temple.[29] It was said that as he moved through the streets at the head of the crowd, he spontaneously composed new (and now presumably unknown) verses of "Vantē mātaram."[30]

Chapter 4

SUBRAMANIA BHARATI AND THE TAMIL MODERN

Newspaperman Thiru. Vi. Kalyanasundaram (Thiru. Vi. Ka.) wrote in his famous memoir of a wondrous encounter with the poet Subramania Bharati. It was 6 April 1919, the first great satyagraha in the Madras Presidency, described in the Introduction. Tens of thousands of people danced their way to the beach in groups singing devotional songs (*bhajans*). It was an extraordinary day. Thiru. Vi. Ka. wrote that the day did not dawn so much as it bloomed (*malarntatu*):

> The air hung with the fragrance of Adigal's [Mahatma's] *ātma sakti* [soul force]. As planned, Royapettai *bhajana* groups and others paraded by the Desabhaktan office. [M.] Subbaraya Kamath and I joined in the procession; by the afternoon we had reached the Guhananda Nilayan of the Sri Balasubramania Bhakta Jana Sabhai. At some point or another Subramania Bharati had joined the procession. As soon as he appeared, our ears were enslaved to his song. I asked Bharati to sing. The great Tamilian began singing the song, "*Muruga, Muruga . . .* " The song—a Tamil song, a Murugan song sweeter than honey—stirred the Murugan in the picture to start moving. It appeared as though the form in the portrait came surging out. The devotees' bodies began to sweat and shake; some fainted; some fell down; everyone was enraptured in joy. And Bharatiyar [Bharati] became the figure in the painting. I saw

> with my eyes and my heart the true unity of the song and the image in the portrait. Then, after a little while, Bharatiyar took his leave and left us. ([1944] 2003, 236–37)

I will return to the dream-like quality of Thiru. Vi. Ka.'s strange meeting later in this chapter, considering the song Subramania Bharati sang and the time in which he sang it. Before that, however, this chapter thinks about Bharati's life, his contributions to Tamil literary and political culture, and the relationships between the two.

But for the moment I suggest that the dream-like quality of this description is not merely an expression of the creative force of Thiru. Vi. Ka. This event occurred only a few months after Bharati was released from jail following an exile of nearly ten years in the French Establishment of Pondicherry. At the time of the satyagraha, Bharati was residing in southern Tamil Nadu in his wife's village and keeping a low profile; he was not engaged in active politics, nor would he do so again. His political contributions had already been written and would be sung for the remainder of the twentieth century in his songs celebrating India, Tamil Nadu, and freedom. As for 6 April 1919, scholars of Bharati believe that he was not actually in Madras. We ask later what it means, if anything, whether Bharati danced the god that day or Thiru. Vi. Ka. dreamed it. Dreamed or not, the account, I argue, says the same thing about Bharati and the Tamil modern.

Poet, songwriter, orator, and activist, C. Subramania Bharati (1882–1921) was the greatest Tamil poet of the twentieth century and remains the national poet of the Tamil people. His language was new. Yet Bharati's new language would not be spun of whole cloth. In perfect accord with his wider ideologies and passions—and as a very icon of universal interpellation—Bharati eschewed the high forms of cultural production available only to a small literary elite and embraced folk language, song, and meters.[1] In particular, he deployed and borrowed from nonspecialist forms of devotional singing, known as *bhajans*, and folk dance and song forms,

FIGURE 4. C. Subramania Bharati

such as *cintu* and *kummi*. Though he spectacularly renounced signs of his own Brahminical privilege—for instance, he sported a mustache and sat down to eat with non-Brahmins—he embraced these two forms, which were quite common within Brahmin families at the time. In this way, his language perfectly models some of the odd contradictions of and intimate connections between linguistic and political modernity: they are new but built with old forms that index cultural continuity through time; they involve signs that are transparent, intelligible to vast numbers of people, and are thus fit for universal interpellation; and they are produced by elite agents who articulate them as elements of the folk.

In this chapter, we therefore interrogate the relationship between poetic language, oratory, and the emergence of the mass political with a consideration of Bharati and a singularly *Tamil* modern. Bharati's poems and oratory embody the universalizing semeiotic introduced by Protestant missionaries with the singular aesthetics of South India—as discussed in previous chapters—to produce a culturally contingent Tamil politics. More than that, Bharati was one of the key agents of that synthesis.[2]

I focus on a set of three speeches and three songs. The first song serves as an introduction to Bharati's vision of Indian society as a force that is both new and ancient. The second song was sung during an event that involved a procession, music, and a large public meeting on Marina Beach on 9 March 1908. It was during this time that Bharati wrote some of his most famous nationalist songs in a simple Tamil set to folk meters and melodies perfect for interpellating a new political agency: the Tamil people. The third song, already mentioned, was reported to be sung eleven years after the second at a crossroads not very far from Marina Beach during a procession of fervent political actors moving toward the first great satyagraha of the Madras Presidency, 6 April 1919. By that time, Bharati had been broken of politics through exile and opium addiction; yet the enigmatic poet was sighted, perhaps dreamed, dancing in and out of events associated with the political form that he had helped establish and that had persisted into the unfolding history of the twentieth century.

Bharati's *Samutāyam* (Society)

Bharati is an uncanny figure. He is very familiar to Tamil speakers as an icon of modern Tamil nationalism and piety. But he is also very strange. By virtue of his songs, his oratory, his writing as a journalist, and his unprecedented political action, Bharati was a fulcrum of history. He stands as the archetype of the Tamil political modern and set out a framework for its unfolding in the twentieth century. In a word, he modeled what became the vernacular politician, the orator to the masses, the central figure of the ritual of the mass meeting that modeled a vision of the mass political (Bate 2009b).

Consider a piece of Bharati's verbal art that demonstrates that uncanniness; in this case, one of his last nationalist songs, "Long Live Indian Society!" (*Bārata samutāyam vāḻkavē*).

Pallavi:

Long live Indian society (*samutāyam*)!
Long live! Long live!
Long live Indian society!
Victoriously! Victoriously! Victoriously!

Anupallavi:

The association (*saṅgam*) of thirty crore [three hundred million] people
will enjoy rights common to all (*mu̲lumaikkup potu uḍaimai*)!
An unequaled society,
a new wonder to all the world (*ulakattukkoru putumai*)!

Saraṇam 1:

Will we continue a culture in which man steals food from man?
Will we henceforth live lives in which man torments man?
Will we see such a life in our lifetimes?
Will we tolerate such a life among ourselves?

(*Pallavi, Anupallavi*)

Saraṇam 2:

A great country filled with uncountable sweet gardens and vast
fields
A bountiful land filled with countless fruits, tubers, and wonderful
things
They will be without number.
They will be without number forever.

(*Pallavi, Anupallavi*)

Saraṇam 3:

We will take a new vow—and we will keep it forever:
If only one human being lives without food
We will destroy the whole world!

(*Pallavi, Anupallavi*)

Saraṇam 4:

"I live within all lives (*ellā uyirkaḷilum nānē irukkiṟēn*)," so said

Lord Krishna
India will bestow the scripture that so casts to the entire world for
all people
Yes, India will give it to the world!
Yes, yes, India will give it to the world!

(Saraṇam 1, Pallavi, Anupallavi)

Saraṇam 5:
All are one lineage, all are one kind
All are one Indian people (*Intiyā makkaḷ*)
All have one standing (*niṟai*), all have one value (*vilai*)
All are kings of this country! We
all are kings of this country! Yes,
all are kings of this country!

(Pallavi, Anupallavi)

Bharati's nationalist songs (*tēsiya gītaṅkaḷ*) were written as lyrics within a number of different genres of singing. This one appears as a *patam*, a form that cycles through a series of refrains (*pallavi*), secondary refrains (*anupallavi*), and verses (*saraṇam*), and thus the song continuously turns back on itself as it moves forward in time. Or, as Davesh Soneji puts it, the song "oscillates between past and present" (2012, 104). Such oscillation laminates the time of narration upon the narrating time, the stories told upon the telling of the stories, producing a peculiar imagination of time that has been called *itihāsa* (Guha 1998). Such an experience of history would have been appropriate within ritual contexts such as those massive public meetings on the broad sands of the Marina in Madras, where they were first sung in the high passions and new spirit of the Swadeshi movement.

Here Bharati worships Indian society (*samutāyam*) as a deity, an entity that encompasses the entirety of India itself. Like a sovereign, she is bountiful and provides for all the people; she is rich and fertile, giving and ample. She is a deity, a Mother as he wrote in some of his other nationalist songs (*tēsiya gītaṅkaḷ*) published in 1907 and 1908, especially his translation of Bankimchandra Chattopadhyay's "Vantē mātaram" (Mother, I bow to thee). We can find analogues of this kind of theme for over a thousand years in the subcontinent in the worship of Siva, Vishnu, and kings who, like gods, make water flow over the land and thus make it fertile and green. The musical form of *patam* is relatively newer, an innovation of eighteenth-century Thanjavur. But one might imagine that the song speaks of ancient themes in what had, by 1907, become a classical genre.

Although familiar, this song is also strange. In the very title of the piece, Bharati evokes the concept of *samutāyam*, a "society." Not a specific society of known individuals, however, but one that is made up of some thirty crore (three hundred million) people (*muppatu kōṭi janaṅkaḷ*). Imagine that, if you can. Since when did numbers attach themselves to populations, especially such vastly imagined populations such as three hundred million? Modern censuses had been conducted by the colonial officials in India beginning with some enthusiasm in the 1820s, exactly the same time that Europe experienced an "avalanche of printed numbers" regarding the new art of statecraft called statistics (Hacking 1982, 281–82; Cohn 1987, 233–34). But besides statisticians, and those who might one day read their reports, why should a poet in the first decades of the twentieth century sing of a population imagined numerically to a crowd gathered on Marina Beach in Madras or publish it so it could be read and sung widely? These three hundred million people form an association, a *saṅgam*, a term that also evokes an ancient lineage in Tamil—the academies or associations of scholars dating back to the first centuries of the Common Era. But such *saṅgams* were scholars and poets, grammarians, people whose names historians know. They were *saṅgams*, we might imagine, in which every member knew—or knew of—every other member.

Bharati sings of a *saṅgam* of millions of ordinary, unnamed people, an abstract *saṅgam* corresponding to an abstract society. Likewise, the members of that *saṅgam*, each unnamed and unknown individual, will have rights. The term *potu uḍaimai* means "general, unrestricted, undemarcated, or common" (*potu*) "property/possession" (*uḍaimai*). For this is a place where if only one person were to go hungry, were to be treated unjustly, then the world itself would be destroyed.[3] No, where we the people, all three hundred million of us, would rise up and destroy it. Here, in this vast, abstract social order, each person is mysteriously related to every other person; we are a part of one family, one lineage, one Indian people (*Intiyā makkaḷ*), where each one is sovereign over himself—"All are kings!"—and bears the same relationship to the larger abstract social order (*samutāyam*), association (*saṅgam*), and people (*makkaḷ*) as any other. So this vast association is one that could never physically instantiate itself in any one place; it is an association that can only (not to say merely) be imagined: an association in which each person holds rights equal to any other, has the same standing as any other, where all are related in some strange way to each other, where the suffering of one is equivalent to the destruction of the whole society—what Bharati sings is a modern social imaginary. And truly, as Bharati stresses in no uncertain terms, India, like this poem, is both a wonder (*putumai*) and a newness (*putumai*) in this world.

The presence of Krishna, of course, imbricates that newness with something old. For the incarnation of Krishna in this song and his citation of one of the key lines from the *Bhagavad Gita* as he articulates this *putumai* suggest that the ideas he articulates here are actually quite old: *ellā uyirkaḷilum nāṉē irukkiṟēṉ*, "I live within all lives."

This is not to say that singing *patam*s to Krishna, a universal being, is strange; indeed, we will later find ourselves grappling with the ubiquity of Krishna in the imaginings of modern political men throughout India during this moment (such as Bal Gangadhar Tilak and Aurobindo; see Singer 1968, 1972; Banerjee 2002; Davis 2015). What is strange, uncanny even, is that Krishna becomes an *avatāram* of India itself, representing the principle of unity that exists within all human beings—"I live within all lives"—and teaching the world that all human beings are one. All are one people.

Such universal values have been articulated before in Indian thought. Here is an ancient line from a *saṅgam* poem recognizable to everyone in Tamil-speaking worlds today: *yātum ūrē yāvarum kēḷir*, "everywhere is home, all are kin." Today, we take this phrase to be a commonplace of modern political and civil belonging. But this is the vision of a renunciate (*turavi*), someone who has given up the ties to home, family, wife, the world (*samsāram*) of the householder. His rootlessness gives him, and only him, the freedom of his impartial universality. There is a kind of particularity in this universal love. And Krishna himself, the *avatāram* of Vishnu in the *Bhagavad Gita*, represents a monism of soul, as it were, a kind of metaphysical underpinning of all reality.

It is a beautiful idea. And it is quite ancient. But it is far from the social order that most people lived within, far from the massively hierarchical complexes of caste, lineage, and status that have characterized Indian society for millennia. It is, in other words, far from the social imaginary that is articulated in this song, a modern social imaginary of an abstract social order of three hundred million theoretically equal human beings, a modern social imaginary that is infused with the idea of Krishna.

This song was penned, it is thought, in Bharati's final years and printed a year after his death in 1921. Sung in political meetings throughout the mass political movement for Indian independence and beyond, this song offers a glimpse into Bharati's uncanny sense of things. It is clearly familiar to political moderns, those who imagine large-scale abstract social orders in which all individuals are, theoretically, the same. It is also strange. For the songs index a very peculiar social milieu and activities for the political modern, for instance, singing praise to God. And the image of God and society is as a charioteer/philosopher offering counsel to a warrior; a cowherd playing a flute; a mischievous baby stealing butter; a young man sitting in a tree teasing girls; a lover who seems always to break his word about meeting us where and when he promised. Bharati's Krishna/*samutāyam* represents a crystalline form of the object I have been seeking to uncover in this book, a peculiarly modern image of social and political order—the abstract society and the equally abstract individual—in the form of a being who can utter an instantly familiar phrase from Indian thought and literature as an element of a modern social imaginary.

The New Spirit

A profoundly precocious child, Subramaniam was given the honorific due a poet, "Bharati," by a council of learned men under the raja at Ettiyapuram in 1897 on the occasion of his marriage.[4] After some time as a tutor for the raja, he worked for a short while at the Sethupathi School in Madurai in 1904, where he was discovered by the leading journalist and Congressman of the day, G. Subramania Iyer, who brought him to Madras, where he worked for the nationalist daily, *Swadesamitran*. Within a year or so, Bharati would begin his own paper, *India*, which took a more aggressively nationalist position. Bharati came to political consciousness as a young nationalist at the outset of the Swadeshi movement discussed in Chapter 3, a period described at the time as the "New Spirit of India" (Nevinson 1908). Many of the key features of the Indian Independence movement were born during this short-lived movement, including economic Swadeshism, which involved the boycott of foreign (*paradeshi*) goods and the promotion of Indian-made (or *swadeshi*) goods, in particular, clothing; and national education, or schools and colleges run not by the government but by nationalist Indians.

Perhaps the most profound invention of the period was the use of vernacular languages and the eschewal of foreign ones in political meetings, as we saw in the previous chapter. For nearly the first time in the Madras Presidency, political leaders systematically addressed non-elite audiences in vernacular—or *swadeshi*—languages, consciously interpellating a new Indian political public. Economic and educational Swadeshism, in other words, would be paralleled by a linguistic Swadeshism. When G. Subramania Iyer began to speak in Tamil during one of the meetings discussed in this chapter, he was interrupted by the audience, imploring him to speak in English, as he was known as one of the most eloquent English orators of India at the time. He replied with the following admonition (according to police notes; punctuation as indicated in the report):

> Gentlemen. The subject which I am going to deal with is Swadeshi and Swaraj. As the subject relates to these, it will not be consistent with our principles to lecture in a foreign tongue. Since most of the audience are not conversant with English and all of you know Tamil. I request you all to listen to it carefully.[5]

At least from the point of view of the activists, if not from the point of view of common folk, there was a clear linkage between linguistic and political modernity.

Also critical to recall from Chapter 3 is that the Swadeshi movement in Madras—if not in Bengal—was mostly led by very young members of upper castes, although not by established political elites. From the perspectives of both official India and established Indian society, these relatively low-status upstarts did not understand how politics was conducted, who one needed to know, to whom one needed to speak. The meetings that they conducted were themselves composed of young people, students in Bharati's meetings on Marina Beach, or "coolies, farmers, and labourers" in the meetings in the bazaars of provincial towns such as Madurai or in the villages of the Andhra deltas. And where they spoke, too, indexed their lack of status. While proper gentlemen of cities and towns spoke a highly cultivated English in halls (such as Pachaiyappa's Hall or Victoria Public Hall in Madras or Victoria Edward Hall in Madurai) that were socially controlled spaces of ritual and social coherence where people of a certain class could gather and discuss the important matters of the day, a bazaar or beach was a space of mixing, of discourse and commerce between people who were very different from each other. Such places were the first sites of vernacular public oratory (Chapters 1, 3). And that "publicness" was a part of their vulgarity, another index of the low status of those who spoke there.

On the Beach

For a little over a year in 1907–8, there was a vast expansion of meetings and processions. Here, the "New Spirit of India" was in full efflorescence in Madras. Bharati and the Telugu speaker Ethiraj Surendranath Arya became the two chief speakers during this time in Madras City—Bharati on Marina Beach and Arya in an open area behind Moore Market in north Madras, described in Chapter 3. Bharati's speeches, at least, were accompanied by nationalist songs and poems, many of which would become standard in the coming decades of the Independence movement: "Bharati's poems and speeches were immediately translated and sent out to the Chief Secretary of the Madras government. The opposition to imperialism in these poems and speeches attracted the attentions of the Government officials" (Kesavan 1991, 79).

The processions and meeting of 9 March 1908 were held to celebrate the release from jail of Bipin Chandra Pal, a prominent Bengali Swadeshi activist. The meeting was said to have about eight thousand people in attendance,[6] a crowd made larger, claimed the acting secretary to the Government of Madras, due to a football match by Presidency College students on the beach that day.[7] There were multiple processions, at least one with music, from "all over to the city" to the foreshore of the south beach, that part of the Marina opposite

Presidency College. The Chennai Jana Sangam had petitioned Commissioner of Police H. F. Wilkieson to process with music, but he refused to do so "for obvious reasons."[8]

An index of how strange the vernacular political oration was at this time is that we have very few transcriptions of Bharati's speeches; those we have were mostly done by police in English translation (Bate 2012b). The sub-inspector who made the translation/transcription on 9 March 1908 noted that Bharati "spoke in Tamil," and his transcript indicates various parenthetical clarifications and ironic bracketing of terms with quotation marks:

> A public meeting was held on the foreshore of the South Beach, Triplicane on the evening of 9 March 1908 in connection with the release of Bipin Chandra Pal. One of the speakers Subramani Barati spoke in Tamil as follows,
>
> When will this thirst for freedom be quenched. When will these fetters of ignorance be removed. Oh Lord that caused the great war of Mahabaratha. Are Plague and Famine intended only to your devoted. Are strangers to prosper while we suffer. Oh Lord of the universe and protector of the good. Is it not your principle to shield the innocent and the suffering! Have you forgotten about the patient suffering?
>
> He further said,
>
> Gentlemen, you have daily seen and heard of people being sent to jail and released therefrom but you never troubled yourself about them. But why have you all assembled here today? You have not come here for honoring a Maharaja or another with grand titles. But it is to celebrate the release of Bepin Chandra Pal [*sic*] today. We have been drawn together here not on account of Pal's character. But we have met here because on account of the faith we have in Swaraj (or on account of the love we have in our country) we are toiling for the welfare of our country. Pal had such views and experienced the troubles that arose from them. All of us too should suffer, according to our might for our principles of swaraj and love of our country. We are prepared to obey the laws framed by foreigners but not always. We will not submit to those laws the moment those foreigners frame

laws which are hostile to our "natural rights." In conformity with the above declaration though, the Commissioner of Police prohibited the playing of music today, since such an order was opposed to our principles, we ignored that order and conducted the procession with music playing. So we should all join and work for (or fight) for our principles of Swadeshi and Swaraj.[9]

The police report noted that the speech was "very vehement and was received with applause and approbation by the audience." Bharati then sang the song mentioned earlier, what we now know as "Enṟu taniyum inta sutantira tāgam" (When will this thirst for freedom be quenched?), a fateful song that would become standard fare during India's Independence movement.

The speech and song were echoed by the venerable G. Subramania Iyer,[10] one of the founding members of the Indian National Congress and *The Hindu* newspaper, as well as the founding editor of *Swadesamitran*. Iyer's speech began with a *longue durée* history of India, a land that was prosperous for thousands of years and had a civilization while "other nations were barbarians and were living in forests." India's wealth and education were such that other nations traveled to India to learn of them and partake of its prosperity. But India's fortunes changed, "as everything under the sun has to experience the vicissitudes of fortune." He said:

> Whenever the country was reduced to such a state, there had appeared great men or mahatmas who had risen above considerations of self and endured all sorts of trouble, reformed the country (the state) and raised it to the level of prosperity. During the reign of the Hindu Rajas, many sages or maharishis appeared and sacrificing their personal welfare worked for the good of the country. Then followed Manu and Manthatha and others who ruled for the welfare of the people. Then came Ramachandra (an incarnation of God) who put down the "Mlechas" and removed all the difficulties from the way of the people. Before the Muhammadan conquest Budha reformed the country when it was in need of reform. It was followed by Sankarachariar, Ramanujachariar and Maduachariar who by their religious discourse and preaching introduced order in to the society. When the people were afflicted with Muhammadan oppression Sivaji came to the front overcame the Muhammadans and ruled the country as Hindu Rajas of old.

He then acknowledges that India has again come to a time when it has been laid low, and he suggests that Bipin Chandra Pal is another mahatma who has been appointed by God to be "a new force" to raise up the people of India. "Moreover," he continues,

> the men who did good to the country till now were not High Court Judges or men with titles or those that drive a pair but only those that had sacrificed the pleasures of the world and had suffered privations and troubles for the way of the people.[11]

That part of Bharati's speech reproduced here models a Protestant appeal to faith, faith in the country and faith in *swaraj*, that is, faith in a generalizable principle of social and political reform. Bharati also holds up Bipin Chandra Pal as an exemplar of suffering because he was true to his faith: "Pal had such views and experienced troubles that arose from them." As a preacher extols his flock to follow the example of Christ, so, too, does Bharati exhort his audience to follow the example of Pal: "All of us too should suffer. . . . We should all join and work for (or fight) for our principles of Swadeshi and Swaraj."

But just as Pal is placed in the position of a suffering God and an exemplar of social and spiritual action, so, too, is he cast in G. Subramania Iyer's speech as an incarnation of God. Only in this speech, God is Vishnu, or to be more specific, the avatar of Vishnu who appears as a savior when mankind falls into dark times—like Krishna of the *Bhagavad Gita*. And Subramania Iyer takes it a step further by placing Pal as an avatar within a historical, linear time frame that includes lawgivers, bhakti saints, Gauthama Buddha, and the Maratha warrior Sivaji. Subramania Iyer concludes, "When we consider [Pal's] actions of the last four or five years, it can not but be said that he appears as though he was reincarnated and has inherited new force."

Both speeches, in short, are fully within the Protestant modern, the first in the rhetorical and aesthetic sense of appealing to the soul, to the sacrifices of self on behalf of faith and a larger purpose; the second as a well-structured oration that casts Hindu ethics and heterogeneous dense time into an ethic that remains constant over the *longue durée* of homogeneous historical time—sometimes called modern time, the time of nations, the time of capital (Chatterjee 2004). And, of course, the speech is universalizable—or nearly so, given the last few restrictions placed on who might be in an evening audience composed of upper-caste men on the beach. From the point of view of the speakers, these speeches were addressed to all Indians, even though, tellingly, most of the activists would not necessarily consider Dalits, Muslims, and women members of the Swadeshi public.

The Tamil Modern

But what of the Tamil modern? What makes this a *Tamil* event rather than merely an expression of a universal (read: European) modernity? No doubt the uptake of the modern form of the sermon, complete with modern themes universalizable to a general public—to a modern social imaginary (Taylor 2003)—qualifies this event as one among so many around the globe that newly interpellated "the people" as a new kind of entity, a new collectivity made up of what Sudipta Kaviraj has called "zero-degree individuals" (1990, 90), those quintessentially modern beings free from the restricting bonds of social categories such as caste, at least in theory.

But is that all? Is the Tamilness of this event reducible only to the Tamil spoken? Is Tamil, then, only a kind of linguistic icon of the idea that modernity was simply translated into new lands, a European form that carries with it European senses and imaginations? In addressing these questions, we turn to the music accompanying the procession and the song that Bharati sung that day. For it is in the musical and poetic elements of language that we discern a vernacular modernity—a *swadeshi* modernity, a Tamil modern. And here lay its power, a power to which the authorities were not insensitive.

H. F. Wilkieson, commissioner of police in Madras, was certain that these meetings represented a grave threat to the British. In a letter to J. N. Atkinson, acting chief secretary to the Government of Madras, he wrote that the "spirit of lawlessness exemplified . . . on the 9th" when speakers "openly defied the law" was not merely a one-off event but rather a "sign of the times":

> That afternoon, many bazaarmen in Triplicane closed their shops ostensibly in honour of Bipan Pal's release, but I have little doubt that it was really a sign of the times: I think it would be a good thing if we could stop the local agitators speaking in public. Though what they say may not be

> very serious still their words are understood by the ignorant mob as purely anti-British.[12]

The open violation of the law that particularly outraged Wilkieson was the playing of music during the procession after he had expressly refused to give permission for it. A High Court *vakil* (lawyer, or advocate), Tirumala Chari, BA, BL, the secretary of the Chennai Jana Sangam, had appeared before him a few days before the event to request permission to process with fireworks and music. "The Sangam," Wilkieson quipped, "is in no sense a musical society."[13] "For obvious reasons I refused to grant a license."[14] Nevertheless, and in violation of Wilkieson's refusal, some members of the procession did have music.

> On 9th March 1908 all the processions started from different parts of the city and proceeded towards the South Beach where a public meeting was convened. The processions were orderly till they reached the Victoria Hostel where music was commenced and used till they reached the South Beach. . . .
>
> After the procession met on the foreshore of the South Beach two of the speakers named Subramania Bharathy and Ethiraj Surendranath Arya in the course of their speeches said that in defiance of the Commissioner's orders they used music and that the audience should take an oath that they must be within the legal bounds of law as far as it did not interfere [unclear] natural rights but when it did so they must infringe the same and break [unclear].
>
> The musicians who played the music are liable to be [unclear] under the City Police Act. If they state before the court that they played the [unclear] their own accord without being engaged either by the organizers of the procession or by the aforesaid two speakers, it will be difficult [unclear] the persons who really abetted the commission of the [unclear] City Police Act. Unsuccessful prosecution would merely make martyrs of the [unclear] positively insignificant men.[15]

Despite Wilkieson's alarm and calls for prosecution, officers at Fort St. George, on the advice of Advocate General P. Sivaswamy Aiyar, were unable to bring

Bharati or Arya to book as they did not yet have the legal tools to prosecute these speeches. The form of the speeches was simply so new that laws had not been written to deal with them; neither did they have surveillance procedures or recording technologies (in this case, shorthand) that would enable them to prove charges of sedition under existing law—laws devised to monitor, record, and prosecute *printed* instances of sedition (Chapter 3).[16]

It is worth paying attention to the fact that Bharati and Arya vehemently objected to being denied permission to play and sing music in procession. A common theme in both their speeches that day was the insistence that a ban on singing constituted violations of their "natural rights." The deployment of the Enlightenment concept masks something singular to their attachment to the music. For it is in the music and poesy of the event that the Tamil modern inheres.[17]

The song Bharati sung, it turns out, became a famous one. Though first published in Bharati's paper, *India*, during the freedom struggle, it was sung for decades in public meetings quite regularly from at least the late 1920s.[18] It was so famous by 1944 that when the great poet Namakkal Kaviñar V. Ramalingam Pillai published his autobiography, *En Katai* (My story), he provided a long discussion of when he first heard of the song and whether the printed versions available were missing verses first sung during Swadeshi meetings in 1907–8 (Viswanathan 1998, 3:123–26).[19] Indeed, it was this song that first drew police attention to Bharati:

> Bharati first drew the attention of the police because he sang songs which imparted a striving for liberty within patriotic sermons, in meetings intended to create a passion for liberty among the illiterate people. The police faced many struggles to take action against Bharati for his sermons on liberty. (3:126)

Viswanathan writes that the poem was first printed in Bharati's *India* on 7 March 1908, just two days before it was first sung on the beach (3:121). Bharati titled it "Sri Krishna Stottiram" (Psalm to Sri Krishna). In translation, it reads:

> When will our thirst for freedom be quenched?
> When will our love for slavery die out?
> When will the chains on our mothers' wrists be broken?

When will our afflictions [*innalkaḷ*] end?
O, Lord of the Mahabharata!
O, Protector of Aryas!
Is it not by you alone that we are victorious?
Is it right that your true devotees should languish without your aid?

Should famine and disease be the fate of your devoted?
For whom else are the good things of this world?
Will you forsake those who have sought your refuge?
Will a mother cast away her own children?
Is it not yours to soothe our fears?
O, Noble Lord! Have you forsaken us?
O, Slayer of evil Rakshasas!
O, Crescent Jewel of Warriors? O, Lord of the Aryas!

Of the many things about this song that warrant analysis, two elements stand out: the key signature/scale, or *rāgam*, of the song and the discursive form in which such a song might be sung. *Rāgams* are something like keys or scales/modes in Western music and have associated with them, at least theoretically, singular sets of emotions or feelings: *rasa*. The *rāgam* in which this song was sung is *kamās*, a *rāgam* sometimes described as "tuneful" or "folksy." Many of the nationalist songs that Bharati composed were set to familiar tunes often expressly considered folksy (*nāṭṭuppuṟa meṭṭu*), at least from the point of view of twentieth-century music specialists such as his granddaughter, Lalitha Bharathi (1986). *Kamās* is often the *rāgam* of shorter, lighter tunes (*kritis*, *tukkadas*), which conclude concerts on an upbeat or happy note. The *rasa*, or feeling associated with this *rāgam*, is said to be *sringara*, or the erotic, which gives it a somewhat playful feeling. This might strike us as odd when the song, and its initial English translation for the police, reads almost like a lamentation of Job. How is this "playful" or "erotic"? And why would a psalm to Krishna be an appropriate accompaniment for a speech on Swadeshi?

These questions lead us to the second thing to be said about this piece: it is quite possible that Bharati was borrowing from another new form in early twentieth-century Madras, the *bhajan*.[20] *Bhajans* involve home-, temple-, or even street-based worship sessions that involve singing devotional—or *bhakti*—songs to personal deities, in particular the beautiful lord Krishna and his consort, Radha, set amid scenes of the old stories, the *purāṇa*s. Among the most common scenes is Krishna's teasing and forsaking the cowherds, the young women (*gopi*s) who pine for his love. Although, in practice, *bhajan*s were restricted to Brahmins, at least ideologically they cut across caste, sect, and lineage divisions among higher-caste organizations. Again, ideally, their practitioners saw themselves as engaging in a universalizing discourse, such as public meetings, that were probably a great deal more restricted than the ideology held. For instance, they were almost always male-only events, at least among the adults.

Regardless, a major theme in *bhajan*s, especially those involving Krishna, was erotic longing by Radha, or more commonly, by the *gopi*s, the cow girls, who longed for his embrace. Men singing these songs cast themselves in the role of the *gopi*s, each hoping to be Krishna's lover. In one song taken from the *Bhāgavatapurāṇa*, Krishna grants each of them her heart's desire and dances with all of them simultaneously. But Krishna is mercurial, fickle, difficult to pin down. He often fails to do what he says, to show up for the secret meeting arranged with his lover. And Bharati actually composed a cycle of songs about Kannan—as both male and female lover, Kannan *and* Kannamma—failing to meet for agreed-on trysts. Here is an excerpt, in translation, from "Kannammā en kātali" (Kannamma, my lover):

> You told me to wait there,
> On the other side of the river,
> In the southernmost corner
> of the Chenbaga garden,
> that you would come there
> with your friend in the pale moonlight.
> You lied, Kannamma! My heart is broken.
> And I see images of you everywhere I look.

In Bharati's discourse, this same feeling of longing is now cast in a nationalist idiom, clearly understood and taken up by nationalists over the course of the freedom movement and into postcolonial democratic politics. And like so many powerful poetic images, this one, too, is polysemous, refracting several possible senses at once. On the one hand, Krishna is the mercurial god who may or may not grant our boons and fulfill our longings. At the same time, while Bharati plays the role of *gopi*, of a pining girl waiting for her fickle lover, Krishna is also cast as the Leviathan, the people who could, if only they willed it so, shake off the shackles of British rule in a day—indeed, such a call to action by three hundred million people was a part of most speeches during this day, 9 March 1908, throughout the Madras Presidency. It was a democratic movement Bharati longed to lead, if only they would rise up and exert the power they had in their hands.

As it turned out, Krishna would fail him.

The Apotheosis of Subramania Bharati

On the day Bharati sang this song, events elsewhere in the Madras Presidency provoked a crackdown that would bring the Swadeshi movement to an end. In particular, Bharati's friend and colleague in the Chennai Jana Sangam, V. O. Chidambaram Pillai (V. O. C.), along with his charismatic companion Subramania Siva, violated a ban on holding a meeting to celebrate Pal's release in Thoothukudi and were arrested a few days later, as I discuss in the next chapter. This arrest sparked a riot during which a district magistrate's office was gutted and a police firing resulted in four deaths and several dozen wounded. Over the next few months, young leaders of the Swadeshi movement across the land were rounded up and charged with sedition (see Chapter 3).

The authorities even went as far as to arrest the venerable G. Subramania Iyer, a shocking turn of events that led to a general outcry among prominent citizens and his rather speedy release after signing a document promising not to print seditious sentiments in his paper. He did not have to admit that he had done so. A few of the younger men begged for leniency and forgiveness for their youthful transgressions, and elders in the communities wrote letters on their behalf promising to take responsibility for them; in some cases the charges were dismissed at the cost of the young men's humiliation. Others received the full brunt of British outrage: V. O. C. was given two life sentences while Subramania Siva was given ten years of rigorous imprisonment, sentences that were reduced to six years each, of which they served every day.

Bharati was never charged for sedition because the authorities failed to move quickly enough against his violation of the ban on music. But fearing for his freedom, he fled to French-governed Pondicherry, where he would remain in bitter exile until late 1918.

And it was indeed bitter. Despite writing many letters to newspapers and British officials, he was never certain he would not be arrested should he return to Madras. Although he continued for a year and a half to publish *India*, Bharati's exile in Pondicherry ultimately broke him of politics. It broke him in many ways. Unable to engage in steady newspaper work, he and his family were reduced to poverty. They often went hungry. He also took to opium, which, at least from his friend V. O. C's account, fundamentally transformed him. He continued to write brilliant poems, many beloved to this day.

Even though he would not engage in formal politics when he finally returned to the Madras Presidency in 1918, there were several reports of him showing up at various kinds of meetings at which he sang devotional songs. Two intelligence reports mention him at labor meetings, some of which would prove to be among the most influential in the development of the mass political in Tamil lands. For these were the meetings that expressly addressed the working man and woman—that called them to the political, "to persuade them into speech and action," as one labor leader put it (Wadia 1921; Bate 2013; see Epilogue). These were the latter-day incarnations of those meetings convened by V. O. C. and Subramania Siva on the beach of Thoothukudi during those forty days of oratorical incandescence just prior to their arrests in 1908, or the Telugu Swadeshi meetings of working men and women—"coolies"—addressed at Madras's Moore Market by Ethiraj Surendranath Arya. So while Bharati had an uncanny ability for showing up at what would become the most important political events of the day, his songs were not pointedly political like his earlier *swadesha gītaṅkaḷ* (national songs). Strangely, he appeared at political events as a nonpolitical actor.

Among the final reports of these strange apparitions is the famous memoir by Thiru. Vi. Ka., activist and editor of the nationalist papers *Desabhaktan* and *Navasakti*. This satyagraha was a political meeting par excellence, a form that would become the very archetype of Indian political action throughout the Independence movement and into postcolonial democratic politics—the essence of the Indian mass political. Reports by nationalists, opposition newspapers, and police all agreed some one hundred thousand people showed up that day. And the stages were set up on the very same spot where Bharati and his comrades gave their speeches and sang their songs eleven years earlier—on the Marina, across from Presidency College.

Bharati did not speak, of course. But he did sing. Thiru. Vi. Ka. describes *bhajan* groups singing and dancing their way to the beach—just as they had eleven years earlier to celebrate Bipin Chandra Pal's release from jail. Only on this great day, the crowds were ten to twelve times larger. Thiru. Vi. Ka. joined a group that passed his newspaper office, and they made their way toward the beach, singing and dancing along with everyone else. In the afternoon, after they passed the meeting place of a major devotional group (Sri Balasubramania Bhakta Jana Sabai) in Royapettah, a few blocks away from the beach, Thiru. Vi. Ka. noticed that "at some point or another Subramania Bharati had joined the procession": "As soon as he appeared, our ears were enslaved to his song. I asked Bharati to sing. The great Tamilian began singing the song 'Muruga, Muruga.'"

Let me break from this description, recounted in full earlier, to speak of this song. This is another hymn, a short song, a folksy *rāga* called "*nāṭṭukuriñci.*" It is almost certainly composed as a *bhajan*, a simple tune with a simple idea that enables a group of nonspecialists to embody the devotional mood in music and song. Again, the song is sung to the beautiful young god Murugan, the son of Siva, a hunter and warrior—and like Krishna, a god of passion. Unlike Krishna, however, Murugan is not so unreliable. The first stanza (*pallavi*) of this tune is as follows:

> Muruga, Muruga, Muruga!
>
> You come riding a peacock
> With your bright spear you come
> And you give us your goodness, worthiness, and praise
> Your penances, your divinity, your quality, your renown,
> Muruga, Muruga, Muruga!

Let us return to Thiru. Vi. Ka.'s description:

> The song—a Tamil song—a Murugan song sweeter than honey—stirred

> the Murugan in the picture to start moving. It appeared as though the form in the portrait came surging out. The devotees' bodies began to sweat and shake; some fainted; some fell down; everyone was enraptured in joy. And Bharatiyar became the figure in the painting. I saw with my eyes and my heart the true unity of the song and the image in the portrait. Then, after a little while, Bharatiyar took his leave and left us. (Kalyanasundaram [1944] 2003, 236–37)

What are we to make of this description? Was it merely the collective effervescence of the moment? Here the quintessential Tamil deity, Murugan, seems to be awakened from his merely representational avatar in a framed print and merges with (indeed, is textually emblematized by) the poet who, more than anyone, spoke the Tamil people. Here, too, is an image of a deity to whom Tamils all over the world perform awesome, trance-inducing austerities to become the peacock vehicle of the god, dancing for hours on end with a palanquin festooned with peacock feathers on their shoulders, swinging above a crowd from hooks piercing the muscles in their backs, as their wives and children dance below them. Their austerities that day had been to sing and dance for miles along the streets in midday sun near the height of the Tamil summer as Bharati danced the god.

Recall that this event occurred only some months after Bharati was released from jail after his more than ten-year exile in Pondicherry and that scholars of Bharati believe that he was not in Madras on the day of the great satyagraha.[21] What does it mean, if anything, whether Bharati danced the god that day or Thiru. Vi. Ka. dreamed it? I do not know.

There were other accounts of Bharati's uncanny presence in political events during that time, ghostly presences that we think were imagined, such as an alleged encounter with Mohandas Gandhi (which was largely reported over much of the latter part of the twentieth century) and a failed speech in Madras where he began singing but did not speak and had to be escorted from the stage (Mahadevan 1957, 119). But whatever we make of these sightings, it is clear that these kinds of austerities, passions, and poesies would be a part of the formation of the Tamil modern from the beginning of mass politics. Ranajit Guha (1973) argues in his essay on the Rowlatt satyagraha that such shows of enthusiasm in the political realm were elements of elite demonstration of their own legitimacy in the face of

British rule. That may be true. But it is also the case that such enthusiasm cannot be reduced to the mere machinations and intentions of elite political will but was the modality in which the political—the modern mass political—would be danced, sung, imagined. Dreamed or not, Thiru. Vi. Ka.'s account offers a truth about Bharati and Tamil political modernity, for the event entered into written history and became an element of truth regarding Subramania Bharati and the forms of politics that followed in his wake.

Conclusion

We might conclude with the speculation that Bharati is one of an entire class of beings around the world during this period. The first nationalist orators around the world were, after all, disproportionately creative verbal artists, poets, and playwrights. This is no accident in two respects. First, structurally speaking, homiletic oratory vies with print as the mass medium par excellence for the enunciation of nationalist time, space, and belonging. And even if there were oratorical traditions prior to missionization in the Philippines (Rosaldo 1984), Madagascar (Keenan 1973; Bloch 1975; Jackson 2013), Papua New Guinea (Kulick 1992), or West Africa (Irvine 1989; Yankah 1995), modern nationalist oratory across the globe seems to have had Protestant forms of textuality at its basis. So, in opposition to print—which theorists such as Benedict Anderson ([1983] 2006) assert was spread by capitalist means of production—modern oratory spread in South Asia, and far more broadly, largely through affective motivations, in appeals to the heart and the imagination and in promises of salvation and of the universalization of concepts of natural or human rights. Orators and poets were the first to articulate this new, queer social imaginary in a way that we understand it today, a modern social imaginary (Taylor 2003). At least it was the orators and poets who articulated and ritually instantiated that imaginary in moments of an odd collective effervescence that became known as public meetings (*potukūṭṭaṅgaḷ*).[22] Creative verbal artists, young, iconoclastic, and beautiful, would stand at the forefront of this process. And poets, I imagine, would have been prominent among this new class of actors.

Second, it is no accident that it would have been poets to effect these revolutions, as poets brought to oratory a language that would contain within its codes the very essences of the truths and beauties felt by the people from whom they arose and to whom they spoke. The poet, young and idealistic, dares to use a new language to speak a people into being.

Combining orator and poet in one person also combined both kinds of poetic world building that have concerned me in this book. The first is Roman Jakobson's (1960) poetic function of language—what he also later called *poeticity* (1987, 368)—that aspect of every utterance that calls attention to the form of the message, which stipulates the form of communicative action being instantiated, the kind of activity being engaged, and the kinds of participants engaging in that activity. The new agency born in this new communicative structure, the Tamil epideictic oration, the secularized avatar of the Protestant sermon, involved the ability to interpellate an entirely new entity, a generalized public, "zero-degree individuals" devoid of class or caste (Kaviraj 1997, 90), yet all Indian—the modern political subject (with all the elisions and erasures such a social imaginary involves). In other words, through the metapragmatic stipulation of a new mode of speaking, the modern political actor—the vernacular politician—and the modern social imaginary of national citizenship were instantiated.

The second mode of poetic world building is the one traditionally understood by the term "poetry," but perhaps not entirely understood as having structuring effects. This includes the relationship language draws between sound, myth, emotion, and the imagination, what we might broadly call the aesthetics of language. Jakobson called this the "palpability of language" (1987, 378). We might also include under this heading not only poetry but rhetoric, the tools of the Sophists so despised by the Platonists yet the fundamental elements of political practice in modern polities. It is through these poetic processes that people's imaginations are lit afire in national passion. And my guess is that worldwide, through both modes of poetic world building, it was poets who disproportionately invoked this passion.

Chapter 5

ELOCUTIONARY INCANDESCENCE

> I came here a wayfarer but was detained to perform *swaraj paṭṭābiṣēkam.* The last thing I say to you is: Gather in thousands.
>
> —Subramania Siva, 4 March 1908, Thoothukudi

For some thirty-five days in early 1908, a group of charismatic orators brought the port and cotton mill town of Thoothukudi to the brink of revolution. Coming at the energetic apogee—and end—of the Swadeshi movement, India's first modern political mobilization described in Chapter 3 (1905–8), Swadeshi activist and entrepreneur V. O. Chidambaram Pillai and an enigmatic ascetic (*sanyasi*) named Subramania Siva led nearly daily meetings of laborers who gathered in massive crowds, estimated by police to number up to five thousand people. The orators lectured on *swadeshi* (self-reliance) and *swaraj* (self-rule), workers' movements around the world, global political history, human rights, the *Bhagavad Gita*, epics such as the *Ramayana*, the dignity of labor, and the divinity of India. Curiously, they spoke a great deal about their own agency in and responsibility for these events.

While established men had delivered Anglophone oratory for some decades in Provincial Congress Committees and other institutions established to engage the Raj in the Madras Presidency, Dravidophone political oratory was a very new thing. Most such oratory was addressed to upper-caste students and professionals in Madras, people who, organizers no doubt imagined, would become the new public of a self-ruling India. The skilled and unskilled mill laborers, dockworkers, service castes, and "coolies" at large who gathered on the beaches of Thoothukudi during those thirty-five days represented people who had been entirely left out of the formal structures of politics, even in most of the Swadeshi movement then efflorescing in what was described at the time as the "New Spirit of India." V. O. C., Subramania Siva, and a handful of others who stepped out of their status positions to address such people were thus imagining and interpellating a new kind of public vis-à-vis the British Raj, on the one hand, and several sets of established and emerging publics in the metropolitan cities, on the other.

These meetings were fateful. First, the workers of the Coral Mills in Thoothukudi peacefully went on strike within several weeks following the start of these meetings, between 27 February and 7 March, and they were awarded higher wages as a result. This is considered among the first such organized labor stoppages in the Madras Presidency (Sivasubramanian 1986).[1] Second, government authorities also took note and acted. While six to nine months of Swadeshi meetings by students and professionals in the city of Madras would pass before authorities began to take action, District Magistrate L. M. Wynch ordered the organizers to desist from their activities less than a month following the onset of the gatherings on 3 February. Organizers were specifically prohibited from holding a public meeting and procession in Thoothukudi on 9 March 1908 to celebrate Bengali Swadeshi leader Bipin Chandra Pal's release from prison. They circumvented the magistrate's orders by participating in a procession and meeting in the nearby district headquarters of Tirunelveli that day and then another brief procession the following day in Thoothukudi. Wynch, outraged by their disobedience, arrested the leaders on 12 March. An uprising broke out in Tirunelveli on the following day, which resulted in a police shooting, four dead, the looting and burning of a number of government buildings (including the magistrate's court and offices), and several dozen arrests (Venkatachalapathy 1987, 18–20; Divan 2008, 9). Officials prosecuted the accused well beyond the limits of the law and sentenced V. O. C. and Subramania Siva to double life (twenty years each, to run concurrently) and ten years, respectively, of rigorous imprisonment (terms that were later reduced to six years upon appeal). Spurred by these events, officials across Madras and India prosecuted other Swadeshi activists; and within a year all speaking activity in Madras had ceased,[2] and the Swadeshi movement was over for the time being.

But their sacrifices were not in vain. Thoothukudi's orators fatefully mobilized a new kind of public imagined within and against the multiple publics that would vie for hegemony in twentieth-century India. The model of political action they imagined was perhaps ten years ahead of its time, a model that would become the commonsense foundation of political action by the late 1910s and early 1920s. Specifically, they anticipated the kinds of crowds organized by leaders of the Madras Labour Union and other labor organizations that effected a fundamental social and structural transformation beginning around 1916 and efflorescing in 1918–19, a structural transformation that enabled modern mass politics to cohere as a possible genre of action (Bate 2013; Veeraraghavan 2013). This transformation was mediated in part, though profoundly, by vernacular homiletic oratory. Spoken to crowds by a new kind of charismatic leader, the vernacular politician, crowd and orator both emerged as actors in a new political public sphere.

I use the term "charisma" pointedly. Max Weber's concept of charisma is tied to the emergence (and routinization) of a particular quality of authority that had force outside otherwise stable patriarchal or bureaucratic modes of power and authority ([1915] 1946, 295–301; [1922] 1946, 245–52). The new leader appeared to stand outside—and against—the older forms of power, those rooted in family ties and bureaucratic office. In this respect, Subramania Siva, a bearded *sanyasi*, a renunciate, was the very image of a charismatic leader (Weber [1922] 1946, 248), dressed as he was in the robes of a figure who, by definition, stands outside the usual relations holding between human beings. V. O. C., the police, and even contemporary scholars write of him as appearing out of nowhere, his authority based not on his station, office, or ties to the community but on his transcendence of such embedded roles through the beauty and power of his words. The power of such a figure is nevertheless inherently sociological despite our sense of his power being sui generis to his charisma or person (Weber [1915] 1946, 294–95).

There is, thus, a genealogy to this kind of action, of the ability of leaders to speak to crowds in this fashion. As I demonstrate in this book, there had to be a socio-aesthetic revolution that would enable a higher-status orator to engage in an oratorical performance before a markedly lower-status audience, a possibility that had existed only a few decades at most.[3] Siva's charisma was not, therefore, only the characteristic of an individual—in this case, of the charismatic abilities of a *sanyasi* who was a gifted orator. Rather, it was the product of a set of social relations produced by an aesthetic of power, one that drew people's passions to a central, ritual figure who embodied a new potential, a new beauty, and a new power. It is this power, inherently sociological, that produces the new agency of the orator and the crowd under an entirely new dispensation in which such gifts might find themselves to be the decisive qualities of central figures in a communal project. The ritual of oratorical performance, of course, developed and deployed by people such as Siva and his contemporaries was the engine of the embodiment and production of this new dispensation. And like rituals everywhere, especially those as powerful as these clearly were, a cosmology was expressed and transformed, complete with the articulation of a new set of values, a new past, and a new future. He became a fulcrum of history. He articulated a vision of a new kind of social order expressed in the very spatial and temporal unfolding of the events themselves.

It was this kind of charismatic political oratory that Subramania Siva and V. O. C. delivered for those thirty-five days or so that became the communicative infrastructure within which the mass politics that characterized the freedom struggle and postcolonial democratic politics throughout the following century would be conducted.

This chapter examines this moment through a consideration of the speeches themselves. We have a number of published descriptions of the labor stoppages and the uprising that occurred during this period, in particular two exemplary and citation-rich accounts by A. Sivasubramanian (1986) and A. R. Venkatachalapathy (1987). Both authors lay out in quite detailed terms what happened during those days, first in the run-up to the labor stoppage itself (Sivasubramanian 1986) and then in the uprising that followed the arrests of V. O. C. and Siva (Venkatachalapathy 1987). What these studies miss, I think, is the infrastructural role oratory played in these events. These writers treat language as disembodied, as statements and attitudes that might have come to workers in Thoothukudi as easily through the press as through the platform. To treat the press and the platform as merely two different means of saying the same thing, however, is to misunderstand the real sensuous activity of communicative practice, the genres of embodied action that communicative forms such as oratory presuppose and entail. For it was not only *what* the orators said that was important but the very *modes* of communicative production in which what was said cohered as a new kind of action. The meaningfulness of their words was dependent first on the ritual genre of communication in which those meanings were embodied as practical activity.

So what I add to Sivasubramanian and Venkatachalapathy's excellent accounts of what happened in Thoothukudi and Tirunelveli over those fateful days is a closer examination of the energetic basis of these events, that is, what must have been incandescent speeches by charismatic orators speaking within ritual events that articulated a "New Spirit of India," one in which every one of those workers would have a vital role to play. For whatever other reasons laborers might have had to gather in these crowds, to strike work, and to gather in anger when their leaders were arrested, the elocutionary charisma generated in these meetings—as well as the imagination of the orators to address laborers as political agents in the first place—must be considered infrastructural processes lying at the heart of what happened there.

The Speakers and Their Speeches

Our sources on these speeches are at once lacking and fulsome.[4] On the one hand, we have mere palimpsests of them, traces left in the accounts of police officers and the memories of witnesses who offered testimony in court. Police representations, in English, of a handful of speeches only begin on 19 February, although authorities reported that both Tamil and English notes existed documenting the fact that Siva began speaking on 3 February. We have no transcripts or reproductions of the orators' speeches in Tamil or in English. We have no Tamil manuscripts of them whatsoever. From one point of view, that of someone trying to figure out what happened and what was really said, we have to treat these records, at best, as no more accurate and complete than a student's notes from a lecture. They were translated and transcribed by agents who were hostile to the orators, trolling for seditious words that might be used as evidence against them in a court of law. And although some appear to be fairly coherent swatches of text that may very well have been spoken by the orators, many very clearly are not complete speeches faithfully transcribed from a recording or even through shorthand notes. Subramania Siva himself objected in a written statement made in the first trial that the "so-called notes of my speeches filed by the prosecution are not true and correct but garbled and distorted. They contain many passages which I never spoke."[5]

A police report suggests that one of the organizers, S. Padmanabha Aiyangar, was taking notes in Tamil shorthand; another claim by Subramania Siva on the evening of 9 March in Tirunelveli was that the activists themselves would take notes in shorthand in the face of police note taking. But we are uncertain what methods the police or activists may have employed because Tamil shorthand had yet to be developed and would not be a usable police procedure for at least another decade (Arnold 1986, 188–90; Bate 2012b). In any event, we do not have these records. And we can hardly take at face value the so-called verbatim accounts of the sub-inspectors and constables who served as witnesses for the prosecution in the sedition trials of the Thoothukudi orators.

On the other hand, our sources are abundant. They offer a great deal of evidence about the kinds of communicative events occurring at the time, along with the ways that people understood these events to be a new kind of action. Officials and activists were aware of the import of these events, their newness, their potential to reorganize the political world in terms of the new modes of action. It is one reason that the activists were so concerned to speak of various kinds of agency: their own, the crowds', and the authorities'. These records, in all their seeming lack, offer a rather fulsome sense of what the authorities and the activists believed they heard, the kinds of impressions that the speeches made on the hearts and memories of the various people who made accounts of the meetings, including police, prosecution witnesses, and sympathetic journalists. So we can say some very definite things about them. We know who spoke, where and when, some rough estimates of the crowds' sizes and social compositions, some of the themes and recurrent motifs within the speeches themselves, and what followed in their wake.

The Orators

Authorities at the time and contemporary scholars credit Thoothukudi native V. O. C. with the leadership of these meetings (Sivasubramanian 1986;

Venkatachalapathy 1987). V. O. C. was certainly the most prominent leader among young Swadeshi activists in 1907–8, due in large part to his audacious founding of the Swadeshi Steam Navigation Company (SSNC). The SSNC was started with two merchant ships to compete with the British-India Steam Navigation Company, first within the narrow Palk Strait between the southern Madras Presidency and Colombo, Ceylon, and later throughout the world. V. O. C.'s ambitious venture inspired Swadeshists across the country with the idea that Indians could compete with British merchant mariners with a homespun navigation company equal to any. When he was not in Thoothukudi or Colombo, V. O. C. was delivering public speeches throughout the Presidency from late 1906 and 1907, seeking support through subscriptions to the SSNC. Swadeshi leader, nationalist, and poet C. Subramania Bharati—whose portrait was sketched in Chapter 4—composed a song honoring his friend's achievement as emblematic of Indian prospects throughout the world:

> *Veḷḷi panimalaiyin mītulāvuvōm*
> *Aḍi mēlaik kaḍal mulutum kappal viḍuvōm.*

> We'll stride the silver snowcapped mountain ranges
> And send our ships across the (three) great oceans (beyond the ti
> of India).

V. O. C. appeared back in Thoothukudi sometime in the first week of February during the heady days following the tumultuous Surat Conference of the Indian National Congress in late December 1907. Upon arrival in his hometown, authorities reported that he "attended and took much interest in, the lectures delivered . . . by Subramania Siva":[6]

> Recognizing the powers of [Subramania Siva] as an orator, [V. O. C.] quickly got hold of him, invited him to his house and commenced with him a campaign of seditious speeches which so inflamed the minds of the populace against the Government authorities and the European community, that they caused the Mill hands of the Coral Mills Company to go in strike on 27.02.08 and ultimately caused the riots at Tuticorin [Thoothukudi] and Tinnevelly [Tirunelveli] on the 13th March. (Government of Tamil Nadu 1982, 422)

While V. O. C. was and still is remembered as the leader of these events, it was clearly Subramania Siva's sudden appearance in Thoothukudi in early February 1908 that kindled the fire that characterized those thirty-five days.[7] Since he was the primary defendant in the sedition trials later that year, inspectors' reports of his speeches are the most extensive and complete of any that we have for that moment. District Magistrate L. M. Wynch wrote that "Subramania Siva has been the worst of the three agitators [V. O. C., Subramania Siva, and S. Padmanabha Aiyangar], but the other two have made speeches similar in tone and have aided and abetted the propaganda."[8]

Subramania Siva was born as Subramania Iyer in Battalagundu, Madurai District (Government of Tamil Nadu 1982, 421). He traveled to Thiruvananthapuram (Trivandrum) sometime after 1902, where, the "history sheet" on him suggests, he, his wife, and his children lived off a *choultry* (religious rest house) for some years as he studied.[9] He appears to have been radicalized into overt political action in 1907 following the arrest of Swadeshi leaders Lala Lajpat Rai and Ajit Singh. He conducted six lectures in Thiruvananthapuram and was then expelled by the princely state.[10] He then showed up in various places in the Madras Presidency, including Madurai and Tirunelveli, where he was said to "tramp the country as an itinerant preacher" (421). The first mention of him in the official record is his lectures on boycott, *swadeshi*, and the formation of a *sabha* (association) at Ambasamudram in Tirunelveli District (421).

> [Finally,] on February 3rd 1908 he arrived at Tuticorin and at once gave a series of lectures extending over a week at the invitation of "The Young Men's Patriotic Association." The police as in duty bound watched him from the first and took notes of his speeches, but until 19.02.08 when the first glaringly seditious speech was made, there was no thought of taking action against him and the earlier notes are lost though the reports based on them are said to be available. (422)

What is clear is that Siva's appearance in Thoothukudi ushered in a new moment. Despite V. O. C.'s many talks in Thoothukudi convincing members of the professional and landed classes to purchase subscriptions to the SSNC, only after the arrival of Siva did events take a very different turn—in particular, a successful strike occurred approximately three weeks after his arrival.

Simply put, he must have been an incandescent orator. Writing in 1948 of Siva's work during that moment in Thoothukudi, the freedom fighter Chidambara Bharati evoked the metaphor of fire, sparks, and flame that appear to characterize Siva's oratory:

> Siva's oratorical fire was kindled. His words were like bombs. He once gave a series of 42 lectures. The first day 100 people showed up, the next day five hundred. Finally, fifty thousand. His lectures kindled the spirit of swadeshi like wind spreads a flame. (*Maturai Jillā Tiyākikaḷ Malar* 1948, 2)

Chidambara Bharati's notion of his speech as being like fire, or like a wind that spreads a flame, appears throughout his short account of Subramania Siva's life (also see Swaminatha Sharma [1959, 199], who describes Subramania Siva as "one who is like fire [*neruppup pōnṟavar*]"; Sivasubramanian 1986). Chidambara Bharati also noted his masculinity and potency (*vīram*), a characteristic that attracted a large number of young men to his martial arts–cum–political school in Madurai in the years before he died in 1925. Photographs of him later in *sanyasi* robes and bare feet, a fighting stick (*silambu*), and a thick black beard show him surrounded by intense and earnest young men.

So while it is difficult to get a sense of his oratory without texts by his own hand or more detailed transcripts, we have a strong sense that it was charismatic, visually and auditorily compelling, and marked by a masculinity that was no doubt deeply attractive to the young men who filled the ranks of the millworkers and others in Thoothukudi.[11] Finally, his ideas compelled the imagination of a world liberated from poverty, oppression, and the loss of dignity in their relationships to a ruling race.

The Location and Composition of the Audiences

The speeches were generally delivered on the beach in the late afternoon as the day cooled into evening, 5:00–6:30 p.m. or so, a moment of both increased energy and leisure for many. The Thoothukudi-based historian A. Sivasubramanian notes that it was unlikely that the meetings would have been held on the broad beach to the north of the port (opposite the mills), as that was the European settlement (including the police lines, the bungalows of the deputy superintendent of police, the sub-collector, and the European

FIGURE 5. Subramania Siva

mill owners).[12] He believes that most of them were held on the beach just opposite Our Lady of the Snows (Tūya Panimaya Mātā), a Catholic church that lies just south of the port.[13]

Other open spaces were used, such as Vandipettai, a place used for parking the carts that brought raw material into the mills and goods out of the ports. They were also said to have orated near the railroad station and Hindu temples (on 22, 23, and 25 February), among several other spots in town. One of these, a vacant lot in the low-caste barbers' quarters that was used for a meeting on

7 March, is notable for what appears to be a democratizing move on the part of the orators. The Swadeshi movement was essentially an upper-class Hindu movement—given the majority-Brahmin representation among the leadership, it would not be unfair to characterize it as a Brahmin movement. But during a meeting held on the beach on 6 March, a day before the strike broke, Subramania Siva made the following announcement:

> The meeting will not be here tomorrow but in the Barbers' quarters. One day it will be in the Parava quarters and another day in the Washermen's quarters. Swadeshi will become indigenous like plague in Tuticorin.[14]

The evocation of the plague here is striking. Was this an error or ellipsis on the part of the sub-inspector who offered an account of the speech? Did he leave something out? Or if he did get this right, what might Subramania Siva have meant by the Swadeshi movement being as "indigenous as the plague"? Was there a motivation for this Brahmin *sanyasi* to imagine contagion in the dwelling areas of the most profoundly subaltern castes of barbers, washermen, and Paravas and to transform his own horror into a novel form of power with which to confront the Raj? Although it is difficult to be sure if he said this, and what precisely he meant by it if he did, an inspector filed a report the following day that a "meeting was held on a vacant site near the Barbers' quarters on the Victoria Extension Road. The gathering was about 3000 strong consisting of different castes."[15]

As this report suggests, these meetings were enormous, some estimated to be between fifteen hundred and five thousand participants.[16] This of course is well prior to the age of public-address systems.[17] It is difficult to know how participants might have been able to hear speeches in meetings that large, but they clearly were participating in some form or another as the following discussion of the chant "*vantē mātaram*" in call-and-response during the meetings indicates. We know, too, that police reported meetings of fewer than one hundred people in the audience. And given what we know about these meetings later on in the Independence movement and beyond, it may very well be that both police and organizers vastly overestimated the sizes of these meetings, which more regularly included numbers closer to one or two hundred rather than one or two thousand people. Regardless of the size of the crowds, police took special care to note that people of diverse castes and classes attended the meetings. We assume that they noted the classes of those in attendance since it was unusual and unnerving to authorities to see such large groups of mill- and dockworkers, "coolies," skilled laborers, and others who might not be considered capable of exercising political or civic judgment. Such concerns were writ large in the deliberations in the trials of V. O. C. and Subramania Siva.

Themes of the Speeches

Although the record of who spoke where and when is incomplete and the transcripts of the speeches suspect, the themes of the speeches are so patterned and so similar to those reported throughout the Madras Presidency during the Swadeshi movement that we can have a fairly high degree of confidence in the topics of the Thoothukudi speeches. Like other speeches for which there are fair records, Swadeshi orators appealed to the concepts of *swadeshi* and *swaraj*, lectured on labor movements and liberation struggles in other parts of the world (including history lessons on the Russian and French Revolutions, for instance), evoked images and stories from the *Ramayana* and the *Mahabharata* (especially the *Bhagavad Gita*), and—during Bipin Chandra Pal's captivity—offered discourses about Pal's sacrifice for the nation.

But perhaps unique to these meetings—and indexical of their strangeness—was the evocation of agency. Orators denied their own agency in provoking sedition and simultaneously asserted it as they attempted to discipline and mobilize the crowds (cf. Guha 1998). These twinned topics suggest a very different kind of audience from those in the metropolitan city of Madras, where students and young professionals—a budding middle class—gathered to participate in the "New Spirit of India." In the Madras meetings, the call was always for the crowd to "take up the bow," to assert the power of their numbers and their nativity in confronting the colonial Other. Crowds in Madras and other locations where the audiences were similar in class and station to the orators also involved music and procession, and by 1907 the crowds regularly sang the nationalist songs of Subramania Bharati that would become standards throughout the Independence movement and beyond. As Henry Nevinson, a European observer of a Madras meeting in November 1907, noted that, despite the size of the crowd, "there was no wild gesticulation, no frantic excess, such as we might imagine in a fanatical East. A Trafalgar Square crowd is more demonstrative and unrestrained" (1908, 126; see Chapter 3). There is no record in the Madras meetings of the same level of reflection on the agency of the orators or the crowds such as we see in V. O. C. and Subramania Siva's speeches. Neither did the police make note of music in their observations of the Thoothukudi meetings, though music was used in the procession and meeting in Tirunelveli on 9 March. These meetings appeared to have a different feel to them, a different unfolding, a different relationship between orator and auditor. The orators' consistent evocation of agency there suggested that they knew very well that they were not addressing people like them but people who were very, very different.

The Appeal to *Swadeshi* and the Call to *Swaraj*

The Swadeshi movement called the people to participate as Indians, to purchase *swadeshi* (Indian-made) clothes and eschew *paradeshi* (foreign) and a fortiori British-made clothes and styles; to eschew English and embrace *swadeshi* languages in print and oratory; and to educate their children in new national colleges and universities where they might embrace Indic philosophical and ethical maxims as depicted in epic and religious literature.

V. O. C.'s speech on 4 March 1908 focused on *swadeshi* industry and how easy it would be to capture industries and markets. As he had been doing for some time, he also made appeals for subscriptions and support of the SSNC. In one moment of the speech, he evoked the image of a barber refusing to shave a "vakil" (lawyer, or advocate) who did not support Swadeshi as a model for shipping and passenger services:

> I heard this morning that a vakil sent for a barber to have a shave. The barber asked him if he was not an anti-Swadeshi, the vakil called him a fool and the barber went away without shaving him. By this I conclude that there is union in this town. If you will take interest in the Swadeshi Company and find out who ships cargo and intends to go by steamer, and request persons going to the British India Steam Navigation Company not to do so, matters will improve very much. [V. O. C., 4 March 1908]

In some reports, the barber was said to have left the unfortunate "vakil" half-shaved, an image both profound in its violation of caste subordination on the part of the profoundly subaltern barber and risible in the image of an upper-status man left in such a ridiculous state.

Likewise, Subramania Siva in that same meeting appealed to their numbers and the ability of the Indian people to shrug off foreign rule and establish *swaraj*:

> We must try our best to obtain Swaraj. Over 30 crores [300 million] of people are trying for it, and will obtain it. If not we will become extinct.... Police officers and other public servants say that they will shoot us, if their officers order them to do so. Are they not Swadeshis? Why should they do so for 15, 20, or 50 rupees? ... While we are slaves under the Government of foreigners we must obey them. Let all the people of India—Europeans and anti-Swadeshis—know, that if anything is done against Swadeshi the God's Shakti will spoil, ruin, and destroy them. [Subramania Siva, 4 March 1908][18]

As the appeal to the concept of *sakti* (power) suggests, Subramania Siva consistently linked Swadeshi and *swaraj* to aspects of Indic philosophy, in particular, the parallel between—or even identity of—spiritual and political liberation (*mukti*). Curiously, that linkage alarmed the authorities to the extent that his call to both *swaraj* and *mukti* on 25 February was cited as one of three instances leading to Subramania Siva's prosecution for sedition:

> I being a sanyasi, must always say, something on religion. People are afraid of death. We must give up fear as there is nothing as death in this world. It is mere "Maya" which does all this mischief and which creates all sorts of fear in human mind. If we die we are born again. The body becomes a corpse; the "atma" [soul] flies away to find its place in some other frame. So, we are born again. The body, when the life goes away, becomes a corpse which is burnt, buried, or thrown away in some way or other. The only reason why we are afraid of death is that we have to leave relations and friends behind. There is Heaven for the good and holy. But don't suppose that the holy alone would get Heaven and not the rest. Don't think that he who does charity would get Heaven only. He, who dies for public good and public cause, is the first man to obtain Heaven, and he is a hero and a man

> in its true sense. Till now we were in "Maya." Now we open our eyes to see Swaraj which we will get soon. [Subramania Siva, 25 February 1908][19]

Subramania Siva seemed to return again and again to the concept of *māyā* (illusion, delusion) and its link to power (*sakti*):

> If anything that is not permanent in this world, such as *maya* [delusion], comes and battles with us will it gain victory over our divine souls? If troubles as large as the Himalayas come and face us, they would not conquer the Atmasakti [the power of the soul] which can not be concealed, separated, or taken away. No one would be able to stand before this Sakti. Bear in mind that it will not be possible to subdue us so long as we do right, work for the cause of the people, and do things which are not illegal. So long as we have strong determination, nothing can be done by the Government or any private body, and if Government interfere with the general public and do harm they will certainly feel the consequences and be ruined. [Subramania Siva, 4 March 1908]

The Appeal to the International

The speeches also made frequent claims about the international order or referred to earlier speeches in which Subramania Siva lectured on the French and Russian Revolutions. Clearly the orators embodied in Thoothukudi what we now know was a key aspect of the Swadeshi movement at large, a strong sense of their links to a larger world of political action and history (Manjapra 2010, 2012; Menon 2012). "In the years from 1903–21," Kris Manjapra writes, "there was no shortage of distant mirrors in which swadeshi activists could see their own revolutionary pursuits reflected back" (2012, 57). And finding reflections of themselves was also the demonstration of a link between the people sitting and standing before them and a larger world around them, as if they could indeed imagine the very same kinds of things occurring around the world simultaneously.[20] In other words, the situation in which they were in, including the relationships of workers to capital or individuals to the state, could be iterable across the planet. Theirs was an implicit appeal to the concept of an abstract social order, if not necessarily the uptake of that appeal on the part of the auditors—indeed, recall Siva's reference to thirty crore people as a novel, numerical epistemization of Society.

Subramania Siva made explicit appeal to transnational *swadeshi* at the moment of calling for a workers' strike just prior to the one breaking out on 23 February 1908. The call to swear allegiance to the movement before Kali terrified the colonial authorities, and this speech was another brought before the courts as evidence of Subramania Siva's sedition:

> Without bloodshed nothing could be accomplished. It is a religious maxim. All Indians should undergo all troubles that might face them. *Yuganter Patrika* was brought to book four times and editor convicted. As Japan was prepared to sacrifice 20,000 people she won victory over Russia. If 5 crores [50 million] of Indians come to sacrifice themselves Swaraj would be theirs. In Johannesburg the Europeans pelted stones at Keir Hardie because he sympathized with the Indian People. Is this civilization? The Indians are not weak people. So in order to obtain Swaraj they should not be afraid of anything. If all Indians whether strong or weak come forward as strong men foreign Government will collapse and Swaraj will be theirs. You must swear before Kali that you would support Swaraj. [Subramania Siva, 23 February 1908]

Assertions and Denials of Personal Agency

As noted previously, perhaps the most singular aspect of these meetings, especially in Madras, was the orators' systematic assertion and simultaneous denials of agency. On the one hand, their denials—especially during the height of the strike itself in early March—were wrapped up in refusals to be subjected to charges of sedition:

> In all my speeches I have curbed my tongue, from giving vent to words that are objectionable, still I am called a sedition-monger. I am not to blame. . . .
>
> I asked you not to use force, but to boycott and to maintain passive resistance. Is that sedition? Though we tried our best not to do anything objectionable, yet we are called sedition mongers. We won't obey the rule of foreigners. We won't pay taxes. We will have our own panchayats and settle matters. If we do all the above we will not be called offenders.

> If any speech is made for the benefit of the public and if any assembly gathers to hear it, it is at once called sedition. I do not care if I am called a sedition monger. Public servants and persons of pomp treat us with contempt, call us sedition-mongers and any names they like. Let us not care for it. Today is Ash Wednesday, so the Inspector told me not to have the meeting opposite the English Church. Simply because we are ruled by Europeans we are not slaves under them. What can I do if 200 or 300 people follow me while going out on the road? [Subramania Siva, 4 March 1908]

In the only reference made of his presence, a junior orator named Sivasubramania Pillai spoke up on the following day precisely on sedition, clearly indicating that the orators were concerned about the charge:

> It is a mass meeting and I am not fit to address such a large crowd. If there be any errors in my speech, I beg to be excused. I am not going to say anything more as everything has been said by Subramania Sivam but with his kind permission I will say one word. "Nothing seditious has been said this evening." [Sivasubramania Pillai, 5 March 1908]

On the other hand, at some moments the denials of their own agency were asserted as they promoted and encouraged the agency of the assembled workers. Some of these appeals were quite similar to what Swadeshi activists were saying all across the land. In another speech that prosecutors would list as evidence against him during his trial, V. O. C. was reported to have delivered a "vehement speech" on 19 February, in which he was reported to have said that

> fear of Europeans was groundless and that, if the three millions of Indians who must die next year of starvation and famine only came to a determination to die at once, the fifty thousand Europeans in India would be no large number for them. All the thirty-three millions in India should join together and earn happiness amicably and with unanimity or die all together in the struggle.[21]

In a departure from wider arguments in the Swadeshi movement, however, orators began calling for active participation and approval by the crowd, including the call and response of the Swadeshi slogan "*vantē mātaram*," especially in the days just before the strike began on 27 February. On 25 February, Subramania Siva claimed that the workers had a voice in the inauguration of the oratorical ritual:

> Gentlemen, I want you to cry out "Bande Mataram" before I commence to give my lecture and also you must recite "Allahoo Akbar" which is a favorite cry of our Mahomedan brothers, which must find its place with our national cry. [Subramania Siva, 25 February 1908]

In one of the last references we have of his speeches in Thoothukudi, Subramania Siva finished by seeking affirmation by the crowd, also suggesting their agency in the great work they had planned:

> The 9th of March will be a memorable day and it should be celebrated with great éclat. Do you consent to this? ([Audience:] Bande Mataram.) We will open the Ayurvedic medical hall. Do you accept this? (Bande Mataram.) We must select at least six persons to go out to preach. The paper Swaraj will commence on that day and the public should assist. Will you do this? (Bande Mataram.) [Subramania Siva, 5 March 1908]

These orators modeled the meetings on those long-standing among elites, meetings that would end with resolutions passed and memorials presented to authorities and publics, often in distant England. The Thoothukudi meetings also resulted in resolutions proposed and passed by the assembled masses, a kind of mass agency. At a meeting of some one thousand people on 17 February, for instance, Subramania Siva presided and V. O. C. proposed the formation of the "Tuticorin Peoples' Sangam" along with some ten other resolutions, including the establishment of a school; "the development of Swadeshi Spirit, unanimity and courage"; the organization of volunteers for preaching Swadeshi among the people; the collection of funds for the SSNC and other projects; and the formation of sub-*saṅgams* in other towns and villages. "The above propositions," wrote a sub-inspector, "were carried unanimously with shouts of *Vande Mataram*."[22]

However, the systematic denial of agency was mirrored by its overt assertion in a great many of the speeches recorded. On 4 March, deep into the strike, Subramania Siva seemed to make an almost schoolmasterly admonishment of the crowd that indexed the kind of agency and authority the speakers understood themselves to embody during these meetings:

> This day being Ash Wednesday there is service in the church and so I would request you all not to shout Bande Mataram. Remember the words Bande Mataram in your hearts and be quiet. We are behaving in an orderly manner up to date and we should also maintain order to-day. You must not clap hands. I will only deliver my speech if you consent not to shout Bande Mataram. Don't feel sorry for my having asked you to do so. I don't want to see persons arrested on plea of disturbance and the lecture spoiled. Don't laugh. Don't talk. Will you consent to this? You had better have your ears open and hear me. [Subramania Siva, 4 March 1908][23]

At several points during the meeting, participants rose up to garland both V. O. C. and Subramania Siva, but they were quickly stopped and silenced by the orators and organizers. Subramania Siva's call for silence and decorum may have suggested that the orators were concerned about the perception of their meetings by people outside the activist and worker community, not to mention their obvious concern that the authorities were becoming increasingly alarmed.

"The Demon of *Bande Mataram*"

Indeed, the last few days of these events in the first week of March found the orators arguing with, admonishing, and sometimes beseeching crowds that had swelled into the thousands. The increased intensity and stakes of the meetings appeared to be weighing on the orators. On 5 March 1908, just two days before the end of the strike, Subramania Siva said that the scheduled speaker, Somasundara Bharati, was ill and therefore he would take his place. He seemed to be driven by the events, his own attempts to control the assembled workers in tension with events driving him forward. "If I don't speak I can't rest," he said. "I feel too weak to speak; I am in a dilemma. However, I will try." District Magistrate L. M. Wynch also noted on 17 March that "the speakers' language became more and more inflammatory as time when on."[24] One wonders if that "inflammatory" nature was in some sense a reading of the intensity of the orators' speeches based on the strike, pressure on them from authorities, or perhaps a situation that had developed into something way beyond anything they had anticipated. Authorities were now speaking directly to the orator activists, warning them of the consequences of their actions, banning them from speaking. And the workers were showing up in ever-greater numbers. The oratorical incandescence of the moment most certainly was an effect of what Émile Durkheim called the "demon of oratorical inspiration" ([1912] 1995, 212),[25] which is nothing other than, as Durkheim suggested, the orator refracting back the energies of the crowd participating in the events. The large crowd and stakes were iconic of each other and articulated in the scale of the rhetoric and ambitions of all concerned. Wynch's sense of these meetings as inflammatory, along with Subramania Siva's own admission of being driven to speak, bear witness to the intensity of the moment, which had grown beyond anyone's control. As Wynch's letter suggests, from the European point of view there was a new and, from their perspective, darker energy among both the speakers and the working classes in Thoothukudi.

It was what one intelligence officer in Madras referred to, echoing Durkheim, as the "demon of bande mataram" that troubled the authorities as much as anything else.[26] Like the speeches themselves, *vantē mātaram* alarmingly crossed social categories and ages, with cheeky youngsters and others directing their cries of "*vantē mātaram*" both to each other and to an unnerved and outraged ruling race. During the trial of Subramania Siva and V. O. C., the chief witness for the prosecution, Jaffer Hussain, claimed that

> after the speeches, I noted a change in the conduct of the people, i.e., there was lawlessness amongst them, they were previously law abiding. They commenced to disobey the orders of public servants. I used to hear shouts of "Bande Mataram" regardless of time and place. They commenced to shout "Bande Mataram" in the presence of Europeans. They commenced collecting in small crowds and going to the houses of Europeans and sometimes threw stones.[27]

Similar reports came from other witnesses. A sub-magistrate (Witness 14) reported that

> after the speeches I heard one evening as I was returning from my office

> to my house a crowd of about 100 rowdies crying aloud, "Bande Mataram, let Swadeshi prosper, let the thalis of the Englishmen's wives be torn off (i.e. let them become widows), hack to pieces the white men, the sons of harlots." This I heard in the first week of March.[28]

And a second-grade pleader of the court (Witness 21) reported:[29]

> Before February and March, people were well disposed and friendly towards Europeans and authorities of Government. After the speeches the people showed signs of dislike, hatred and disloyalty. I move freely among the people. I gathered my impressions from conversations with different people. Crowds going to hear the preaching shouted "Bande Mataram, let Swadeshi prosper and foreigners be damned." These cries were uttered especially by the lower orders.

Something had changed and dramatically so. And the authorities were becoming more and more concerned.

The Procession on 9 March

Officials began to become seriously concerned about these meetings sometime after the speeches on 19 February by both Subramania Siva and V. O. C. And their concerns turned to alarm as it appeared on 26 February that a strike was imminent. A temporary suspension of the meetings occurred on 27 February, and a private meeting was held the next day. Circulars signed by Shanmugam Sundaram Pillai also appeared on 28 February. One referred to stopping all meetings and told the people that they need not be in the least afraid to assemble in public to discuss public matters. Another announced a meeting in the signatory's residence at which Subramania Siva and V. O. C. would speak on *swaraj* and warned government officials to keep away or there might be a breach of the peace. A third announced a lecture on the beach by S. Padmanabha Aiyangar of Madras. V. O. C. attended this lecture and at the close said that there would be a meeting that night in a private house and that he was arranging for meetings to be held on a private site where more than five thousand people might assemble.[30]

The meetings in Thoothukudi were getting louder, larger, and more intense every day. As we have seen, in that short, incandescent period between

11 February and 8 March 1908, these two young men, V. O. C. and Subramania Siva, orchestrated a major labor stoppage and brought the city to the brink of revolution through their larger and more frequent public meetings. Given the size and organization of the meetings, District Magistrate Wynch banned the planned meetings and procession in Thoothukudi on 9 March, which was the day that the Bengali Swadeshi leader Bipin Chandra Pal was to be released from prison.[31]

Subramania Siva and V. O. C. obeyed the letter of the law, but not its spirit, and conducted a procession and meeting in Tirunelveli instead. The meeting began at the Nellaiyappa Temple in the center of Tirunelveli town. It had a celebratory character. Following the same route of the god during the Tai Poosam festival, the procession carried a picture of Bipin Chandra Pal mounted on an elephant, first around the temple and then along the Nellaiyappar High Road to the Tai Poosam *mandapam* in the broad, sandy bed of the Thamirabarani River. There they gave several speeches that were written down by the sub-inspectors. One gets a distinct sense of very young men in defiance, a sense that these men were challenging their overlords within a framework both familiar and strange to them, the vernacular oration couched within the larger idiom of the temple festival and procession.[32]

The Uprising and Official Murders on 13 March

Displeased that they had circumvented the ban with daily meetings and concerned "that the 2 [V. O. C. and Subramania Siva] accused could no longer with safety be allowed to be at large,"[33] District Magistrate L. M. Wynch and Sub-collector and Joint Magistrate Robert Ashe arrested Subramania Siva, V. O. C., and S. Padmanabha Aiyangar on 12 March. The arrests set off "a riot of serious character" the following day in Thoothukudi, Tirunelveli, and Thachanallur.[34] In Tirunelveli, all shops were closed in a show of defiant support, Church Mission Society's College was attacked (the protesters compelling the college principal to say the words "*vantē mātaram*" three times), and the principal of Madurai Diraviyam Thayumanavar (MDT) Hindu College was stoned. Every public building but the sub-registrar's office came under attack: municipal offices, the court, the post office, the police station (where weapons were destroyed, prisoners freed, and the building lit on fire), and the oil depot (which burned for two days). Documents were burned and telegraph wires severed (Venkatachalapathy 2010). In Thoothukudi, the Coral Mills again went on strike for a week, along with workers from Best and Company, municipal workers, butchers, and horse-cart drivers.

In Vandipettai in Thoothukudi, on the afternoon of 13 March, a large protest meeting was conducted (numbering, by some estimates, four to five thousand), despite official prohibitions. Sub-divisional Magistrate Ashe arrived in the evening with armed forces to disperse the meeting. Assaulted by, as the *Tinnevelly District Gazetteer* described it, "a large and disorderly mob," the deputy superintendent of police unsuccessfully ordered the meeting to disperse (cited in Venkatachalapathy 2010, 41). Met in response with pelted stones, the police fired into the crowd. No one was killed. In Tirunelveli, by contrast, District Magistrate Wynch dispersed the riot by deploying the Reserve Police who, on orders from Wynch, shot into the crowd, resulting in the deaths of four individuals. As the Tirunelveli journalist Che. Divan has noted in his extensive writings on the so-called Tinnevelly riots, the four dead were not only the upper castes and classes of Tirunelveli town. They were a non-Brahmin priest from a nearby goddess temple, a boy who worked in a bakery, a Muslim man, and a Dalit. They resembled in many ways the publics that were anything but those imagined by the metropolitan leaders; rather, they were the public that would become normative by the end of the century, well after Swadeshi had run its course.

In the wake of the riots followed dozens of arrests and prosecutions (in Thoothukudi, thirty-six rioters were arrested and thirty-two convicted). V. O. C. and Subramania Siva were tried and sentenced to twenty and ten years, respectively, of hard labor. The magistrate was enraged at the young men's insolence and terrified by the unknowable of the vernacular public meeting and the violence that they attributed to their speech.[35]

Seditious Chronotopes and the Chain of Signs

There was no doubt in the minds of the authorities that the events on 13 March 1908 stemmed directly from the speeches and organizing activities of V. O. C. and Subramania Siva (rather than the official action of arresting the activists). They singled out specific speeches given by Subramania Siva on 19, 23, and 26 February and 1 and 5 March as "calculated to create disaffection and enmity between classes." Likewise, they specified 19 and 23 February and 3 March as "about the worst specimens of [V. O. C.]'s speeches."[36] Strangely, or perhaps not strangely at all, the seditious elements of these speeches were due as much as and seemingly more to the *form* of the speeches themselves than their denotational content. Judges consistently maintained that meetings held outside amid what they considered a "mob" were grounds for bringing charges against the accused for sedition under Section 124A of the Indian Penal Code and for promoting "hatred or contempt between different classes of His Majesty's subjects" under Section 153A.[37]

The prosecution had first to prove that they said the words that they were accused of saying. Neither V. O. C. nor Subramania Siva denied that they did, in fact, speak on 9 March at the Tai Poosam *mandapam* in Tirunelveli. Even their own defense attorneys admitted that their behavior that evening was not beyond reproach, that "the accused [V. O. C.] it appeared, laboured from a sort of disease which compelled him to speak on that occasion."[38] They did, however, claim that the words they spoke were not the words presented by the prosecution. District Magistrate Wynch supplied the advocate general of the Government of Madras notes on a number of the speeches in question, requesting sanction to prosecute the three men.[39] Wynch also claimed that "full reports of [the speeches] have been sent to the C.I.D. and should have been printed at the time and be in the hands of Government." He continued:

> Notes of the speeches have been made in Tamil by Sub-Inspectors and S.H.O.s [sp?] and by the Town Inspector in English. It is from these notes that the reports have been compiled which have been furnished to the C.I.D. The original notes have been filed in my court.[40]

V. O. C. and Siva's lawyers also objected in appeal that the police officers' notes of the speeches were filed as "evidence." This, say the judges, was not the case:

> No one, of course, would suggest that these notes were, in themselves, evidence. What happened at the trial was this. The police-officers using their notes for the purpose of refreshing their memory give evidence in accordance with their notes. The learned Judge did not record the whole of this evidence but only such portions of it as the prosecution relied on. He then allowed the notes themselves to become part of the record in the

> case. This, it seems to us, was done quite as much in the interest of the accused as in the interest of the prosecution.[41]

In responding to objections by the defense, the additional sessions judge who presided over the trial of V. O. C. and Subramania Siva, Arthur F. Pinhey, focused more on the sign vehicles than the content:

> The offense made punishable by section 124A is the bringing or attempting to bring into hatred and contempt, or exciting or attempting to excite disaffection towards His Majesty or the Government established by British Law in India in one or more of the ways specified by *words spoken* or *written* or by *visible representations* or by *signs* or other wise. Where the allegation is that the offence has been committed by means of a printed newspaper article, as was the case in 22 Bombay, the exact words are beyond dispute and can easily be proved by filing with the complaint a copy of the article complained of. Where, as in the present instance, the allegation is that the offence has been committed repeatedly in a series of speeches of which no short hand reports are available, the Magistrate taking cognizance has to rest content with a less specific allegation in the complaint. In the former case the issue "What were the words used?" does not arise. The exact words are known. In the latter it does and the question has to be answered in general terms after hearing the oral evidence of the witnesses who heard the speeches and who observed the effect that they had on the audience addressed. Speeches addressed to an assembled mob may have a greater and a more immediate effect than a printed article in a paper, which appeals to solitary individuals under less exciting conditions and it would be unsafe to hold that the more dangerous and persistent criminal should go scot free unless the exact words used were set forth and that too in the original complaint. In the present instance the District Magistrate elicited by his examination of the complainant under section 200, Cr.P.C. the fact that notes of the speeches had been taken by some of the police witnesses especially deputed for the purpose, and that some of the notes themselves as well as extracts had already been filed before himself a fortnight earlier in certain proceedings taken against the accused under section 108 Cr.P.C. The effect of the speeches had been such that the most serious riots had ensued on the arrest of the speakers. In view of

all these circumstances I am unable to hold that the District Magistrate had no complaint of facts before him to warrant him in taking cognizance of the complaint Exhibit U.[42]

Judge Pinhey's sense of how an "audience" becomes a "mob" (cf. Guha 1973, 110) appears entirely based on the *mode* of communication and its mixed character. Speeches to "an assembled mob" are quite different—and at an altogether different civilizational level—than newspaper articles that are read "individually" under "less exciting conditions."[43]

The *Swadesamitran* newspaper picked up on this point explicitly in its critique of the proceedings:

He [the Judge] would like to tell them that if a man actually made a speech and excited hatred, contempt or disaffection he committed an offence whether he intended to do so or not. On the other hand if they intended to excite feelings of hatred contempt or disaffection by their language, it did not matter in either case the offence was complete. So that in making speeches one should be very cautious in these respects. Before His Honour would read to them the actual speech with which the accused was charged he would tell them that in England political speeches were common. Political speeches in this country were a novelty to him. There was no lawful occasion as for as [*sic*] His Honour could see for any man in this country to make a political speech. People in England had votes. In England a political speaker made public speeches because the chances were that he was addressing his constituents to secure their votes. There fore a speaker in England might say that he was persuading his audience to exercise their constitutional power in his favour at some future time. There was no such thing as that in this country. The masses of Tinnevelly and Tuticorin had no votes.[44]

Swadesamitran continued to bring to the fore both the judge's assumed ideology of space, time, and sociality (sociochronotopes) of the communicative event and the circular logic of the decision:

For instance, it they objected to the new Press Bill and wanted to get its provisions altered they could not get it altered by addressing a mob in the

> Tinnevelli river bed. Therefore the chances were that when a speaker addressed an audience consisting of a mob in that country he would be doing so only to persuade the crowd to exercise their physical power as human beings, and that was a dangerous thing.[45]

Of course, even in cases involving printed sedition, words written on a page were no less problematic than words spoken. For the words to bear meaning of a specific sort of sedition within a court of law, prosecutors had also to establish a chain of signs and practices that led from the legal responsibility of the publisher to the writing of a text, the printing of the material, and finally to the production of translations and the storage of the text artifacts that, from one authorized hand to another, reached the court as evidence.

A brief example from the case against Subramania Bharati's paper, *India*, which was published by M. Sreenivasa Iyengar, helps illustrate the point. The record of this case begins with depositions by Inspector of Police S. Bavanandam Pillai, Intelligence Department, Madras City, who solemnly affirmed that he was who he said he was and that he filed as evidence three articles in the *India* from 2 May, 23 May, and 27 June 1908. He continues with a clerk in the office of Commissioner of Police Neelamaga Charry, who solemnly affirmed that he was who he said he was and that he witnessed M. Sreenivasa Iyengar sign a declaration that he was publisher and printer of the *India* on 18 November 1907. The Tamil translator of the government then affirmed that he received three copies of the newspaper, that he was the subscriber, and that the copies presented here bear the initials of his clerk who first received them in the office. "I know his initials," he added. And then he made a declaration before the court in the simple present indicating the timelessness of the truth he reveals as he speaks:

> I see the issue of the 2nd May. There is an article "Stories from the Mahabharrata." I made a translation of it. This is it. I have signed it. I see the issue of the 23rd May. I find an article entitled "Of the many robberies this is also one." I made a translation of it—this is it. It is signed by me. I see . . .[46]

The prosecution proceeds to call several postal workers to confirm the signature of Mr. Sreenivasan and the one on the declaration; it calls other postal officials to attest that the newspaper was mailed in one place and delivered in another. The deposition is shot through with performatives—transactions, signings—and articulated in the timeless present—"I see the issue," "I find the article"—characteristic of ritual language,[47] which, of course, it is: an alchemical ritual of tying the words spoken in one place and time to words being evaluated in another. The entire chain leading from legal propriety to printing, distribution, reception, and translation is attested to in these oaths, all demonstrating and securing a link between seditious words spoken in the heat of political engagement and those presented before the court and the accused standing right there in the docks.

In Thoothukudi, by the same token, there was a slippage that had to be reconstructed: between the immediate effect of the speeches on the audience and the riots that occurred after the arrest of the speakers several days later. The magistrate thereby attributes and performatively secures the root cause of the riots to the speech through a chain of signs rather to the action of the state per se. As far as the chain of signs that leads to our knowledge is concerned, the chain itself, without any content, becomes sufficient ground to assume that seditious content existed in these speeches for the government. If there had been no seditious talk, why would District Magistrate L. M. Wynch have gone to the trouble of deputing police officers to produce notes of the speeches and file the extracts? It was the *chain of signs*, rather than the denotationality of the signs, that damned V. O. C. and Subramania Siva to six years of rigorous imprisonment.

Conclusion

Everyone—organizers, authorities, and eyewitnesses—was in agreement that the speeches lay at the heart of these events, much as the judges who so harshly prosecuted V. O. C. and Subramania Siva maintained. We agree. Oratory provided a communicative matrix in which the work of politics could take place among the complex of castes, classes, races, and statuses that found themselves interacting in Thoothukudi during this moment. The oratorical events carried with them a distinct form of agency, of spatiotemporal unfolding, and social order. The speeches, in their denotational as well as interactional textuality (Silverstein and Urban 1996), enabled organizers and participants alike to share a single meaning of the world at that moment, to clarify the social world of Thoothukudi within the larger context of a global struggle for the dignity of labor and the divinity of India, and finally to marshal the potential of organized collective action. The orators, especially Subramania Siva, served as charismatic ritual centers for some thirty-five days of collective effervescence embodying the New Spirit of Swadeshi. Contrary to official condemnation of these events, the Thoothukudi orators did not provoke the uprising as much as vividly embody a world, an ethos, and a fantastic potential whose foreclosing would prove intolerable to large numbers and categories of people in Tirunelveli and Thoothukudi.

V. O. C. and Subramania Siva's imaginings of what might be a relevant political public was nearly unprecedented in the Swadeshi movement. There were some others working with specific subaltern publics in the Madras Presidency: we have incomplete police reports of Ethiraj Surendranath Arya, who offered several dozen Telugu addresses to "coolies" and laborers in an open area behind the Moore Market in Madras and, significantly, on at least two occasions, to workers in Perambur, a textile mill neighborhood of Madras, the birthplace of the Madras Labour Union some ten years later (for Bengal, see Sarkar [1973] 2010).[48] A number of young Swadeshi "preachers" made a series of itinerating speaking tours in 1907 and 1908 to bring the gospel of Swadeshi to farmers and others throughout the Kistna (or Krishna) and Godavari deltas.[49] But in no other instance did organizers systematically address one set of workers in one limited locality for a sustained period of time to achieve specific results, as did the Thoothukudi orators.

The explicit attention to agency in these speeches—and the effects of these speeches on the audience—suggests a key difference from the speeches delivered on the beach and on the *maidans* (open grounds, evening bazaar spaces) of Madras or almost anywhere else in the Presidency (with a few isolated exceptions, as mentioned earlier). There the speeches were accompanied, almost as a rule, by music, poetry, and procession. In marked contrast to the working-class audiences of the Thoothukudi meetings, those who participated in the peaceful procession in Tirunelveli on 9 March (which provoked the arrest of V. O. C. and Subramania Siva) were the provincial counterparts to the men who gathered on the beach in Madras, youngsters of the upper castes and classes of the district capital. In Tirunelveli, they sang and danced; they carried an image of their deity—Bipin Chandra Pal himself—along the processional route of the Tirunelveli's sovereign deity, Nellaiyappa, an avatar of Siva. These were very different publics indeed, those who did not require admonition or explicit direction from the orators and those who were seen to require just such direction. The former would become the normative public of the Indian Independence movement, whose massed bodies enthusiastically processing in the streets singing songs and attending speeches would simultaneously be signs of elite political hegemony, as Ranajit Guha maintained (1997, 100–102), as well as signs of their own participation in a global struggle. The latter, contrarily, would always be problematic for the leaders; it was necessary for such lower classes to embody the passion for Swadeshi that leaders could then, in turn, rally for their own legitimacy and power. Yet they were always seemingly in need of shepherding lest they get out of hand.[50] They were a public whom later leaders would come to treat with a great deal of ambivalence, not unlike V. O. C. and Subramania Siva did.

While there are moments of ambivalence in the speeches Subramania Siva delivered, moments when he was clearly concerned about the nature of the crowd and their enthusiasms, he appeared to understand very well the power of the forces he was channeling. Like the mixed group of subaltern folk who suffered the official murder of the police on 13 March in Tirunelveli, the men assembled before Subramania Siva during those thirty-five days represented a public that would become generalized by the mid-twentieth century, long after Swadeshi had run its course. He called to a crowd of mixed caste, class, and station; he universalized the notion of the elite political man who could, under these modern times, be any man, Everyman. This call to the crowd was ten years before the formation of the Madras Labour Union, which would come to redefine workers' agency and subaltern agency in the public sphere. And of course, crowds, thousands processing through the streets and attending speeches, would become the very model of political performance and communicative practice over the Independence movement, starting around 1918–19, and also in postcolonial Tamil Nadu.

When Subramania Siva called to the workers gathered before him on 6

March 1908, in one of the last fragments of oratory we have from him prior to his fiery appeals in court, his words were prophetic. I like to think that the sub-inspector who took these notes that day got his words exactly right:

> I came here a wayfarer but was detained to perform *swaraj paṭṭābiṣēkam* [the coronation of *swaraj*]. The last thing I say to you is: Gather in thousands.

Epilogue

HOME RULE, THE LABOR MOVEMENT, AND LINGUISTIC AND POLITICAL MODERNITY

After it was shut down in 1908, vernacular political oratory would not be heard again until late 1916 and 1917, leading eventually to the great satyagraha of 1919 described at the beginning of this book. Police and judicial attentions under the India Press Act of 1910 moved from a concern with "sedition" from 1911–12 to one with "obscenity" by 1913–14. Starting in 1914, the Fortnightly Reports from the secretary to the Government of Madras showed virtually no interest in "politics" (*la politique*) per se until late 1915, when notice began to be given to the increasing activities of Theosophical Society leader and political activist Annie Besant and her nascent Home Rule movement. As far as the political (*le politique*) is concerned, reports from the beginning of 1916 concentrated on the war effort, prices of basic commodities, and Muslim reaction to British enmity with the Khalifat. In one Fortnightly Report, the chief secretary to the Government of Madras dismissively predicts that Annie Besant's activities will not be supported by the people. Over the course of the year, however, his mocking tone turns to concern and then to genuine alarm as the movement grows by leaps and bounds; Besant is nearly deified in her reception around the Presidency, and subscriptions to her newspaper, *New India*, explode to more than ten thousand, eclipsing even *The Hindu*.

Her movement began with a transformation of some thirty-four theosophical lodges—in provincial towns and centers throughout the Presidency—from strictly religious and philanthropic organizations into an outright political machine.[1] Mostly coming from the educated classes, several thousand students, *vakils* (lawyers), and landowners participated in its meetings, which were still conducted in English, as were the great public meetings that Besant held at Gokhale Hall in Madras throughout the movement.

But by December 1916 and early 1917, Besant was calling for a new kind of political action that involved vernacular pamphlets and the "itineration of Home Rule preachers," very much like what had happened some nine to ten years earlier in the Andhra deltas and parts of the Tamil-speaking lands of the Madras Presidency. The Government of Madras in Fort St. George saw the connection immediately: "Hitherto the district reports have for the most part pictured the Home Rule movement as confined to the younger *vaikils* [*sic*] and students in the central towns, but in the report from Guntur district for the past fortnight the Collector lays stress upon the activities of the league in the delta villages of Tenali Taluk."[2] Just a few months later, in March 1917, the Home Rule League's main office issued a notice to the members of the Theosophical Society: "It is proposed by Mrs. Besant that a more vigorous campaign must begin throughout the Tamil districts of the Presidency to form as many branches of the Home Rule League and enlist as many members as possible. To do this, fluent speakers in Tamil are required."[3] Besant's involvement in the Provincial Congress Committees, too, seemed to spur on calls to vernacularize meetings and thereby persuade more and more categories of people into speech and action.[4]

The Madras Presidency Association

This was the crucial moment when the non-Brahmin movement began to formally organize itself in the establishment of the pro-British/anti-Congress Justice Party, on the one hand, and the formation of the pro-Congress Madras Presidency Association, on the other. The Justice Party continued to hold Anglophone hall meetings, while the Madras Presidency Association established itself in its very first meeting by passing a resolution declaring that henceforth all meetings in Tamil-speaking areas would be conducted in Tamil. Thiru. Vi. Kalyanasundaram (Thiru. Vi. Ka.), wrote of that meeting:

> The Trichy-Tanjavur conference was organized on behalf of the Madras Presidency Association and met in Tanjavur on 20, 21 April 1918. Under the Presidency of Indian Patriot editor Diwan Bahadur Karunakara Menon, many resolutions were passed in that conference. One of them involved Tamil. I seconded the motion which stated that, henceforward, the Tamilians' mother tongue must be spoken in public meetings, that foreign tongues are not to be spoken, and that if anyone should speak in a foreign tongue, the general public would reserve the right to rebuke him.... Of all the revolutions [*puraṭci*] of my life, this was the first. ([1944] 2003, 202)

In this period, the Andhra movement also started to formally demand separate political accommodation for the furtherance of Telugu-speaking people; at the May 1917 Ganjam District Conference there was a major split between the Oriya and Telugu speakers over representation; and one even begins to read from this period of the return of some of the vernacular lecturers of the Swadeshi movement.[5]

The vernacular had arrived in a big way, and vernacular oratory was back. The authorities were becoming worried and began to compare these times with the Swadeshi movement, taking action accordingly.

The Labor Movement, 1917–20

This time it would be different, however. First, the people engaging in these lectures and organizations were not upstart young men without standing but established politicians and respectable people. The Madras Presidency now had all-India figures of status, such as Besant and her two chief lieutenants in the Home Rule movement, George Arundale and B. P. Wadia. This time they were not going to be so easily dismissed or crushed.

A second difference was that now they not only reached out to the lower classes and appealed to their nationalism and devotion, as during the Swadeshi movement, but they also tied their politics to issues of direct concern to ordinary people, especially to the economics and dignity of the new proletariat toiling in the cotton mills around Madras. The biggest transformation, and probably the key element in the establishment of vernacular oratory, was the formation of the Madras Labour Union, as well as other unions that arose immediately thereafter, in 1918. The Labor movement started, flourished, and became established precisely because of the direction of vernacular oratory to the workers.

It is important to briefly examine what kinds of actions and communicative practices were engaged in prior to the formation of organized labor institutions. Work stoppages, strikes, workers' riots, and other disturbances are as old as industrial forms of production in India. The managing agents of the Buckingham and Carnatic (B&C) Mills in Perambur, Madras, reported a strike just a few months after opening their first textile factory in 1878. They continued to report major strikes at intervals of every two years throughout the 1880s, a figure consistent with reports from other factories surveyed in an 1892 Royal Commission on Labour report (Veeraraghavan 1987, 88–89). Modes of protest frequently took the form of idling, theft, sabotage, and throwing spindles at managers, sometimes with riots involving thousands, violence directed at supervisors, and destruction of factory property or the personal property of their tormentors. Workers' demands were sometimes monetary but often had more to do with assaults to their dignity by their European managers, overwork, the denial of previous privileges, or what were perceived to be unjust dismissals of fellow workers. As Dipesh Chakrabarty has noted, the kinds of industrial violence that followed often took the form of personalized vengeance precisely because the form of colonial authority practiced in the mills—a kind of *maa-baap* system of parental despotism[6]—was personalized, excessive, and bore the marks of terror (1989, 170–77). The forms of struggle against this system of unreasonable power were met with unreasonable violence, and managerial terror, in turn, met with workers' vengeance (182). These all continued well into the twentieth century.

What was born with the organized labor union, then, was a different mode of communicative practice, even as a paternalistic system continued to operate by other means. The direct oration to the workers constituted a new mode of action that would be fateful indeed. The formation of an organized union was the result of a conscious, deliberate move by a series of different groups to address the workers directly. It began, curiously enough, with the ethical and humanitarian idealism of a Perambur-based merchants' philanthropic and religious organization, the Sri Venkatesa Gunamrithavarshini Sabha (SVGS). Run by two small shopkeepers in the Perambur area—cloth merchant G. Chelvapathi Chettiar and rice merchant G. Ramanjulu Naidu—the SVGS sponsored weekly discourses by religious orators such as Thiru. Vi. Ka., who was by then well-known for such oration, and N. C. Kannabiran Mudaliar, a Vaishnava preacher of some renown. Just as the Besantite Home Rulers based their organization initially on the infrastructure laid down by the Theosophical Society, it is no coincidence that the fateful move to address workers came from a group organized around oratory, in this case Vaishnava sermons and literary discourses (Chettiar 1961; Souvenir 1963; Murphy 1981).

As providers of goods to the local workforce, Chelvapathi Chettiar and Ramanjulu Naidu were well aware of the plight of the workers, their sub-subsistence wages, inhumane living conditions, and the constant humiliations and degradations they faced as the lowest-status workers in an apartheid-like social situation.[7] Over the course of several months in late 1917 and early 1918, the SVGS moved from sponsoring strictly religious discourses to ones addressing the need for an organized labor union (Veeraraghavan 1987, 119–23). It began on Vijayadasami Day (mid-October) in 1917, when the SVGS organized a small meeting of some thirty workers who were addressed by N. C. Kannabiran Mudaliar on "a few victorious passages from Mahabharata" and the need for a labor union. Thiru. Vi. Ka. participated in meetings of this sort for some months thereafter, and his memoir states that with every speech more workers showed up.[8] After the enthusiastic reception of Kannibiran Mudaliar's proposal for a labor union and the successes of Thiru. Vi. Ka.'s speeches, Chelvapathi and Ramanjulu decided to organize a public meeting of workers.[9]

The first meeting was held at Janga Ramayammal Gardens on Statham's Road, Perambur, on 2 March 1918. By all accounts the meeting was massive: the police estimated that one thousand B&C workers—"most were coolies"—showed up, but Thiru. Vi. Ka. said that "many thousands of workers thronged the meeting, filling the *maidan*, the walls and the trees" ([1944] 2003, 352); Chelvapathi claimed that ten thousand came, but that number seems high. In any case, the meeting was most likely the single largest event of its kind ever in the Madras Presidency, and certainly nothing close to it had ever been organized specifically for workers. The only meetings that might have rivaled it were those that V. O. Chidambaram Pillai and his colleagues had organized for workers in Thoothukudi in 1908 (Chapter 5).

The meeting was chaired by V. E. Sudarsana Mudaliar, an honorary magistrate, and the main speakers included Thiru. Vi. Ka. His speech, and the reactions to it, serve well to illustrate the crossroads of, and emerging contradictions between, religious philanthropy and political organization. Chelvapathi described it as "a powerful speech in chaste but simple Tamil" (Veeraraghavan 1987, 120–21). Police reported that Thiru. Vi. Ka. "spoke on the need of organizing labor at Madras. In doing so he emphasized the fact that labor plays an important part in the prosperity of a country and how India is becoming poorer day by day by the industrial exploitation of foreign countries. . . . He placed the picture of Mr. Gandhi's life before them and exhorted them . . . to follow his example. They should all be loyal, constitutional and do their work with truth in one hand and fearlessness in the other, thinking that service to man is service to God because man is but a moving temple to God."[10] According to Thiru. Vi. Ka., he spoke about "the history of the labor movement in Western countries, the dignity of economic liberty, and the necessity of a labor union. The workers were brimming with a sense of new possibility" ([1944] 2003, 352).

Clearly, Thiru. Vi. Ka. saw his purpose as addressing the political, economic, social, and even spiritual challenges facing the workers as a whole. However, the chair, Mudaliar, was displeased with his remarks and in his closing speech rebuked Thiru. Vi. Ka. for what he felt was an overly political oration: "The Chair, for his part, had come with the expectation that this was going to be some kind of religious speech. He was a government employee. He began to rebuke my speech. The uproar made by the workers, who had gathered like the sea, reached all the way to the stage. Mr. Chelvapathi Chettiar [in his vote of thanks] cut and felled the Chair's rebuttal decisively. . . . The workers' honor had been protected. And the question of when a new 'Labourers' Union' would be formed circulated widely among the workers" (Kalyanasundaram [1944] 2003, 353; see also Veeraraghavan 1987, 120–21).[11]

Given the success of the first public meeting, Chelvapathi Chettiar and Ramanjulu Naidu took the next step of approaching the highest-profile persons they could find who might be sympathetic to their cause. They spoke with a number of prominent politicians, including Congressmen, about joining them as leaders, but no one was interested in the plight of "lowly, illiterate labourers" (Murphy 1981, 82). Finally, they turned to Annie Besant and her people, and though they went to the Theosophical Society headquarters in Adyar with the hope of luring Besant herself, she was out of the office that day and they chanced to meet one of her lieutenants, B. P. Wadia.[12] In the end it was he who, despite his own ignorance of the mills, the workers, and the overall condition of labor in India, immediately understood that labor would be a key ally in their larger struggle for home rule in India. "The educated classes in India," he wrote, "have so far failed to realize the great value of the Labour movement as a factor in the general political advancement of the country. Without the masses there can be no true Democracy" (Wadia 1921, xvi).

The first meeting with Wadia was held at the Janga Ramayammal Gardens in Perambur, at 5:00 p.m. on 13 March 1918. Five hundred people attended. Tellingly for our purposes, the police report of this meeting spends a significant amount of time on the codes deployed, the languages spoken, the quality of that language, and the work of translation:

> Mr. B. P. Wadia presided. Mr. T. V. Kalyanasundaram Mudaliyar (editor of *Desabhaktan*) explained to the audience that Mr. Wadia did not know Tamil and so he would speak in English and after his speech Mr. Kalyanasundaram Mudlr. would translate into Tamil so that the whole audience might understand what Mr. Wadia said. Mr. Wadia then addressed the audience in English and laid stress on the fact that they were all sparks of the Divine Being and so they are all equal. . . .
>
> Mr. Kalyanasundaram then translated into Tamil the ideas mentioned by Mr. Wadia . . . and pointed out how influential the labour movement was in England. He also referred to the success achieved by the mill hands at Ahmedabad by the kind intervention of Mr. Gandhi.
>
> Mr. Kurnivala, a Parsee on the staff of "New India" next spoke in broken Tamil and compared the laborers to the feet and hands of a man's body and the mill owners to the head and said that if there are no feet and hands the head would be worth nothing.[13]

Most reports mention translations not at all or, at best, very little, and the attention paid here to translation and the broken Tamil of speakers is no doubt an index of just how strange and significant this kind of meeting was to the policeman observing it. Unlike the Swadeshi speakers of ten years earlier, who were youngsters and upstarts, students and people without status, B. P. Wadia was a major political personality whose internment (house arrest) the previous year along with Annie Besant had only boosted his fortunes and made him a pan-Indian political hero. For men of that stature to not only take an interest in the welfare of the common man but also actually commit to addressing him in the vernacular (albeit translated by Thiru. Vi. Ka.) was extremely rare if not unprecedented.[14]

From the establishment of the Madras Labour Union on 27 April 1918 onward, Thiru. Vi. Ka., along with Chelvapathi and Ramanjulu, spoke at Perambur and "wherever workers were" (Kalyanasundaram [1944] 2003, 354). The major vernacular politicians of the day, including many who had been active since the Swadeshi movement and many others who would come to dominate politics over the next several decades, all fanned out to help organize new unions.[15] The result was an explosion of labor unions, many within months, most within one year. By April 1920, there were some eleven major unions, and another ten to fifteen organizations of workers organized enough to issue collective bargaining statements and go on strike.[16] Thiru. Vi. Ka. lists the Madras & Southern Maratha Railways Workshop Workers Union, the Tramway Workers Union, the Madras Electric Supply Corporation Workers Union, the Kerosine Workers Union, the Aluminium Workers Union, Domestic Servants in European Homes, Barbers, Conservancy Workers, Rickshaw Drivers, Police, Postmen, the Southern Railway Workshop Union in Nagapattnam, and the Textile Workers Unions in Madurai and Coimbatore (354).[17] All of these organizations and more emerged within two years of the founding of the Madras Labour Union. It was a fundamental transformation in social organization, as if the entire society suddenly phase-shifted from one state to another, providing the basis for a new mode of action on the part of workers as well as new relationships to owners. A necessary condition of that shift was the new interpellative power of the vernacular oration to persuade the people into speech and action, a new infrastructure of communication whose origins have been at the heart of this book.

A final point to note is that while these unions were started at the instigation of elites from "outside" the workforce, over the course of the following year workers themselves began to address meetings, first the skilled laborers such as weavers, carpenters, clerks, and so on, and later some of the ordinary workers (Veeraraghavan 1987). We see numerous reports over the course of 1919 and 1920 of meetings from which the leaders were absent or in which members of the general workforce countered their recommendations.[18] A meeting of the Tramway Workers Union of 1919 was chaired by Thiru. Vi. Ka. and featured speeches by old-time Swadeshi activists such as V. O. Chidambaram Pillai and Subramania Siva. A meeting ten days later, chaired by another Swadeshi speaker, S. Padmanabha Aiyangar, included other current and former politicians of note. But workers at both meetings heard speeches by Mohaiuddin Sahib, a former Tramway employee, and Vasudeva Ayyar, a secondary school teacher. The secretary of the union, Sriramulu Nayudu, reported on responses authorities gave to the grievances the workers presented. But they were no longer responding only to the luminaries of the union, the heroes of the past, or important figures of the nation (B. P. Wadia and his co-Theosophists and Home Ruler George Arundale) or of the Madras Presidency (Thiru. Vi. Ka.), but also to a tramway driver, a schoolteacher, and a clerk.

Finally, George Arundale, a man of all-India stature, chaired a meeting of the Madras Labour Union in February 1920. As was the wont of the responsible elite liberals, Arundale cautioned prudence and patience on the part of the workers and counseled them to wait for negotiations to go through among their leaders and elected representatives. He "repeatedly exhorted [the workers] to refrain from strike. He even threatened to sever his connection with the Union should they be hasty." To this, a worker named Natesan rose on the platform and presented a tableau that is striking when we consider the career of vernacular oratory over just fifteen years: "One Natesan, a weaver, followed Mr. Arundale. He told the men that Mr. Arundale's preaching were no longer of any use to them. . . . The only successful course now therefore left open to them was to strike. Natesan's speech is said to have created a more favorable impression than that of Mr. Arundale's."[19]

The ability to speak, though still highly restricted, was being extended, as all people were being invited to the political through being interpellated, called, via the vernacular press and the vernacular platform and through being invited to interpellate the public itself.[20] By the end of 1919, as Wadia had called for just one year earlier, the masses had finally been "persuaded to speech and action."

Interpellative Infrastructure and the Birth of Modern Tamil Politics

Political men faced the common man of 1916 and 1917 and began to address him directly. Their address called the people into being as a new category of social action, a new estate, and a new agency. By 1919, at least, the common man began to stand up alongside, and sometimes against, his master, and began to speak back with greater force than ever—Natesan the weaver being but one case in point.

When we consider what constitutes political action in general, we invariably must account not only for the ideas and the people engaging those ideas but also the real-time practices and actions of those people that are, invariably, couched within very particular communicative modalities. Writing, printing, and the circulation of printed texts throughout a limited vernacular geography have been the usual foci of analysis in considering the political practices that constitute the large-scale social imaginaries such as the public or the nation (Habermas [1962] 1991; Anderson [1983] 2006; Blackburn 2003; Taylor 2003; Venkatachalapathy 2012). As I have argued, we must also add homiletic oratory, which has generally been forgotten in the genealogies of such imaginaries. Perhaps chief among the reasons is that it is an embodied form of action rather than a new technology such as printing, the telegraph, or the internet, and its embodiment has suggested to people that it is therefore natural and panhuman, that people must have always orated.

As we have seen, this was not the case in South India. In fact, this equally invented form enabled politics on a new level, mass politics of the kind that came to dominate twentieth-century India and the empire of orators of Tamil Nadu in particular (Bate 2009b). Whereas Indic models of textual authority resulted in a kind of identity, or consubstantiality, of text and person, in modern or sermonic oratory the object was to effect some kind of change, to transform the world and the hearers from one state in a linear chain of becoming to the next, just as the Protestant sermonizer attempts to transform the souls of his auditors from a state of being lost to one of salvation. Oratory embodied a new kind of agency with entirely new models of textual authority and social order, from religious discourses to new forms of education and, of course, to political action.

The history of Tamil oratory, then, is also a history of the social and cultural transformation of the practices, statuses, and agencies of the population that enabled new kinds of political and social action. The vernacular oratorical revolution that I outline in this book entailed a new kind of agency on the part of an entirely new genre of political actor, the vernacular politician, who could now turn toward and evoke the participation of people formerly thought to be irrelevant at best and irrational and dangerous at worst. In that interpellation, it was Tamil oratory that enabled the production of a new Tamil people whose agency came to define twentieth-century Tamil politics.

What does it mean for the definition of politics, then, to say that in 1918–19 "the people" emerged as an agentive category in politics? If we say that the people became relevant to politics, then what were the people doing prior to that point? And who was engaging in politics? If a riot broke out between two communities, was that not politics? Or was it something else? When laborers attacked their supervisors and charged out of the factory floor, was that not politics?

I think it was political (*le politique*), but I do not think they were a part of what we call politics (*la politique*), that is, the particular realm of action in which people directly face the state, an activity that is called politics itself. Elites of the time, such as Wadia, clearly understood that inviting the masses "to speech and action" was, in fact, calling them into politics. Politics (*la politique*) was enabled not only by the rupture of historical events and the emergence of factions such as Gandhian satyagraha, nonviolence, or the massive events that shook India at the end of World War I (such as the infamous massacre at Jallianwalla Bagh on 13 April 1919), which are said to have transformed the nationalist movement into a fully fledged mass movement. These events had to occur within some kind of sociocultural context in which they could cohere as events that large groups of people would recognize as relevant to them and then mobilize appropriately (see Sahlins 1991).

More pointedly, as I have emphasized, these events emerged at a moment in which mass politics was possible due to the infrastructure of new communicative forms. There could have been no mass politics without the presence of such interpellative networks, without the interpellative infrastructure of the mass meeting and "public" oration. Such an infrastructure provided a practical basis of action within which new kinds of agency and agents, that is, the vernacular politician, produced new kinds of effects. Such an infrastructure provided a practical basis of action in which a speaker could call an audience and the audience would return his gaze and recognize itself as such. Without the interpellative infrastructure of the public address, the forms of politics that emerged in 1918–19, and for the next hundred years, could not have occurred.

But they did not emerge just as they pleased—the new modern, social, political forms were modern, but they were also Indic, and as time passed, the more twentieth-century politics became Tamil politics itself, the more Indian those forms became (Kaviraj 2005a, 2005b).

Afterword

ORATORY AND THE ORIGINS OF POLITICS

Sudipta Kaviraj

This is literally an afterword—words that come after what Bernard Bate left behind in his unfinished book. We lost in Bate a remarkable scholar, with rare gifts and uncommon modesty. Bate's work is, for two reasons, of unusual importance for those who wish to understand politics as a live activity. First, he chose for his scholarly analysis a feature of political life that is obviously of profound significance yet that few have subjected to serious examination: language in oratory. Second, he analyzed this aspect of politics with amazing skill and subtlety. In this afterword, I follow the steps in the development of Bate's argument to mark its points of departure and arrival, with a few occasional comments and some suggestions about the wide range of its implications.

General Themes

Several overlapping themes are studied in Bate's book. They all exist inextricably connected in the lifeworlds of real history but require analytical distinction for proper analysis. His main subject is the political speech—the orator, his text, his style, his persona, his context, the consequences he leaves behind (and in all but one case—the Vellala woman in Madurai that Bate discusses in Chapter 3—they were men). Unless these various features of a single speech are distinguished by careful analytics, it is hard to understand how the speech works its effect on history. But this book is also a study of the birth of modern politics, the creation of a new Tamil language, the origins of Tamil peoplehood, the first steps toward an Indian nationalism, and the fateful transformative process of decolonization. As a scholar, Bate is exceptionally scrupulous and reflexive.[1] All these varying aspects of speech and its history are clearly distinguished, carefully defined, and examined with rare precision of both analysis and locution. Students of politics should give this work close attention because few others have produced such a thorough study of Indian political oratory and its historical world.

Bate's work is remarkable because of the understated methodological complexity with which he approaches political modernity. It appears to start unsurprisingly from a study of American Protestant missionary work in Sri Lanka and follow its line of evolution to Tamil Saivite oratory into modern Tamil politics. Actually, his methodological approach to this history is remarkably complex: he claims that writing the history of the political modern is full of surprises. That modernity is a historical phenomenon that starts in the West is a conventional truism; but Bate shows that if we break a platitude like "modernity" down into its constituent practices, the connections become surprising.[2] In doing so, Bate's work makes a startling "world-historical" claim: all modern politics, especially those associated with nationalism but not that alone, deploy a communicative infrastructure generated by innovations made by Protestant intellectuals of Europe during the "revolution of the saints,"[3] but they were then generalized across the world. Protestant leaders offered a strikingly different form of religiosity or form of the sacred from that of previous Catholic Christian faith. Bate follows scholars of the Protestant revolution to claim that "the revolution of the saints" brought in a new, more epistemized understanding of religion, based on a more explicit "theory" of the presence of God in the world than earlier Catholic conceptions.

A central part of this epistemized form of religion was the idea that knowledge of God came through the knowledge of texts. Religious texts such as the Bible were thus to be disseminated to ordinary people, who were encouraged to become literate and read them directly. In doing so, the mediation of God would be demystified, his intention and compassion epistemically available to all. Protestant theologians believed, correctly, that the consequences of this religious transformation would be revolutionary. Assisted by the print revolution, this would make the texts available to everybody: instead of being esoteric, texts would be democratic and widely available. People would be transformed by this new practice from religious dupes into coparticipants in an ennobling enterprise, bringing dignity to the life of all human beings.

Bate suggests that this initial Protestant religious subject—who is interpellated as a rational ethical being through epistemic practices such as text circulation and sermonizing—turns into the subject of modern politics.[4] Bate, it is true, is not directly concerned with the theological apparatus, which he largely allows to stay in the background. He concentrates on the peculiar Protestant conception of textuality because he believes that it led to the creation of modern social imaginaries such as the public sphere. Implicit in Bate's work is an argument parallel to Jürgen Habermas's analysis of the public sphere in Europe, where an initially literary public sphere turns quickly to fashion a political public sphere that works, in turn, as the precondition for national mass politics.[5] Bate believes, however, that each trajectory of modernity is historically unique. He turns to tell the story of the Tamil public sphere.

Protestant Critique of Tamil Textuality

When American Protestants started missions in the Tamil country in Sri Lanka, these textual practices of Protestantism had been long practiced in the West. They simply brought with them standard textual practices of Protestant religiosity into an alien textual world. These clashed so fundamentally with the conventional textual conventions of the Tamil lands that Protestant missionaries were forced to articulate, increasingly explicitly, a profound critique of traditional Tamil textuality.

The Tamil cultural world was rich in textual traditions, but at each point, their constituting principles collided with the new principles of the Protestants. Traditionally, religious texts were prized and bore immense cultural prestige. But the way that prestige worked made these texts highly esoteric and restricted. Texts were brought into animation but in highly controlled, strictly hierarchical sacred spaces. Texts were presented in theatrical incantation inside temples, where ordinary people's task was not to understand them as ethical texts and practice their normative rules in everyday lives but to submit to their mystique and aural enchantment. Texts existed very differently in enchanted and disenchanted worlds, just as religiosity and the sacred meant utterly different things.

Protestant textuality, therefore, offered a profound challenge to Tamil textuality and the social order that sustained and expressed it. Introduction of a religion of disenchantment therefore entailed several interconnected processes of "universalization" (that is, making things more universally accessible). Primarily, in Bate's view, this meant three things: (1) creation of a more universal religious message in a more universalizing language, (2) delivered unrestrictedly to ordinary people without discrimination or hierarchy, and (3) delivered in more universalizing spaces such as bazaars. The Protestant sermon, because it came from outside as a competing religious theory, had to be delivered not merely in the cloistered settings of the Protestant churches where only those already converted to their religion came to attend. As a competitor, it had to seek settings that were more open, where it could call ordinary people who were not already Christians to the message of Christian salvation. What went on in these settings, Bate shows us with great care, was entirely opposite to the activities of conventional Tamil textual practice. Texts were truly animated in Hindu temple contexts, presented aurally and aesthetically rather than—to the Protestants' eyes and ears—through rational argumentation and referential discourse. Protestants offered an opposite kind of animation in which the messages of the text, based on supposed clarity of rational reasoning, would persuade people of its truth—a universalizing textuality addressing a universal subject.

Protestants were suspicious of the poesy of religious speech because they suspected correctly that the communicative structure of a society was linked to its social structure and endorsed it. Therefore, they sought to convey the message of their texts through a new mode of textual animation: homiletic oratory, carried out into a non-Christian world through a call to the Word of God. The Protestant critique, carried out through oratorical textuality, identified the defining feature of Hindu textuality, rote memorization, as draining the words of their rational persuasive power (a rhetoric of reason) and replacing them with a kind of imposing, paralyzing, unquestionable rhetoric of gravity captured in recitation and incantation. In both cases, Hindu and Protestant, textuality seeks expression through an embodiment, what Bate calls in the Introduction "emblematization." But they do so through entirely opposed models: one captured in the ceremonial setting inside or in front of temples, in incantatory recitation of fixed texts that could not be altered and did not need to be rationally understood; the other embodied in the speeches delivered in the free space of bazaars where Protestant missionaries were calling all people, irrespective of caste and status, to the reasoned message of their democratic God.

Tamil Appropriation of Protestant Oratory

All over India, a few decades of Western education began to produce what Rabindranath Tagore jestingly called the "preceptor-killing disciples of Western savants" (*javan panditder gurumara chela*),[6] who turned the intellectual skills they learned from Western colonial teachers against colonial culture. In the Tamil country, the most remarkable products of Protestant education began to use their skill at this new oratory designed for a new public sphere to defend and propagate not Protestant but traditional Saiva doctrines. Within a short time, such defections and the evident inability of the missionaries to show large numbers of conversions convinced the mother institutions to call the enterprise a failure and, in some cases, to shut them down. But the "failure," Bate shows, was a great historical paradox. Saiva disciples who came out of this training gave up Protestant religious doctrines but not the new communicative infrastructure. Embracing the Protestant modes of textuality, they made it utterly dominant by transplanting it inside Saiva religious practices. It was a very successful failure, because, as Bate writes in the Introduction, "while Protestantism had failed, Protestant textuality emerged as dominant."

However, Bate's own detailed analysis of the career of Arumugam Navalar, the first non-Christian to use Protestant homiletic speech styles with unparalleled success, shows a more complex construction. Navalar, Bate shows, incorporated into his typical form of oratorical interpellation of audiences not just the epistemized use of "rational" language but also something that should be called rhetorical or, better, a corporeal element drawn from the textualities of the Tamil tradition. Bate shows that an important, often dominant element of older Tamil textuality was the presence of something sonic, a bodily rather than mental ("a sonorous poesy") use of *alankaric* elements within a high form of enunciation. If Protestant oratory sought to persuade people simply by reason, this added a supplemental aspect, bodily and rhetorical, that produced a far more potent effect.

What Bate describes for Tamil was a common process observed in many vernaculars across the subcontinent. Vernacular languages across North India were usually derived from Sanskrit and shared a vocabulary stock. Ingenious users of such languages, while negotiating the demands modernity placed on language, often derived a sonorous high rhetorical style from Sanskrit textual practice, both in their use of vocabulary and in the sonorous enunciation of Sanskrit incantative modes. Similarly, Navalar added a supplement drawn from earlier Tamil textuality to elevate the character of his oratorical prose. Remarkably, the subtle innovation in this enhancement is that a feature normally associated with high-style, and heteroglossic, verse was now cleverly shifted to (vernacular, increasingly monolingual) prose. Identical moves are found in the rise of high-modern Bengali in authors such as Bankimchandra Chattopadhyay. A highly Sanskritic vocabulary serves to lift the tone of Bengali prose precisely at a time when proficiency in Sanskrit quickly declined.

The new oratory crafted by figures such as Navalar found a historic opportunity for widespread public use with the Swadeshi movement. Vernacular oratory exploded in the Tamil country, altering the relation between the speakers and their addressees and the field that contained and defined them both—a new kind of public sphere, based on an entirely altered definition of the public. Formerly, the "public" considered relevant for the elitist and arcane activity named "politics" consisted of the doubly educated—in vernacular and in two "high languages," Sanskrit, but more critically in English, the language required to deal with intricacies of colonial law and governance. The Swadeshi agitation suddenly turned politics into an increasingly universal field, open to everyone, and therefore a sphere where interpellation of the people was possible only in the vernacular.

It is here that Protestant textuality and modern South Asian politics meet, where new forms of oratorical discourse and textuality are put to use in the interpellative creation of a new public—open, abstract, secular, universal. As Bate details, audiences became universalized in containing people from low castes, women, and laborers—all excluded by both the sacred and the colonial definitions of public space. As noted, the Protestants also advocated a shift from a sonocentric language that wanted to impress by its mystical aura to a logocentric one that wished to convert by the power of rational argument. Saiva orators who followed them had a different relation to the premodern Tamil high language, selectively absorbing the stylistic devices from the older language in their embodiment, incorporating memorization and recitation (meaning a lofty enunciation). After all, political speech, too, contains repetition and poesy, which no audience finds unpleasant. Like the repetitiveness of the invocation of the sacred, political speeches also invoke principles considered true or good in an ethical sense. Repetition of these values, instead of being unpleasant, comes to be heard as enhancement. Political speeches also have incantation-like elements—incandescent phrases such as "workers of the world unite," which came to be paralleled in the emerging world of Indian nationalism by "Vantē mātaram."

The Non-archive of Oratory

Bate's history is also unusually reflective about its archive. Paradoxically, the orators have been hidden by the archive itself, Bate notes with subtlety. This is an interesting observation that requires greater reflection. Any analyst of politics would be struck simultaneously by the significance of oratory and its strange elusiveness. A great speech obviously makes an instant impact on political life. But, ironically, once it is over as a physical, corporeal event, precisely because of its essential corporeality it becomes impossible to recapture or re-present, unlike many other types of acts that constitute political activity.

This peculiar elusiveness becomes apparent if we compare the histories of writing and speaking. Consider two significant speeches at the time of Indian independence—Jawaharlal Nehru's "tryst with destiny" speech and Babasaheb Ambedkar's valedictory address to the Constituent Assembly. Nehru's speech was recorded and filmed. Because of the poor technical quality of recording, some of the corporeal event is certainly lost. But we can access with some accuracy the actual—*eigentlich*—event of history. By contrast, Ambedkar's speech is impossible to reconstruct *in full.* Because it was not filmed and recorded, we have lost forever the corporeal speech-event. All that we have is a textual record of the speech. The speech was forever altered by the archive: its effect on history and its capture by historians would remain permanently as *a piece of writing*—which it was not. The archive has hidden the orator, not in the sense that Ambedkar is not known, nor in the fact that his speech is not recorded, but in the more profound sense that the character of the historical event has been perpetually and irreversibly transformed by turning the live speech into a written text. If this is true of the well-archived speeches of the greatest historic significance, we can imagine what the relation between the speech and the archive is for more ordinary instances of significant oratory and for the earliest moments in the history of oratory before sufficient recording technologies were devised (including shorthand, as Bate discusses). The orators play the most effective conative role in bringing people to politics, but either there is no archive for this fundamental activity or the archive precisely hides the orators. In the archive, orators have been turned into text-producing agents. Records exist, of course, as Bate notes, sometimes in surprisingly large volume. We have a lot of evidence of their contexts—what led to the speech and its consequences—what came after, with very little about the speech itself. Orations do not have any reliable recorders. And even when they exist in their degraded textual form, the recordings or texts do not capture the corporeal phenomenology of the lectures—the live, contingent, utterly momentary gestures for persuading, convincing, converting someone to a political view. Moreover, usually they are transcribed by agents hostile to the speaker—leaving to historians such as Bate to practice a particularly hard form of "reading against the grain." In a strange paradox, the police were the only archivists of the poetry of rebellion. What the speech was really like in case of a fiery orator such as Subramania Siva (discussed in Chapter 5)—what linguistic sparks lit the flame—the historian has to construct not through strict evidence but through imagination.

Bate's important historiographic argument—to underscore the point—is that though oratory played an immense role in the creation of modern Indian politics, it is relatively forgotten in history. Because writing is permanent and oratory is transient, oratory leaves no trace: it is hard to discover and record both for the policeman and for the historian. Writers find a place in history;

orators are largely forgotten. Even when they are remembered, their productions are misremembered as texts. In case of figures like Subramania Bharati, for example, they are forgotten as orators, remembered affectionately as poets. If history is to capture what actually happened, the actual happening of oratory is strangely depleted in our historical recall. Its specificity gets smudged into the generality of the conventional claim that nationalist ideas spread by way of the "press and the platform," reinforcing our disregard of the fact that they were two separate modes, requiring distinct skills with quite divergent conative effects. Speech is more of an affective force than writing, leading people to a visceral emotion of collective anger, leading to collective action. Political action, we tend to forget, is not a step produced by simple ratiocination but requires something affective as a supplement.

Bate raises another interesting question about these early oratorical meetings: as the numbers grow too large—reaching thousands, without loudspeakers—the lecture must have been a highly complex aural event. Large sections of the gathering must have been too far away from the speaker to hear clearly what was being said. If they could not hear the lecture, why were they there? What, if not listening, were they doing? Orators seem to have become figures who took part in a complex public performance that transcended the initial attraction of a rousing speech. Mass meetings were becoming new rituals of political belonging: people joined them to show their support for an increasingly larger and abstract yet deeply meaningful cause.

From some parts of the truncated archive, Bate is able to piece together segments of the actual oratorical statements. Some oratorical flourishes Bate records are similar to textual polemics by Bengali authors such as Ram Mohan Roy. Often they saved the worst vitriol for their polemics against Christian missionaries, sometimes launching into a comparison of portrayals of God in different faiths and characterizing the Christian God as the meanest of them all. Some features of this oratory diverge from the Protestant model. They start using religion not as denotational but evocational, to use a characterization from Valentine Daniel that Bate admires, using "mood" rather than mind.[7] Serious political arguments are interspersed with mythological stories, which, as observers reported, seemed to lift the hearers out of their present historical time into a strange mythic time of heroic deeds. Yet evocation of that mythic time was a detour: the speech invoked them primarily to relate to their own present time in an altered, charged fashion. And they did so, according to Bate's analysis, through another interesting transfer: as we noted earlier, by fashioning a new kind of Tamil for politics that was highly refined, beautiful, yet meant for the open public sphere. Anyone could speak that language if he had the talent, had learned and practiced it. So it was a beautiful language but in a way that was entirely opposite to the refined language inside the temple: it was not high-caste, not sequestered inside a sacred space, not ennobled by elitism.

As a careful analyst, Bate also notes some features of intonation and poetics, in how the speech sounded. Oratorical speech was nothing like the beautiful language inside the temple—measured, predetermined, preformed, highly structured. Political oratory, by contrast, was flowing, animated, full of surprises, although at the same time these features repeated and expanded and heightened a single theme, its political message. Effective oratory involves an aural punctuation—high and low notes of the tone, varying speeds of delivery of words, the deliberateness of pauses, the finality of endings. Punctuation also introduces into writing something that is crucial in speaking. Bate notes that these separate uses of language must be understood in the context of a larger economy of linguistic functions—reading, writing, speaking. These are not simply variations of each other, leaving the textual content unaffected. Each one had different forms, styles, and they were calculated to produce very different effects with words. Historically, this was the time of emergence of modern silent reading, which must have heightened the contrast between the silence of reading and the sonority of speaking. As reading becomes silent, that is, devoid of aural qualities, sonic qualities come to ornament orality even more strikingly. Oratory becomes a new kind of oral performance in which formal features of linguistic refinement—such as punctuation and pronunciation—become significant. And alongside this, new political ideas were emerging, ideas that demanded and formed a new kind of public sphere that people attended in unprecedented large numbers. New political ideas and ideals—nationalism—were conveyed to these masses in this new language of oratory. The British Indian Empire at the turn of the century became, in Bate's memorable phrase, "an empire of orators."

The Oratory of Swadeshi and the Emergence of a Demonic Demos

Changes in oratory signaled larger historical changes in the political world of India. The injustice against which the orators wanted the Tamil people to show their outrage did not happen only in the Tamil country but also in distant Bengal. Tamil people were exhorted to rejoice, for example, at the release of a Bengali leader and orator himself, Bipin Chandra Pal. Through the Swadeshi movement sweeping across India, the rise of modern oratory produced two new figures that concern Bate: the common politician and the common people the politician represents. The measure of the importance of the politician was not his high status either in caste or colonial terms but his ability to rouse the common people against an unjust partition of their country. In his discussion of Swadeshi, Bate briefly comments on the history of the Madras Mahajana Sabha, the association of the eminent of Madras. Elite groups such as the English-conducted Mahajana Sabha often derided the upstart vernacular politicians about their ignorance of how politics was conducted; they did not expect that the conduct of politics itself was itself changing. Groups of *mahajana*s were not aware of their looming obsolescence: they were about to be replaced by a different collective actor, who could also be called the *mahajana*, "the great people": the political arrival of the masses.[8]

Historically, the effect of the Swadeshi episode was short-lived because, Bate feels, the idea of an Indian nation was too abstract. In fact, the government's repressive actions revealed both the power and the elusiveness of vernacular oratory. Vernacular newspapers—the other vehicle of the language of the people—were vulnerable to government pressures, threats, and legal controls. To read vernacular newspapers and journals, their audience required literacy. Oratory was free of these limitations; thus, in many parts of India, not just in Tamil Nadu, it was oratory that kept the fire of the new expansive, supralocal, post-Swadeshi nationalism burning despite the colonial state's repressive efforts to extinguish it.

Since political life is truly a "field," a reliable picture requires portrayals from different sides or points of view. Bate's history provides a powerful example and masterful account of the record of oratory and change in the culture of speech from a fascinating testimony of an English observer, Henry Nevinson.[9] To colonial administrators and British observers such as Nevinson, political change across this period appeared invariably as a dark, ominous development, a sudden change in atmosphere that was impossible to escape and a threat that could suddenly erupt anywhere. To him the masses were the mob, always unpredictable, irrational, volatile, hard to identify and control. Mobs could form suddenly and melt away and could threaten order and stability.

Preferred spaces for the new language and the mass meetings they conducted were beaches, bazaars, and schools—places noted for miscegenation that were open to everybody and where exclusion was hard to practice. As the specter of this new mass nationalism began to spread, British observers sensed a dark alteration in the atmosphere. When speeches were not being made in the bazaars, British inhabitants of cities were startled by little boys crying "*vantē mātaram*," a chant that carried a demonic spectral quality, a dark spirit that lurked everywhere and could suddenly materialize in unaccountable forms that were impossible to police. Boys shouting "*vantē mātaram*" were hard to punish; yet, if they went unpunished, that seemed an invitation to more general defiance and a positive end to the colonial order. For Nevinson, even scenes of nature became infected with the rising anxiety, colored by human affect: "the sky was full of the deep and ominous colours of an Indian sunset in the rains."[10] Great historical experiences are all-encompassing.

Nevinson was struck by some features of the speeches he had heard. The cadence of the speeches was slow and steady, with sobriety and clarity, marked by a tone of solemnity—very much, observed truthfully, like speeches made regularly in England that demanded extension of human rights, which were taken for granted in British politics. Speakers were not demanding something unusual or uncommon. They were demanding a human right granted to free people as a matter of course. Often these meetings ended in great emotion, with songs and the ever-present cry of "*vantē mātaram*." The speeches were entirely sober and rational, Nevinson noted; "the thunder comes from the cry of bande mataram."[11] In the slow movement of the world of language, the colonial ideology of orderly improvement was coming apart. At this time, immediately after the first wave of Swadeshi enthusiasm, incendiary speech makers would often deny making those speeches when facing trials and possible long sentences. But soon this would change. In a trial a decade later, the leader of the national movement would stop the public prosecutor's argument and claim that he had, indeed, made seditious speeches, sometimes more seditious than the ones cited by the prosecution, and further, that he wanted the judge to give him the maximum sentence. Mass politics became possible, Bate argues persuasively, because of the new communicative infrastructure. This was the inauguration of a new stage in political modernity, and this modernity was truly Tamil and Indic.[12]

Bharati and Modern Tamil Language

It takes poets to make the language catch fire. They can impart to languages a musical force that no other users can. Poets extend the boundaries of what is semantically possible. Not surprisingly, poets have enjoyed a particularly close relation with nationalism everywhere. When a new unprecedented collective emotion takes hold of their people, they are the only ones who can provide them with the words that bring this emotion to speech. But modern poetics is complex and moves in different lines. A highly significant development in modern poetry is the slow abandonment of older forms of poesy, such as alliteration, explicit ornamentation, and other features that marked older forms of the poetic. As reading becomes increasingly silent—a scene of semantic enjoyment of the solitary sophisticated reader—modern poetry moves away from conventional rhetorical forms.

Yet political modernity makes entirely opposite demands on poetry as well. Nationalism everywhere requires a new kind of poesy as a vehicle of its collective emotional effervescence. Leading poets in all modern traditions have provided this vehicle through poetry and musical composition. Bate selects the poetic corpus of Subramania Bharati as the paradigmatic figure of modern Tamil poesy, particularly of its collective emotion. Unlike the increasing cerebrality of the other poetic tradition, this tradition foregrounds the corporeal in language and the expression of collective emotion, indeed, its musicality.

Bate notes a gradual expansion of the rhetoric and repertoire of defiance. Demonstrations, as they become more frequent, acquire additional features, such as processions and music. These, for him, are steps in the same path that vernacular oratory opened. They were modeled in some senses on the

Protestant appeal to faith, but the faith is now typically Indian and Tamil. Appeals are made to Indian images of God; in Bharati's case, to the avatar of Vishnu when the world falls into dark times, partly because the *Mahabharata* and the *Bhagavad Gita* literally invite this evocation.[13] The iterative promise of God's future comings makes this a trope with obvious appeal for nationalist writers.[14]

Here, too, Bate emphasizes the deep connection between music and language, because music cannot affect people if it is not in the language that is not learned. English can convey the clarity of rational argumentation but not the burst of the collective emotion. But this music, as Bate reads it, is both old and new. It invokes the presence of Krishna as a charioteer and philosopher—but now not to a lone warrior of an ancient society but to a newly formed people in the living present. In Bate's subtle description, it laminates the time of the narrating over the time of the narrated event. Searching for rousing tropes to communicate this unprecedented emotion, poets across India used similar devices. Rabindranath Tagore, a self-consciously "secular" writer, uses the same trope without overt reference to the Krishna figure in the national anthem. Evocations of the Krishna theme are indirect but discernible in the anthem, though in passages that are not standardly sung:

> *patana-abhyudaya-bandhura pantha yuga yuga-dhavita yatri*
> *he cira-sarathi taba rathacakre mukharita patha dina ratri*
> *daruna viplava majhe taba sankha dhvani baje sankata-duhkha-trata.*
> . . .
> *ghora-timira-ghana nibida-nishithe pidita murchita deshe*
> *jagrata chhila taba abichala mangala nata nayane animeshe*
> *duhsapne atanka Raksha karile anke, senahamayi tumi mata*

> The path is uneven—rising and falling, the traveler journeys through the epochs
> O eternal charioteer, the path resounds to the rumble of your chariot wheels
> In the middle of terrible destruction, your conch sounds, rescuer from calamity and suffering.

. . .

In the dense darkness of the night, when the country was sick,
senseless,
Your steadfast will to auspiciousness in your unblinking kind eyes
In times of nightmare, of deep dread
You saved us in your lap,
Our compassionate Mother.

Clearly, in Tagore's poem the chariot and charioteer have been modernized in crucial ways. The path of history is not indefinite nondescript time; it is a path of rise and fall consonant with a modern conception of historical time. The wheels of the chariot do not merely make circles in the bloody field of a great battle. They rumble along a linear path. And the charioteer's conch sounds not in a meaningless battle but in the great revolutions of history. Tagore is writing in the cultural context of Bengal, marked by the simultaneous presence of both the Vaishnava and the Shakta traditions, and the semiosis of the figure alternates between masculine and feminine forms. In one stanza, the figure is like Krishna, as in Bharati, but in the second, it is reminiscent of Devi. But significantly, it is very different from the fighting image Bankimchandra Chattopadhyay produced in his song "Vantē mātaram" in his 1882 novel *Anandamath* through an overlay of Kali and Durga. Tagore invokes a feminine figure of sustenance and care for the distressed. In times of destruction and distress, this androgynous God delivers as a charioteer and comforts as a mother. God has become mortal in a world of mortals, representing the *samutāyam* (society), what Tagore using an adjacent *tatsama* term calls the *samuha*. Features of this God are all related to his or her ability to comfort the collective people: *janagana*, celebrated in cascading adjectives, which ring with God's qualities but also the people's presence: *janagana-mana-adhinayaka* (leader of the people's mind), *janagana-mangaladayaka* (creator of the people's welfare), *janagana-aikyavidhayaka* (maker of the people's unity), *janagana-pathaparicayaka* (guide to the people's path), *janagana-duhkhatrayaka* (rescuer of the people from suffering). The final adjective in Tagore's poem, *sankata-duhkhatrata* (rescuer from calamity and suffering), does not explicitly incorporate *janagana*, but it is not hard to understand whose *sankata* (calamity) and *duhkha* (suffering) that God is incarnated to relieve. All parts of India rang with this new language found in Swadeshi, a new affect that has now found a new expressive poetry that was increasingly common to all vernaculars.

This new poetry is musical and is meant to be set to music. In Chapter 4, Bate offers a memorable account from a writer who took part in one of these processions that broke into music—a Bharati song evoking the other warlike god, Murugan. The author remembers his own vision in which at a climactic musical moment the icon in the picture seemed to come alive and start moving. He seemed to remember that Bharati was in the procession, when historical evidence makes that implausible. In Bate's analysis, Bharati's association with his music generated this illusion. Whenever his music was really sung, people had an excusable illusion, when remembering that event much later, that the poet was present. Though, after his return from long exile in Pondicherry, Bharati stayed away from direct political activity, in which he had become politically irrelevant. Nevertheless, his music, always ineradicably political, continued to work its magical amplification of collective affect.

The crowds in the meetings had changed, both in terms of numbers and of class. A hundred thousand turned up at a meeting, as lower castes and working classes began to join the new throngs of "the people." Led by rebellious young members of the upper castes, a section of the elite itself broke off from conservative politics and began to embrace the "vulgarity" of the people, eventually dissociating the popular from the vulgar and the stigmatized and turning their support into the noblest badge of honor. This is a characteristic feature of revolutionary movements speaking a recognizable language merging anger and hope, captured in Bharati's phrase, "if one person goes hungry, we'll destroy the world."

Bharati spoke the Tamil people into existence, according to Bate, combining the orator and the poet in a single person in a heroic act of poetic and political world making.

What This Incandescent Elocution Achieved

Politics originates surprisingly. I have argued that in Bengal it originated in comedy, in satire that allowed authors to say what was unsayable under colonial power.[15] In most historical settings, nationalist politics owe their original impulse to literature.[16] In the Tamil world, however, Bate shows that it originated in the *spoken* word, in oratory. Oratory is evidently related to a conative process—the creation of collective emotions that results in a disposition to collective action. Undemocratic representative politics of colonial times gave rise to segmentary publics and highly restricted and tightly controlled spheres of political action (by caste, class, gender). The Swadeshi movement began to rupture these boundaries, inviting ordinary people from all castes and incomes into the expanded conception of politics of a nationalism driven by the masses, "the people," the *janagana*. Multiple publics, which were separate and mediated their relation with the colonial government independently, began to merge into a nationalist public and turned the public sphere of political activity into a field of exchange of moves and maneuvers between the colonial government and an increasingly unified and defiant people.

Locations

The evolution of oratory shows the sequence of spaces for political gathering. When the activity of politics remained restricted only to the earlier definition of the colonial *mahajana* elites, their proper spaces were the new kinds of collective forums—for example, town halls, and halls meant specifically for meetings of that kind—such as the Albert Hall in Calcutta, the scene of the great oratorical occasions for leaders such as Surendranath Banerjee. With Swadeshi there is a clear historic shift to spaces that were outside these stuffy theaters of colonial elegance and arrogance, mostly in fields and *maidans*, or bazaars, sometimes in compounds of schools controlled by the local native groups rather than the state administration. As the crowds swelled, these moved to the spaces that figure prominently in Bate's story: bazaars, but also fields, beaches, parks. After a few decades, technology makes it possible for vast numbers to actually hear what was being said in these huge public meetings, with the introduction of public-address systems. They make even soft-spoken and mild-mannered speakers like Gandhi audible to these vast audiences of thousands who joined the nationalist meetings.

Bate is careful in presenting even this story of space and analyzes not merely the inevitable logic of larger numbers but also at times critical decisions made by the speakers to select spaces with symbolic value. In one instance, speakers decide to have a meeting in front of the barbers' quarters in the town. Another remarkable feature of the story is the slow rise of an awareness that traditional social belongings such as caste and community hindered the growth of this new consciousness of a people. It is remarkable that organizers of meetings and demonstrations not merely wanted to make the people inclusive by symbolically assembling in "lowly" spaces but also by exhorting followers to chant "Allahu akbar" alongside "*vantē mātaram*" and, also notably, that speakers urged their followers not to shout and break the calm for Christians on Ash Wednesday. In the tragic Tinnevelly shooting incident after the advent of mass politics that Bate discusses in Chapter 5, this mixture is reflected in the dead: a non-Brahmin priest, a working-class boy working in a bakery, a Muslim, and a Dalit.

Themes

Bate's analysis of the content of the speeches reveals something interesting that he did not, unfortunately, have time to elaborate. He notes the major linguistic paradox of Indian nationalism: India could not be united and energized by the use of a single Indian language. Ironically, the only pan-Indian language that worked as the language of the elite was English. The intractability of this linguistic difficulty is reflected in the repeated attempts by Congress leaders to raise the question and the partial answers offered and debated periodically. Hindustani was supported by figures such as Gandhi and Nehru but was opposed, ironically, by advocates of Hindi, who, presumably, were not opposed to the idea of a common Indian language but objected to Hindustani being elevated to that status. They would not have objected to Hindi occupying that place instead. In my own work, I have felt that this was resolved in practice by obviating the question of which *single* language should be the means of pan-Indian communication altogether and working through the ubiquitous existence of a diglossia.[17]

As Bate shows, politics before the rise of the masses was marked by an elite cosmopolitanism that used English as its means of communication. But this pan-Indianism was quite different from what emerged from the period of Bate's history. English was the apt means of communication at that stage of politics because the communication involved elites of different regions—all fluent in English—and because their primary interlocutors were the British rulers.

The rise of mass politics after Swadeshi, and the dawning realization after the emergence of Gandhi that only increasing mass mobilization could prise open the colonial grip on sovereignty, altered the orientation of political activity. Instead of speaking to the state, speaking to the masses become the critical persuasive act, for which the vernacular was the only linguistic means. In the next phase of the nationalist movement, the discourse of most important leaders was bilingual and split in its address. They persuaded their mass followings in the vernacular but conducted their proceedings in the All-India Congress sessions in English.

This picture of the grid of communication remains true. But Bate's detailed analysis of the content of oratory adds a new aspect to our understanding of how Indians did not speak the same language but understood each other. Bate reads Nevinson's hostile but meticulous description of the speeches to grasp a new and critically significant point. This can be grasped only by giving attention to vernacular speech making. Political persuasion happens through speeches that are primarily a set of "utterances"—what structuralists would call *parole*—the purely adventitious combination of words in accidental sentences. But clearly, the language, the utterances of the political movement, must carry some larger ideas repetitively. Otherwise, speeches would melt in the air. What allows them to leave an intelligible residue of understandings and ideas? What allows a second speech to build on a first—in particular, when the subjectivity of the speakers is in some ways transcended so that the same theme can be carried in unconnected speeches by hundreds of orators in discrete occasions and settings? Bate's work shows clearly the emergence of common concepts and tropes. Themes of *swaraj* (self-rule) and *mukti* (political liberation) become increasingly recurrent during the Swadeshi agitation. But that shows what the masses or the nation desired. Could the nation achieve these objectives against the overwhelming power of the British Empire?

Writers and orators in all vernacular settings—Bate offers instances from Tamil, and similar examples can be easily drawn from Bengali—converge in finding unsuspected sources of "strength" in the people. The song "Vantē mātaram" itself invokes that unrecognized strength, but in a locution of hesitancy—"*abala kena ma eta bale*?" (Why are you called weak, despite such vast strength?)—which it seeks to override in a resonant incantation following immediately: "*bahubala-dharinim namami tarinim ripudalabarinim mataram*" (I bow to the Mother who has immense power, who is the rescuer, and who stops the enemy hordes). In subsequent nationalist thinking, this theme of seeking the sources of the strength of the ordinary people fixes on concepts of *sakti*, particularly *atmasakti* and *satyagraha*, especially through Gandhi's insistence on the use of the noncognitive meaning of the word *satya*—where existence itself is meant to carry weight. This is also reflected in the chanting of numbers. Bate's work shows that although the vernaculars were distinct and separate and although India was becoming more of a monoglot world, a complex of ideas and concepts was forming that transcends the boundaries of the vernaculars. People speaking vernaculars might not understand each other's language, but they all understand the meaning of *swaraj* and *satyagraha* and that the people have an immense *sakti*.

A second form of rising common intelligibility was potentially more problematic. In the rising language of emotion, commonly intelligible tropes—both linguistic and iconic—began to circulate and assume semantic significance. Many of these tropes—the icon of the sustaining and defending mother, the charioteer who can see the path in epochal darkness—were obviously prior religious figures. But in being used for nationalist emotion, these had to be disembedded from their earlier dense moorings of religious semantics before they could be deployed in the service of secular politics. Yet they remained potent religious imagery—with the possibility that for some this imagery would intensify the affect of such tropes and images. For others, however, such imagery and affect would remain distant and alien. Organizers of the meetings that Bate discusses show a clear awareness of such dissension by using Islamic chants and desisting from singing on Christian days of silence. But these tropes always retained this ambiguous potential.

Representation/Identity

Bate's scholarly focus was entirely on the question of oratory and the emergence of the Tamil modern and nationalist politics, at the same moment and through the same act. In closing, however, I want to mention several other themes implicitly analyzed in this rich tapestry of analysis of the spoken language.

The first theme is representation. It is sometimes seen that two forms of representation—political and artistic—are often intertwined in historical events. Bate's study of the origins of nationalist politics in fact deftly weaves these two arguments about the representative process. Though this is not his main preoccupation, his historical account reveals how the story of modern politics unfolds through forms of representation. Evidently, the colonial state's ruling process depends heavily on a device of representation that has nothing to do with democracy. It is simply a colonial extension of a process by which the ruling power nominates representatives of groups it believes it has to address and communicate with in its exercise of quotidian power. Even colonial authority has to elicit concerns before it formulates policies and gathers responses afterward from social groups of various kinds, religious, regional, occupational. A system of nominational representation of these groups was put in place in the period of high colonial rule, which worked through its restrictive public sphere. Participation in this public sphere was controlled by class, caste, gender, and language, as we have noted. Representatives of regional elites communicated with colonial authorities in English and observed an intricate etiquette of deferential conversation with the ruling powers. It is this structure of representation that was overthrown and transformed by the Swadeshi movement and the first uncertain moves toward popular politics that Bate chronicles with careful attention. The new politics altered the terms of representation, despite desperate disapproval and hostility from the colonial state.

In the course of a few decades, the terms of political exchange between British colonial authorities and their Indian subjects were utterly transformed. The Indians, earlier seen as a dispersed collection of elite islands in a vast illiterate society that had no self-recognition gradually conceived themselves as a people who were represented to the colonial authorities by their own chosen politicians, defying and undermining the process of nomination. It is not the state that selected who it wanted to converse with in the political sphere. Rather, it was the people who decided by their demonstrative acts who their representatives were. How could the state decide who were the representative of the people? Within a surprisingly short time what was obvious and taken for granted was turned into an absurdity. This constituted a fundamental shift in the process of *political representation*, and the state was obliged by the force of popular mobilization to accord this new idea a recognition by installing a limited form of elective representation in the 1930s.

What makes Bate's narrative singular is the clarity with which it grasps and presents to our view the connection of this process with a process of *imaginative representation*. This second process is imaginative in two different senses, both crucial for an understanding of nationalist politics. First, the idea of a people—which included all social groups, castes, classes, genders—was a matter of conception, when it was purely imagined, even as actual social conduct did not follow the logic of this conception. But by acting on this imagination, a group of political actors, orators in their vanguard, slowly made this real. They realized it, turning it from an imaginative idea—much like a fictional figure in literature—into a social fact.

This translation into the real was not inevitable; it depended on real, contingent, small but world-constituting acts by politicians. Surprisingly, some of these acts were simply using charged words—an intangible flow of oratorical ideas. But such oratorical acts and acts of politics these incited—meetings, demonstrations, exile: the enormous repertoire of defiance of colonial power—required concrete shapes, forms, ideas, images. This is what imagination in the second sense—arts, novels, poetry, music, paintings—provided, allowing for concrete images around which this new imagination could congeal. The people had to be represented to themselves for them to believe that they existed as a real collectivity before the questions of their political representation arose. Oratory—passionate use of words to suggest political ideas, images that realized the nation—played an irreplaceable role in this process of presenting the people to themselves.

Second, Bate's history also shows us some features of this imagined community of people. Starting from separate religious groups—Protestants, Saivites, and so on—this idea of the people expands to break its restrictive boundaries. On one side, it begins to include lower castes, poorer groups, women, anyone who spoke and aesthetically responded to Tamil. But the rejoicing at the release of a politician from faraway Bengal after Swadeshi, as we noted previously, indicates the forming of a larger entity. It indicates the first stirrings of an improbable Indian people to whom the Tamils belonged. This larger belonging did not cancel out Tamil identity but encompassed it even if it stood uneasily with it (as Bate's first book, *Tamil Oratory and the Dravidian Aesthetic* indicates).[18] Bate's work gives us an invaluable and surprising history of this elusive but critical moment because of the surprising object he seeks to capture: the dancing words of oratory.

NOTES

Abbreviations of Archival Sources

ACM TR	American Ceylon Mission Triennial Report
CID	Criminal Investigation Department
DIG	Deputy Inspector General
DO	Demi-Official Letter
DSP	Deputy Superintendent of Police
FR	Fortnightly Reports
GO	Government Order
GOI	Government of India
HFM	History of the Freedom Movement volumes in the Tamil Nadu Archives
TNA	Tamil Nadu Archives

Foreword

1. Bernard Bate, "Arumuga Navalar, Saivite Sermons and the Delimitation of Religion," *Indian Economic and Social History Review* 42, no. 4 (2005): 469–84.

2. Bernard Bate, "Nāṟpatu Vayatu Matikkattakka Vēḷālap Peṇ—Tamiḻaga Cutēci Iyakkac Coṟpoḻivāḷarkaḷ Kuṟitta Kuṟippukaḷ" [A Vellala woman about forty years old—notes on orators in the Swadeshi movement in Tamilagam], *Matruveli* (Tamil Nadu) 2 (2009): 49–53. http://www.keetru.com/index.php?option=com_content&view=article&id=457:2009-09-13-%15-38-47&catid=918:09&Itemid=166.

3. Bernard Bate, *Tamil Oratory and the Dravidian Aesthetic* (New York: Columbia University Press, 2009).

4. Published originally in *Thamarai Jeeva Sirappu Malar*, April 1963. Since then it has been included in a number of Sundara Ramaswamy's collections of essays but especially a volume of the same title, *Kattril Kalantha Perosai* (Nagercoil: Kalchuvadu Pathippagam, 1998). Jeeva, as he was popularly known, was a forceful orator who fashioned a distinct style markedly different from the Dravidian style that was becoming hegemonic. His style, too, had its imitators. See D. Jayakanthan, *Oru Ilakkiyavathiyin Arasiyal Ninaivugal* (Madurai: Meenakshi Puthaka Nilaiyam, 1974).

5. Also see Bernard Bate, "Swadeshi Oratory and the Development of Tamil Shorthand," in "Swadeshi in the Time of Nations: Reflections on Sumit Sarkar's *The*

Swadeshi Movement in Bengal, India and Elsewhere," ed. B. Bate and Dilip Menon, special section of *Economic and Political Weekly* 47, no. 42 (2012): 70–75.

6. However, I was struck to find archival confirmation of some legendary oral history. Va. Ra. (V. Ramaswami Iyengar), the famed biographer of Subramania Bharati, recalled Ethiraj Surendranath Arya ridiculing cowardly Indian men in a public meeting: "O, Indians why do you sport a moustache? Even prawns have them?" A CID policeman reported Arya's speech at Moore Market on 5 June 1908 in the following words: "Even prawns had long moustaches and that a man's courage could not be judged merely by the length of his moustache."

7. Thiru. Vi. Kalyanasundaram Mudaliar, *Tamil Thendral allathu Thalamai Pozhivu* (1928; repr., Chennai: Poompuhar Pathippagam, 1997), 13–14. This book was first published in 1928 and had seen four reprints by 1947.

8. *Kudi Arasu*, 5 November 1933.

9. Mudaliar, *Tamil Tendral allathu Thalamai Pozhivu*.

10. S. Satyamurthy, *Satyamurthy Pesugirar* (1945; repr., Chennai: Tamil Pannai, 1946), v–vi.

11. Ranajit Guha, "The Prose of Counter-insurgency," in *Selected Subaltern Studies*, ed. Ranajit Guha and Gayatri Spivak (Delhi: Oxford University Press, 1988), 46.

12. A. Madhaviah, *Padmavathi Charithiram* (Chennai: People's Printing and Publishing House, 1928), 3:121. This chapter was written sometime in 1925.

13. Kalki, *Palattril Oru Pagarkanavu* (Chennai: Vanathi Pathippagam, 2007), 33.

14. See Amanda Weidman, *Singing the Classical, Voicing the Modern* (Durham, NC: Duke University Press, 2006), 59–60, 86–93. As late as in the late 1950s police reports of political speeches indicated the use of loudspeakers. See, for instance, the bulky file on Periyar's speeches in the Tamil Nadu Archives: GO 73, Public, Gen-B, 8-1-1958.

15. Soda water bottles also doubled as missiles and weaponry in political street fights. By the turn of the millennium packaged drinking water in plastic bottles had displaced soda water.

16. T. M. Deivasigamani Achari, *Medai Tamil* (Chennai: Sadhu Acchukoodam, 1949).

17. For its influence on singing in Carnatic music, see T. M. Krishna, *A Southern Music: The Karnatik Story* (Noida: HarperCollins, 2013), 408–12.

18. See P. Saravanan's magisterial compilation of the polemical tracts, *Arutpa Marutpa Kandana Thirattu* (Nagercoil: Kalchuvadu Pathippagam, 2010), and my extended introduction to the volume. For an incisive new study of Ramalinga Swamigal, see Richard Weiss, *The Emergence of Modern Hinduism: Religion on the Margins of Colonialism* (Berkeley: University of California Press, 2019).

19. Maraimalai Adigal commanded high speaking fees, as much as five hundred

rupees or more, and made demands—such as a separate house to lodge, hot-water baths, freshly clarified ghee, unbroken raw rice—in keeping with his star status. Despite having a squeaky voice, he more than made up for it with his erudition. (Indicative of his popularity were invitations for two long speaking tours of Sri Lanka.)

20. Extant Tamil historiography tends to have a strong Saivite bias. The "pravachana" tradition in Vaishnavism would also need to be kept in mind, though this tradition does not seem to have taken a political inflection. The unrivaled commentator and polemicist Prativadi Bhayankaram Annangarachariar (1891–1983) is known to have delivered a weekly discourse at Chennai from 1931 to 1964 without a break. For the collected lectures, see Annangarachariar, *Bhaktamrutham* (Chennai: Oriental Press, 1947). See his autobiography for descriptions of his discourses: P. B. Annangarachariar, *Thansarithai Churukkam* (Kanchipuram: Sri Ramanujan Veliyeedu, 1970).

21. Kalki's "Prasangangalum Prasangigalum" was published in two parts and appeared originally in *Ananda Vikatan*, 12 February and 14 March 1931. It is now included in Kalki, *Palattril Oru Pagarkanavu*, 1–38; and Thodarban [Ma. Su. Sambandan], *Sirantha Pechalargal* (Chennai: Tamilar Pathippagam, 1947 [shoddily reprinted by Manivasagar Pathippagam in 1997].

22. The Dravidian style of oratory was both lauded and derided for using excessive alliteration. A prominent critic was none other than Periyar himself. See *Viduthalai*, 16 October 1958. Periyar, as we know, used a colloquial register in his speeches.

23. A prominent exception to the trend was K. Kamaraj, Congress leader and chief minister, who relied on his organizational skills. On the platform, he was known to be brief and brusque, often responding with the words "*ākaṭṭum pākkalām*!" (Okay, let's see!), which could be interpreted in any number of ways.

24. Not incidentally, Deivasigamani Achari was the son of T. M. Mookan Achari, the first delegate to move a resolution in a vernacular language (Tamil) on the occasion of the Indian National Congress's third session in Chennai in 1887.

25. This exchange was immediately transcribed and published in 1943 as *Thee Paravattum*.

26. A textile dealer by profession, Anbu Pazhamnee was a bibliophile, dealer in secondhand books, and officiating priest in Tamil/Saiva marriages. I used to meet him regularly in the 1980s. He said that he wrote out Anna's speeches in longhand and had the text approved by him before sending it for printing.

27. Anbu Pazhamnee and K. V. Veeraraghavan, *Anna Pechu: Vettri Ragasiyam* (Chennai: Arivu Pannai, 1949).

28. Anbu Pazhamnee and K. V. Veeraraghavan, *Pecchu Kalai* (Chennai: Tamil Puthakalayam, 1950).

29. A. K. Parandamanar, *Pechalaraka* (Chennai: Malar Nilayam, 1955). This book still remains in print.

30. Parandamanar, 4.

31. Parandamanar, 7.

Introduction

1. DO no. 1190 W-1, 21 Apr. 1919 (FR), TNA, "History of the Freedom Movement" 71, 14–17; Kalyanasundaram (1944) 2003, 236–37.

2. A sub-inspector wrote: "The messages of Messrs. Gandhi and Subrahmanya Ayyar [*sic*] were read and translated into the vernacular." DO no. 306-c, 7 Apr. 1919, TNA, GO 222, Public, 24 Apr. 1919; also reproduced in "History of the Freedom Movement" 63, Home Rule.

3. DO no. 306-c, 7 Apr. 1919, TNA, GO 222, Public, 24 Apr. 1919.

4. DO no. 306-c.

5. DO no. 306-c.

6. [Editorial note: This opening section was taken, and redacted, from Bate 2013, 142–45.]

7. [Editorial note: The previous two sentences and the title of this section are from "SPS Fragment_the-press-and-the-platform.docx," with additions from Bate 2013, 160–61.]

8. [Editorial note: This paragraph is from Bate 2013, 161.]

9. [Editorial note: One anonymous reviewer of the manuscript points out that there was, however, a long tradition of premodern religious discourses that predated homiletic oratory in South India and would have addressed the laity in some public way. As Srilata Raman notes (pers. comm. with Francis Cody, 9 September 2020), for example, Śrīvaiṣṇava hagiographies called *guruparampara*s composed from the twelfth century onward are explicit about how the teachers of the community gave public discourses to the laity that explained theology and the sacred texts of the community; similarly, there are the *harikathā* traditions of South India, particularly recorded from the seventeenth century onward, which combined dancing, singing, and public performance of purāṇic tales through multilingualism to inspire an ethical devotionalism (Soneji 2013). Bate's point here, however, is the distinctness and newness of homiletic sermon vis-à-vis such examples, both in its imagination of its address and composition of its audiences, as well as its aims, rhetorical strategies, and language ideologies.]

10. Universal interpellation was a practice associated only with the lowest-status people—indeed, the drum (*paṟai*), an instrument of the lowest caste (*paṟaiyar*) due to its polluting leather (Sherinian 2014), stands as emblem of what was considered a vulgar act: the calling out to all indiscriminately. Its voice or "roar" (*murasu*)

spoke to all without distinction, a feature that led *murasu* to become the name of some early Tamil newspapers, texts printed to be broadcast to the world. To be a leader, on the other hand, such as a king or even a district- or village-level official, was to be relatively taciturn in speech, even silent (Bate 2009b); it certainly did not involve anything as vulgar as directly addressing a crowd. [Editorial note: This note is from Bate 2014, 551; and Bate 2013, 162.]

11. [Editorial note: This paragraph is from "Bate_2016-03-01_Swadeshi-Bharati_Berkeley_FINAL.docx," 10.]

12. [Editorial note: The previous two sentences are from "SPS_Fragment_the-press-and-the-platform.docx."]

13. [Editorial note: The previous two sentences are from "SPS_Fragment_the-press-and-the-platform.docx."]

14. [Editorial note: This is not to say that texts did not address audiences across communities prior to missionization. For example, seventeenth-century South Indian theological debates "addressed—and indeed spoke on behalf of—a religious public unconstrained by the walls of a monastery, the vows of asceticism, the hierarchies of lineage (*paramparā*), or the boundaries of any single religious institution" (Fisher 2017, 20). But there is little evidence to suggest that such address was universal in the sense Bate argues, for later Protestant textuality and speech meant to move audiences of lower-status people as political actors regardless of their religious background.]

15. [Editorial note: The previous three sentences are from "Bate_2016-03-01_Swadeshi-Bharati_Berkeley_FINAL.doc," 12.]

16. [Editorial note: This sentence is from "Bate_2016-03-01_Swadeshi-Bharati_Berkeley_FINAL," 12.]

17. "Poeticity is present when the word is felt as a word and not a mere representation of the object being named or an outburst of emotion, when words and their composition, their meaning, their external and inner form, acquire a weight and value of their own instead of referring indifferently to reality" (Jakobson 1987, 378).

18. In the anthropology of language, the poetic function has been described under terms such as "framing" (Goffman 1974) or "metapragmatics" (Silverstein 1976, 1993), a regimenting function of language that, in practice, draws a relationship between words and actions, denotationality and interaction. More broadly, poetic functions of language stipulate the emergence of social structural being-in-time through the regimentation of actors, agency, space, and time—what we call, following Mikhail Bakhtin (1981), "chronotopes." Such regimentation occurs constantly throughout any communicative process. Consider the chronotopic phase shifts in social order that occur before and at the onset of an oratorical event of some kind, say, a lecture (Goffman 1981) or a sermon. The lecturer or organizer

calls the event to "order" and quite abruptly who speaks, who attends, shifts suddenly and dramatically into a new mode of becoming, the sociotemporal qualities of which are well understood by all involved. It is the poetic function of language that provides that stipulating, framing effect between one sociochronotope and another.

19. [Editorial note: The previous three paragraphs are from "Bate_2016-03-01_Swadeshi-Bharati_Berkeley_FINAL," 10–12.]

20. [Editorial note: This sentence is from "Bate_2015-06-15_Swadeshi-Bharati_WRKG.docx," 23, with references supplied by Bate 2014.]

21. [Editorial note: This sentence is emended by language from "Bate_2016-03-03_Swadeshi-Bharati_WRKG.docx," 1.]

22. Even in 1836, when the missionary pioneer Daniel Poore wrote of his work in the American Ceylon Mission in Jaffna, it was commonplace to call science the "handmaid of religion" (ACM TR 1839, 9).

23. Robert Frykenberg, following Christopher Bayly (1996), writes of the Halle Pietist contribution to the formation of the "public":

> By "information revolution" I mean that enormous process by which information in India was transformed from something almost entirely and exclusively "private" into something increasingly "public." What, from ancient times, had been something held strictly within the bounds of those "sacred and secret" ties of birth and blood, something to be guarded and treasured as each family's most precious heritage, was gradually "revolutionized" and transformed into something open, something inclusive and common to all people, regardless of birth, gender, age or condition. Not until this process had reached a certain stage of broadening, intercultural social communication—not until a social mobilization of what, in previous works, I have called the "small hard pieces" (of birth groups and communities) had reached a certain continent-wide reach and density—could ideology, in any modern sense, begin to play a stronger role in "public" life. Only then, with the increase of "social communication" and "social mobilization" across caste and communal and regional barriers, could increasing numbers of people take part in a gradually developing political system which was constitutional, representative, and democratic. (1999, 7–8)

Frykenberg's insight, built over forty years of inquiry, is tentative in its use of terms such as "social communication," "social mobilization," or, importantly, "public," for reasons that are unclear. Regardless, as we discuss later in the book, the claim that things moved from the "private" to the "public" needs to be troubled to the extent that the Indic phenomenology of sociospatial order and action did not oppose the public to the private but rather opposed the interior (*akam*, *ghare*) to the exterior (*puram*, *baire*). See Chapter 1 for more discussion. [Editorial note: This note is from "Bate_2016-03-01_Swadeshi-Bharati_Berkeley_FINAL.docx," 11.]

24. [Editorial note: This is not to say that denotation or rational argumentation was completely unimportant, especially in didactic works such as the *Tirukkuṟaḷ* or Cittar poetry, but to emphasize the degree to which the performative traditions to which these texts belong struck Protestants as tainted by their reliance on the authority and aesthetics of sonic power.]

25. [Editorial note: The previous three sentences are from Bate 2013, 162, emended by language from "Bate_2010-09-27_Political Tamil and the Tamil Political_WORKING.doc," 20.]

26. [Editorial note: The second half of this sentence is taken from Bate 2013, 147, 158, as well as from "SPS_Four Moments.docx."]

27. [Editorial note: The discussion in this and the next section has been heavily redacted from the original draft of the Introduction, given redundancy with materials covered in Chapter 1.]

28. A longer account of the events surrounding its teaching begins with—and focuses on—the restrictions of the social relations and handling of the text:

> The Scanda Purana is in the hands of but few persons in the Country excepting those immediately connected with the Hindoo Temples, as it is generally thought unsafe to have the book in the house, lest it should be in some way defiled.... Nearly two years ago, it was thought expedient to indroduce [*sic*] the reading of this Purana in the Seminary. As soon as our intention was made known, the principal Tamul teacher who has been connected with the institution from its commencement, respectfully remonstrated against the measure. He urged that the Scanda Purana is one of the most sacred books used in the Country—that it should be taught only in sacred places—that the Mission premises are, in the estimation of the people, very far from sacred—that it would not be possible to perform on them those ceremonies which ought ever to precede, accompany, and follow, the reading of that book—that the members of the Seminary were not fit persons to be instructed in the Purana, and finally, that he could not subject himself to the odium that would be cast upon him by the people, for thus teaching it.

The teacher apparently relented to teaching the text to one student after a portion of the *Kantapurāṇam* was secured from Nellore, the site of the Kandaswamy (Murugan) Temple and a major Saivite center.

29. "Letter from Dr. Anderson, No. 3," *Missionary Herald* 51, no. 9 (September 1855): 257–60.

30. Examples of this sort are copious in any of the major Dravidianist speakers, such as Ariñar C. N. Annadurai or Kalaiñar Mu. Karunanidhi (Bate 2009b). Even

the embodiment of knowledge through the memorization and recitation of text was resurrected by Dravidianist politicians, who combined the precolonial textual emblematization—indexing and iconically instantiating consubstantiality of person and text—with the sermonic form in oratorical discourse. Memorization and poesy became key elements of the very character of the interpellation of the Tamil public sphere, of its leaders and its people. In short, both textualities came to inhere at once.

31. [Editorial note: This paragraph was moved from earlier in the original draft of the Introduction.]

32. R. Suntharalingam claims that the towns visited were Cuddalore, Chidambaram, Tirichinopoly, Tanjore, Kumbaconam, Mayavaram, Negapatam, Madura, Tinnevelly, and Tuticorin (1974, 181). He cites the "Proceedings of the MNA on the Resolution of the GOI on Local Self-Government," 1–26.

33. Roja Muthia Research Library (RMRL), *Kāṅgiras Vinā Viḍai allatu Ittēsattil Varuṣa Varuṣam Kūḍivarum Kāṅgiras Janasabaiyin Sarittiram*, 3rd ed., composed by Mu. Veeraragavachariyar (Chennai: National Press, 1888. Pe. Cu. Mani claims that this was an expanded version of G. Subramania Iyer's *Suya Arasaṭci Vinā Viḍai* of 1883 (2005, 19). A. R. Venkatachalapathy (pers. comm.) suggests that Pe. Cu. Mani read of this tour in Gurumalai Sundaram Pillai's 1907 biography of G. Subramania Iyer.

34. See GO 923, 4 July 1908, Judicial, Confidential, cf. "Enclosure I" (CID No. 563, 24-6-08), in which G. Subramania Iyer insists on addressing a crowd on the beach on 9 March 1908 in Tamil despite the crowd's call for him to speak in English. Cf. Viswanathan 1998, vol. 3.

35. [Editorial note: This paragraph is from "SPS_Four Moments.docx"; and Bate 2013, 148.]

Chapter 1

1. [Editorial note: Bate here is emphasizing the Protestant perspective. As one anonymous reviewer notes, there were strands of religious Indic thought that emphasized the denotational function of the word rather than the sonic sacrality of the Vedas or mantric-based ritualism that characterized Protestant encounters with Indic religious thought. In Hindu ethics, for example, the long history of the interpretation and influence of the *Bhagavad Gita*, starting from the eighth century commentary of Śaṅkara, and the concern with how to understand *niṣkāma karma* (disinterested action) demonstrate the importance given to denotational meaning (similarly, on how the Jātaka tales were meant to be heard, read, and understood as ethical fables for cultivation of a moral life; see Hallisey and Hansen 1996).]

2. Whereas high-status textual practice did not appear to deploy sermonic forms, lower classes/castes engaged in a number of different genres of generalized interpellation. See, for instance, Clarke-Decès 2005.

3. It is actually the third most prominent Indic text: the *Tirukkuraḷ* is by far the first with thirty-two citations; the Telugu *Vemanar* is the second with twenty-three citations; and the *Nālaḍiyār* is third with sixteen.

4. [Editorial note: *Trivarga* refers to the ethical doctrine of the three goals, or ends, of life: right conduct (*dharma*), material gain and rule (*artha*), and romantic or sexual love (*kāmā*).]

5. For a startling example of the vitriol with which the Christians attacked Indic religiosity, see Winslow and Vedanayaka Sastri's notorious tract *Kuruṭṭuvaḻi* [The blind way] (Jaffna: Jaffna Tract Society, ca. 1845).

6. The following three verses are taken from Pope 1893, 181, 125, 18. [Editorial note: References in the main text of the *Nālaḍiyār* are to the chapter number and quatrain number in that chapter in Pope's text.]

7. That it was famous even in the mid-nineteenth century is suggested by the fact that it is the only *nālaḍi* left unnumbered in the original Tamil edition as well as in the English translation of 1869.

8. For a more complete discussion of the Dravidianist paradigm of political oratory, see Bate 2009b.

Chapter 2

1. Today, an inscription within the Vannarpannai Sivan Temple marks the spot where Arumugam first gave his sermon.

2. For alternative views that inform this chapter, see Warner 1990; Hall 1996; Silverstein 2000.

3. The earliest Tamil homiletic I have found is James Duthie's *Homiletics* (1885). Also see the Introduction and Chapter 1 for discussion of the 1865 text published by the American Mission Press in Madras, H. M. Scudder's *The Bazaar Book, or, Vernacular Preacher's Companion*, which provides models of Tamil sermons for use by catechists, or "native assistants," in the marketplace or street.

4. For outlines of Navalar's life and Saivite reformation, I rely heavily on Dennis Hudson's (1992a, 1992b, 1994) work, especially the 1992 works. One of the best biographies available of Navalar was written by his grandnephew, T. Kailasapillai ([1918] 1955). For a more hagiographic biography, see Muttucumaraswamy 1965. A 1979 death centenary volume lists some 267 works in Tamil and English regarding Arumuga Navalar's life and works. See Kailasapathy 1979.

5. That Bible is now known as the "Tentative" or "Percival Version" among Christians, but it is more commonly known in Tamil as the "Navalar Version." See Kulendran 1958.

6. Karthigesaiyer—Robinson's "faithful moonshee"—was, in fact, one of the key members of Navalar's group and went on to become an important Saivite intellectual and activist in his own right.

7. [Editorial note: As noted in Chapter 1, it is the Protestant textual ethic that insists on this distinction and the priority of *logos* over the sonic qualities of language.]

8. [Editorial note: The article by T. P. Meenakshisundaran cited by Muttucumaraswamy ("Ceylon Tamil Poets") was included in a collection of Meenakshisundaran's articles in Meenakshisundaran (1954) 1978, in which it was retitled "Āṟumugam Nāvalar." Thanks to V. Govindarajan for help locating this reference.]

9. For a longer discussion of the history of oratory in Tamil literature, see Bate 2000, 2009b.

10. Cited as "Mr. S. Sivapadasundaram" in his brochure titled "Arumuga Navalar," in V. Muttucumaraswamy 1965, 49.

Chapter 3

1. [Editorial note: The phrase *vantē mātaram* comes from the eponymous Swadeshi-era Bengali poem written by Bankimchandra Chattopadhyay in his 1882 novel *Anandamath* and taken up by the Swadeshi movement by the end of the nineteenth century.]

2. [Editorial note: The previous two sentences are taken, in redacted form, from "Bate_2009-11-01_SpeakingSwadeshi_WORKING.doc," 1.]

3. [Editorial note: This sentence is from Bate 2012b, 70.]

4. [Editorial note: The previous three sentences are from "Bate_2009-11-01_SpeakingSwadeshi_WORKING.doc," 1–2; and "Bate_2009-05-29_Notes on Speaking_RMRL.doc," 1.]

5. GO 923, 4 July 1908, Judicial, Confidential, cf. "Enclosure I" (CID No. 563, 24-6-08), in which G. Subramania Iyer insists on addressing a crowd on the beach on 9 March 1908 in Tamil despite the crowd's call for him to speak in English. Cf. Viswanathan 1998, vol. 3. Also see discussion in Chapter 4.

6. [Editorial note: Marina Beach has continued to be a major site of protest and the manifestation of "the people" into the twenty-first century, as witnessed in the 2017 "Jallikattu" protests.]

7. "History Sheet" of Ethiraj Surendranath Arya," CID Madras, 21.5.09.

8. "Copy of a report on Madura made by a C.I.D. inspector, dt. 9th November 1908," in TNA, CID Report, November 1908–December 1908, vol. 4. This report is typical of many during this period for its contempt for the Swadeshi movement. The British police and government officials disdained the Swadeshists for their successes—and for their failures. The *vakil*s of Madurai, the inspector wrote, were no trouble to officials as their "sole aim and object was to please the collector and District Judge and thus to get some more practice." There were about five Swadeshi shops, indicating that some people were supporting their ideology with real money. But the Swadeshi shops were operating with only a few hundred rupees of

capital, says the inspector, so they are really more pathetic than any threat to British commerce. And perhaps the surest sign of how "dull" Madurai was in terms of Swadeshism was the stature of its lecturers. See? A mere woman gave an oration last April. In including her in the report to index just how uninteresting Swadeshism in Madurai was at that time, the inspector provided a startling fragment that indicated not only how women might be written into history but out of it as well. [Editorial note: This note was taken, in emended form, from an English-language version of Bate 2009a; "Bate_2009-06-04_A Vellala Woman in Madurai.doc," 1, 2].

9. [Editorial note: The second half of this sentence is taken from "Bate_2009-06-04_A Vellala Woman in Madurai.doc," 2.]

10. The Vellala woman may have been a Jaffna Vellala, as Jaffna Women's Sangam had been formed in 1906.

11. "History Sheet on Ethiraj Surendranath Arya," in TNA, GO 1473, Public-Confidential, 21-07-1913.

12. [Editorial note: The previous two paragraphs are emended with excerpts from "Bate_2009-05-29_Notes on Speaking_RMRL.doc," 5. Also see Bate 2012b.]

13. M. No. 655, dt. 25-6-07, in GO 1407–1408, 10-8-1907, Judicial, Confidential. [Editorial note: The second half of this quote is provided in "Bate_2009-11-01_Speaking-Swadeshi_WORKING.doc," 8.]

14. "History Sheet on Ethiraj Surendranath Arya," in TNA, GO 1473, Public-Confidential, 21-07-1913.

15. See "History Sheet of V. O. Chidambaram Pillai," CID Madras, 19 June 1909, prepared by J. T. W. Filson, personal assistant to DIG of Police, CID, and Railways. In TNA, CID Reports 1908–9, vol. 5.

16. F. B. M. Cardozo letter, dt. 25 June 1907, CID 1907, Unrest File No. I, 114–15.

17. F. B. M. Cardozo letter, 117.

18. Krishnamachari, TNA, GO 2000, 29.11.1907, Judicial.

19. [Editorial note: This paragraph is taken from "Bate_2009-11-01_Speaking-Swadeshi_WORKING.doc," 1–2; and "Bate_2009-05-29_Notes on Speaking_RMRL.doc," 3.]

20. In their minds, these were not audiences composed of discerning men capable of engaging in rational-critical discourse (one assumes). Perhaps here, too, the imaginary of the public sphere was entirely as Habermas ([1962] 1991) originally imagined it. Elite men in the beginning formation of the bourgeois public sphere saw themselves as engaging in precisely such discourse, unaware that their rationality was already deeply compromised by the blindness to their own privileged position.

21. See Subramania Bharati's article, "Sober Madras," published in *India*, 2 March 1907 (Viswanathan 1998, 2:458–60), for a discussion of the *Madras Times*'s charge

that the speakers in a recent public meeting lacked the "appropriate status" (*takka antaṣtu*) necessary to carry on an august discussion of the political matters of the day. The *Madras Times*, Bharati reported, also wrote that the audience was composed of "little boys" (*siru kulantaikaḷ*). Bharati disagreed with that characterization and suggested that the reporter, Rao Bhahadur N. S. Rajagopalachariyar, get his eyes checked as soon as possible.

22. [Editorial note: The *Maturai Jillā Tiyākikaḷ Malar* is also discussed and cited in Pe. Cu. Mani 2004, 149.]

23. [Editorial note: The previous two paragraphs are taken from "Bate_2009-06-04_A Vellala Woman in Madurai.doc," 1–2, with emendations from an earlier version of Chapter 4.]

24. "For the DIG," letter dated 5 October 1907, TNA, CID Reports, vol. 1, pt. 2, September 1907–August 1908.

25. M. No. 3463, Judicial Current, n.d. (probably June 1907), in TNA, CID 1907, Unrest File, vol. 1, pt. 1.

26. [Editorial note: The previous two paragraphs are from Bate 2012b, 72, with some emendation from "Bate_2009-11-01_SpeakingSwadeshi_WORKING.doc," 10.]

27. [Editorial note: This sentence is from "Bate_2009-11-01_SpeakingSwadeshi_WORKING.doc," 10.]

28. V. Ramaswami Iyengar described some of them in *Makākavi Bāratiyār* (1944, 49); V. Ramalingam Pillai's ([1944] 1955) *En Katai* has some mention of Bharati's speeches.

29. [Editorial note: This paragraph is from "Bate_2009-11-01_SpeakingSwadeshi_WORKING.doc," 13.]

30. [Editorial note: The most recent draft of Chapter 3, based on a 2011 talk delivered to the Department of Anthropology, Stanford University, 28 October 2011 ("SPS-Ch03_2011-10-28_SpeakingSwadeshi_Stanford.pdf"), ends with a bullet-point list of "Notes and Thoughts." Similarly, a 2009 version ("Bate_2009-11-01_Speaking-Swadeshi_WORKING.doc," 10) has a penultimate section with a list of "Problems and Opportunities for This Research," which the 2011 version refers back to but does not include. Given their interest to scholars working on this topic, we have included both here, though certain aspects of each were also integrated into the body of the text in the 2011 draft and in the main text of this chapter.]

Problems and Opportunities for This Research:

1. The archives are deteriorating. Materials seen ten years ago are now gone. I don't know what anyone will do about that.

2. We do not have the original speeches in Tamil for most of the speeches. There are some in the *Swadesamitran* and in the *India*, but the vast majority

of these speeches are only portions of the speeches made by the police and translated to English.

a. This is a major problem for obvious reasons.

b. But not so obvious is that the English translation might sound a great deal different than the original, even indexing entirely different semiotics (cf. Viswanathan 1998, 120–32).

3. There is little thick description of the events. Police focused on what was said, the denotationality of the speeches, for that was what enabled prosecution.

a. I want to know what they looked like: How did they begin and end? What were the speaking orders of the orators? What kind of space did they occupy?

4. Similar question: How did people project their voices so that they could speak to thousands of people?

a. What did a meeting on the beach look like if it had no public-address system?

b. Beaches, for instance, have very bad acoustics, especially if the wind is blowing in the wrong direction.

c. The meetings I have seen on the beach without P.A. systems seem to be very small, circular, and tightly packed groups of people standing or sitting.

5. There appears to be little secondary writing on these events in Tamil by contemporaries.

a. Thiru. Vi. Ka's *Vāḻkkai Kuṟippukaḷ* stands out as the single most important of these.

b. V. Ramaswami Iyengar described some of them.

c. Namakkal Kaviñar's *En Katai* has some of the Bharatiyar speeches.

d. Who else wrote of these things? Who else described them?

Notes and Thoughts:

I would propose that some of the problems above can be solved by looking beyond the actual speeches themselves and attempting to gain clues about them via an exploration of the communicative ecosystem:

1. Theatre (*Harikathā*?)

2. Bhajanas: They appeared to be connected with the Swadeshi meetings; several such were reported in Triplicane.

3. Songs/poems: I am lucky in this project that Bharatiyar was associated with the Swadeshi movement as he laid down a great deal of material during those years that was directly related to this project.

4. E.g., the speech on the beach on 9 March 1908 to celebrate the release of Bipin Chandra Pal from prison. According to the CID report of this meeting, Bharati began it with an invocation that could almost come right out of some Hebrew lamentation in the Old Testament:

   a. "When will this thirst for freedom be quenched. When will these fetters of ignorance be removed. O, Lord that caused the great war of Mahabharatha. Are plague and Famine intended only to your devoted. Are strangers to prosper while we suffer. O, Lord of the universe and the protector of the good. Is it not your principle to shield the innocent and the suffering! Have you forgotten about the patient suffering?"

   b. Of course, it is not an Old Testament lament, even though it is rendered thus in English.

   c. Rather, I'm sure most of you recognize it is the very familiar "Eṉṟu taṇiyum inta sutantira tākam" (When will my thirst for freedom be quenched?) to which Bharati gave the title "Sri Krishna Stottiram," probably first sung that very night.

5. Processions:

   a. The routes of political processions followed the routes of religious ones. (Tirunelveli Nellaiyappa procession to Tai Poosa Mandabam; the processions around Meenakshi Amman Koyil began on the north side of the temple in front of the Mottai Gopuram and processed along the Masi streets; the processions from different points in Madras to the [Marina] Beach; Bharati and Ethiraj's meetings were, I think, almost always associated with Bhajanas.)

What did they do? (The music, bhajanas, etc.)

Chapter 4

[Editorial note: This chapter is based on a combination of a draft version, "Bharathi and the Tamil Modern" ("SPS-Ch05_Bharati-and-the-Tamil-Modern_2011-01-12.pdf") and a version of a 1 March 2016 talk, "Bate_2016-03-03_

Swadeshi-Bharati_WRKG.docx," with additions and emendations from other versions, as noted.]

1. An index of his youthful passion, talent, and democratic impulses comes from a memory passed through the family of the anthropologist Arjun Appadurai and recorded in a transcribed interview of his father, S. Appadurai Aiyar, by Carol Breckenridge. Arjun Appadurai's paternal grandfather was a court Brahmin at Ettiyapuram, where his reputation did no honor to the family. His dissolute life ended early, and his wife and son were left destitute in the Brahmin neighborhood (*agrahāram*) of Sivalaperi, a dry, dusty town near Tirunelveli with few charms and fewer prospects. S. A. Aiyar remembers as a small boy, sometime in the first decade of the twentieth century, that he met Bharati, his father's first cousin, while he and his mother were visiting Tirunelveli. He had hitched a ride with Bharati back to Sivalaperi on an oxcart. The driver asked the poet to sing a song, and Bharati improvised a new song on the spot, singing of driving in an oxcart to the town of Sivalaperi: "Sivalaperi kaṇḍēnē!" (I beheld Sivalaperi!). When reflecting on this story with me, two elements struck Professor Appadurai about the character and life of Bharati as told by his father. First, there is something remarkable about this young quasi-aristocrat willing to sing a song at the request of a humble oxcart driver. Likewise, he had no aristocracy of topic for his poem; he was willing to thematize as "humble and trivial and dusty a place as Sivalaperi" in the same tones, even the same words, as those *pirabantam* singers who sang of great gods such as the lord Parthasarathy of Tiruvallikeni (or Triplicane), where Bharati lived during his days in Madras: "Tiruvallikeni kaṇḍēnē!" The story speaks not only of Bharati's gifts as a poet but also of his inherent democracy, egalitarianism, and goodwill. These traits are very much apparent in his later work, in his songs, and in his overall dealings with his fellow beings.

2. [Editorial note: The previous two sentences are from "Bate_2013-11-03_Swadeshi-Bharati_NMML.pdf," 1.]

3. Cf. Qur'an 5:32: "If any one killed a person, it would be as if he killed the whole of mankind; and if any one saved a life, it would be as if he saved the life of the whole of mankind."

4. See P. Mahadevan 1957, 17, though there is debate about this date. Go. Kesavan (1995), among others, suggests it was in 1894. [Editorial note: The editors were not able to fill out the references by Bate to Go. Kesavan.]

5. GO 923, 4 July 1908, Judicial, Confidential, cf. "Enclosure I" (CID No. 563, 24-6-08), 5.

6. "History Sheet of Ethiraj Surendranath Arya," CID Madras, 21.5.09.

7. DO, dt. 12.3.08, Atkinson to Bradley, TNA, GO 1729, 29.12.08, Jud.Confl.

8. DO, dt. 12.3.08, Atkinson to Bradley, TNA, GO 1729, 29.12.08, Jud.Confl.

9. "Enclosure I" [CID No. 563, 24-06-08], GO 923, Jud.Confl., 4.7.08.

10. It is unclear whether G. Subramania Iyer immediately followed Bharati or whether the latter's speech was followed by Ethiraj Surendranath Arya (as stated in "History Sheet of Ethiraj Surendranath Arya," CID Reports 1908–1909, vol. 5). Iyer, as the highest-status person in attendance, was probably the final speaker of the evening.

11. See Viswanathan 1998, 3:301–3, for a complete transcript of this speech.

12. DO, dt. 16.3.08, TNA, GO 1729, 29.12.08, Jud.Confl.

13. DO, dt. 14.3.08, TNA, GO 1729, 29.12.08, Jud.Confl.

14. DO, dt. 12.3.08, Wilkieson to Atkinson, TNA, GO 1729, 29.12.08, Jud.Confl.

15. DO, dt. 12.3.08, TNA, GO 1729, 29.12.08, Jud.Confl.

16. [Editor's note: Also see Bate 2012b on the development of Tamil shorthand in relation to these events.]

17. And, of course, oratory was but one of the major forms of communicative practice that was being radically transformed during this period, in addition to music and dance. [Editorial note: This note is sourced from an oral-talk version of this chapter, "Bate_2016-03-03_Swadeshi-Bharati_WRKG.docx."]

18. The independence and, later, labor activist Madurai Mayandi Bharati (1917–2015) recalls singing the song in the late 1920s and early 1930s (see Chapter 3).

19. Viswanathan (1998, 3:123–26) believes that V. Ramaswami Iyengar (Va. Ra.) and Namakkal Kaviñar V. Ramalingam Pillai's memories are at fault and that there were no other verses.

20. This is a strange thing to say, but this particular form of *bhajan* was introduced as another form of cultural modernity in the early twentieth century and has been traced back to Maratha King Serfoji II's court in Thanjavur (late eighteenth, early nineteenth century) along with a whole host of other early-modern communicative forms—not least being the *kathakalakshebam* textual discourses and *Harikathā* theater (Peterson 2011).

21. [Editorial note: A. R. Venkatachalapathy (2008), however, in *Bharati Karuvūlam* has shown that Bharati was giving a talk in Chennai just ten days after this.]

22. [Editor's note: The previous two sentences were taken from "Bate_2016-03-03_Swadeshi Bharati_WRKG.docx," 3.]

Chapter 5

1. The claim is somewhat misleading as strikes were occurring from the very first years of the establishment of large industrial operations in Madras in the 1870s, in particular at the Buckingham and Carnatic Mills in Perambur and other major sites. Sivasubramanian's (1986) claim that these are the first organized and planned labor stoppages is perhaps more accurate. Also see Veeraraghavan 2013.

2. "History Sheet on Ethiraj Surendranath Arya," in TNA, GO 1542, 3 October 1911, Judicial-Confidential.

3. Here, we might also consider shifts in addressivity and audience composition in arts such as Bharatnatyam.

4. While District Magistrate L. M. Wynch reports that English notes of the speeches were made by various officers and filed in his court, in addition to being furnished to the CID through reports made from them, both the court and the district magistrate's office were burned down on 13 March 1908. No account of any notes has been reported since then. See L. M. Wynch, DO, dt. 17 March 1908, TNA, GO 478, 24-03-1908, Judicial Confidential; Venkatachalapathy 1987, 18–20.

5. Paragraph 4, Exhibit S, Criminal Appeals Nos. 491 (V. O. C., 2nd Prisoner) and 503 (Subramania Siva, 1st Prisoner) of 1908, High Court of Judicature at Madras, Wednesday, the fourth day of November, 1908.

6. "History Sheet of V. O. Chidambaram Pillai."

7. The record is contradictory. The court records claim that speeches occurred nearly daily from 3 February; however, the "History Sheet" claims that Siva presided over meetings at the Thoothukudi Beach "on the 11th, 16th, and 19th February." Regardless, we do not have a record of anything he said prior to a few excerpts of a speech he gave on 19 February, recorded in the "History Sheet."

8. L. M. Wynch, DO, dt. 17 March 1908, TNA, GO 478, 24-03-1908, Judicial Confidential.

9. "History Sheet on Subrahmanya Siva."

10. TNA, GO No. 1542, 3.10.1911, Jud.Confl.; see also "History Sheet on Subrahmanya Siva" and "History Sheet of V. O. Chidambaram Pillai," CID Madras, 19 June 1909, prepared by J. T. W. Filson, personal assistant to the DIG of Police, CID, and Railways, TNA, CID Reports 1908–9, vol. 5.

11. Cf. Hansen 1996 on the wrestler's body and his masculinity; and Van der Veer 2001 on masculinity and "muscular Hinduism."

12. Professor A. Sivasubramanian accompanied me on a tour of the port and mill areas of Thoothukudi in January 2009, where we thought about where these events may have taken place.

13. The beach opposite that church today was narrowed with the construction of a large jetty to the south that altered the currents and pushed the shoreline inland. But in 1908 it would have been a broad, open space free of the thornbushes and plastic flotsam that clogs it today.

14. Unless otherwise indicated, all speeches are drawn from TNA, GO 1542, 3.10.1911, Jud.Confl.

15. TNA, GO 1542, 3.10.1911, Jud.Confl.

16. Chidambara Bharati's claim noted in the main text that Siva's third meeting drew fifty thousand, one suspects, is quite understandable hyperbole appropriate

to the jubilation of the years immediately following independence. There are no reports of meetings exceeding five thousand participants.

17. The first working public-address system was unveiled in 1915 in San Francisco by Magnavox; A. R. Venkatachalapathy reports that specifying "mic sets" in announcements of public meetings became common only in the 1930s (pers. comm., April 2014).

18. As in Bharati's song analyzed in the previous chapter, here, too, the notion of thirty crores acts as an index of a novel numerical imagination—indeed, epistemization—of society (see Kaviraj 2010).

19. In the written statement Siva issued prior to his first trial he wrote:

> I am a Sanyasi. My mission is to propagate the principles of Mukthi and also the ways to attain it. Mukthi for a soul is freedom from all foreign bondages. Mukthi for a nation is freedom from all foreign control, that is, Absolute Swaraj. Accordingly I preached to my countrymen the gospel of Swaraj and also the ways to attain it viz., Boycott—boycott of all that stands in the way of my nation's attaining Swaraj—, Passive Resistance and National Education. (Paragraph 2, Exhibit S, Criminal Appeals Nos. 491 [V. O. C., 2nd Prisoner] and 503 [Subramania Siva, 1st Prisoner] of 1908, High Court of Judicature at Madras, Wednesday the fourth day of November, 1908)

20. Cf. Benedict Anderson's ([1983] 2006) notion of "unbound seriality," the evocation of a homogeneous space and time in which different moments in history were linked and in which we might see parallel social systems, parallel cosmologies, and a shared human condition based on an abstraction of ourselves in a *social* world. For a critique and complication of this concept, see Chatterjee 2004, 3–8.

21. "History Sheet of V. O. Chidambaram Pillai."

22. "History Sheet of V. O. Chidambaram Pillai."

23. "Tuticorin Inspectors Reports, Meeting on the Beach on the 4th March 1908," TNA, GO 1542, 3.10.1911, Jud.Confl. See also "History Sheet on Subrahmanya Siva" and "History Sheet of V. O. Chidambaram Pillai."

24. L. M. Wynch, DO, dt. 17 March 1908, TNA, GO No 478, 24-03-1908, Judicial Confidential.

25. [Editorial note: In *The Elementary Forms of Religious Life*, Durkheim writes, "It is by this trait that we are able to recognize what has often been called the demon of oratorical inspiration," indicating that the phrase was a common one (in French at least), or at least not particular to Durkheim ([1912] 1995, 212).]

26. M. No. 3463, Judicial Current, n.d. (probably June 1907), in TNA, CID 1907, Unrest File, vol. 1, pt. 1.

27. TNA, GO 1542, 3.10.1911, Jud.Confl.

28. TNA, GO 1542, 3.10.1911, Jud.Confl.

29. [Editorial note: In the Madras Presidency, a second-grade pleader is a kind of lawyer in the middle of the colonial legal hierarchy.]

30. "History Sheet of V. O. Chidambaram Pillai."

31. [Editorial note: This paragraph is emended with excerpts from "Bate_2008-2009_Misc Writing 2008-09.doc," 30.]

32. Similar events occurred across the Presidency. In Chingleput, a group of men associated with the Satya Vratha Sangam of Kanchipuram petitioned the inspector of police and were given permission to "process through the streets with music." As the leaders of the Sangam, including Venkata Aryan, were leading men of the town, the police had no reason to deny them permission. But the event was noteworthy to the police for it involved a procession similar to that described in Tirunelveli, which also forefronted the performance of worship to Bharatmata:

> In an empty chair was placed a picture of India, executed by the artist Ravi Varma and below this picture as a likeness of Bipin Chandra Pal. These two pictures were decorated with flowers. The meeting began at 5 P.M. and ended at 7:20 P.M. In the picture of India was a representation of the goddess Kali.

Venkata Aryan offered prayers in Sanskrit for India and worshipped the picture with flowers and fire. Flowers also were distributed to the people, who threw them on the picture. Venkata Aryan then pointed out Kali and said: "The name of this goddess is Buru Devi. The country of India is her body. We are all living in her womb. We should therefore consider her body, i.e. India as our mother and should say 'Vande Mataram' meaning that we bow to our mother." On saying this, he repeated the words "*vantē mātaram*" in a loud voice and the assembly took up the cry. Then he pointed to Pal's picture and cried out "Bipin Chandra Pal Ji," meaning "success to &c." (Written report of DSP Chingleput, 21-03-08, TNA, CID Reports, vol. 1, pt. 2, September 1907–August 1908, 78–83) [Editorial note: This note was taken from "SPS_Fragment_events of 9 March throughout the Presidency.docx," 1.]

33. GO 1542, 3.10.1911, Judicial Confidential, 423. [Editorial note: This section (The Uprising and Official Murders on 13 March) was only skeletally sketched in Bate's various drafts of the chapter and is composed by the editors based on these sketches, supplemented with primary and secondary sources that Bate would have had access to (e.g., GO 1542, 3.10.1911, Judicial Confidential; Asha 2009, 154–81; Venkatachalapathy 1987, 2010). Specific passages are taken from "Bate_2013-05-02_Tutukudi-oratorical-incandescence.docx"; "Bate_2013-11-01_Tutukudi-oratorical-incandescence.docx"; and "Bate_2014-05-29_Elocutionary-incandescence_Chicago.docx."]

34. GO 1542, 3.10.1911, Judicial Confidential, 423.

35. The fallout for Robert Ashe was considerable as well (Venkatachalapathy 2010). Within a month of the riots, Ashe was transferred to Godavari District, though he returned in August 1910 as acting collector of Tirunelveli. In the interim,

and in response to the events of 1908, a group of militant nationalists had organized, their efforts culminating in Ashe's assassination by R. Vanchi Aiyar on 17 June 1911 at the Maniyachi train junction. Fourteen were arrested and charged with conspiracy (nine of whom were convicted and sentenced), while two others who were part of the conspiracy committed suicide (in addition to Vanchi Aiyar, who shot himself immediately after the murder) and one escaped, never to be found. Following the murder, the colonial government put increased pressure on nationalists they felt to have supported the conspiracy, including Subramania Bharati, who had already fled to Pondicherry, as discussed in Chapter 4. The murder was determined by government authorities to have had "a direct causal link with the political events in the district [of Tirunelveli] in 1908" (Venkatachalapathy 2010, 40), including the imprisonment of V. O. C. and Subramania Siva and the ensuing riots, but also the blame that Ashe later took for crushing V. O. C.'s SSNC. Venkatachalapathy (2010) argues that while Wynch was ultimately in charge of the events that transpired in 1908 and was a major target of local critique, despite his complicity in the events, Ashe's death was the result, in part, from being in the wrong place at the wrong time; Wynch was furloughed, and Ashe was posted as the acting collector at the time.

36. L. M. Wynch, DO, dt. 17 March 1908, TNA, GO 478, 24-03-1908, Judicial Confidential, 11–12.

37. "The Tinnevelly Sedition Trial: Amazing Summing Up by the Judge," *Swadesamitran*, 6 June 1908 (translation), CID Report cited in TNA, HFM 79, 136–43.

38. "The Tinnevelly Sedition Trial."

39. L. M. Wynch, DO, dt. 17 March 1908, TNA, GO 478, 24-03-1908, Judicial Confidential.

40. L. M. Wynch, DO, dt. 17 March 1908. Of course, those notes and any other evidence of the speeches would have been lost when the district magistrate's office and court burned down on 13 March 1908.

41. Criminal Appeals Nos. 491 (V. O. C., 2nd Prisoner) and 503 (Subramania Siva, 1st Prisoner) of 1908, High Court of Judicature at Madras, Wednesday the fourth day of November, 1908.

42. Judgment by Arthur F. Pinhey, Esq., Additional Sessions Judge, Tinnevelly District, 7 July 1908, in the case against V. O. C. and Subramania Siva, GO 1542, 3.10.1911, Judicial (Confidential), in Government of Tamil Nadu 1982, 414–15.

43. Of course, the judge's imagination of what constituted "newspaper reading" had very little to do with the ways that newspapers were (and are being) read in the Tamil country—and perhaps across India. Newspaper reading, far from being a solitary, individual affair, was more likely carried out both silently and out loud amid others in places of gatherings, such as tea stalls. See Bate 2009b; Cody 2009.

44. "The Tinnevelly Sedition Trial."

45. "The Tinnevelly Sedition Trial."

46. "The Tinnevelly Sedition Trial."

47. For a clear discussion of the proximal (versus distal) and tenseless quality of ritual language, see Silverstein 2004, 36–39.

48. "History Sheet on Ethiraj Surendranath Arya," in TNA, GO 1473, 21 July 1913, Public-Confidential. The very first notice of him by police, in fact, was a speech he delivered in Perambur, 14 April 1907, for the Fellow Workers Society. For discussions on the Perambur labor union, see Bate 2013; Veeraraghavan 2013.

49. A police inspector and several deputies took at least two tours of the delta regions of Kistna (or Krishna) and Godavari Districts in 1907. "Proceedings of a Swadeshi Meeting," in CID Report, 1907, Unrest File, vol. 1, pt. 1, 179–90; "Letter, Confidential," dt. 18.7.1907, CID Report, 1907, Unrest File, vol. 1, pt. 1, 204–14; "Report," 5.12.1907, CID Report, 1907, Unrest File, vol. 1, pt. 1, 567–73; DO dt. 10.11.1907, CID Report, 1907, Unrest File, vol. 1, pt. 1, 577.

50. See Amin 1988, 304–5, for a discussion of nationalist understandings of the correct role between elites, masses, and the figure of Mohandas Gandhi in North India, ca. 1921–22; cf. Chatterjee 2004 on the distinction between civil and political society.

Epilogue

1. David Washbrook writes: "As the president of the Theosophical Society, she controlled an organization with several thousand members, which linked the presidency capital to every large mofussil town. When she converted this to political purposes, she was able to inaugurate her movement with prepared support and a sophisticated structure of command in as many as thirty-four separate localities" (1976, 290). See also DO 105 W-1, 17 Jan. 1917, TNA, FR 1917.

2. DO no. 4788 W-1, 18 Dec. 1916, TNA, FR 1916.

3. DO no. 846 W-1, 1 Mar. 1917, TNA, FR 1917.

4. DO no. 1051 W-1, 17 Mar. 1917, TNA, FR 1917.

5. K. Krishnaswami Sarma, who had been jailed for three years of rigorous imprisonment, was found again to be "delivering Sunday lectures in Tamil on the Beach at Madras in which he has contrasted the past glories of India with its degradation in recent times" (DO no. 1250 W-1, 2 April 1917, TNA, FR 1917). Other prominent members of the Swadeshi movement generation, such as V. O. C., Subramania Siva, and G. Harisarvathama Rao, would also begin to attend labor meetings.

6. [Editorial note: The *maa-baap* (mother-father, from Hindi) system refers to a mode of governance metaphorically based on absolute, paternal authority.]

7. A particularly ugly story about one of these humiliations involved a man de-

nied permission by a superior to answer a call of nature. The worker soiled himself at the gate, was beaten by white managers, and was forced to clean up after himself. Chelvapathi Chettiar worked to publicize the story in the *Indian Patriot* and other local newspapers, provoking the outrage of the reading public. See Souvenir 1963.

8. Though we have no reports of the content of those lectures, see Kalyanasundaram [1944] 2003, 352; and Souvenir 1963, 36.

9. We have an unusually rich variety of sources for this meeting: the City Police, who had stationed a sub-inspector in Perambur to report on the situation (TNA, GO 342, 18 Apr. 1919, Public [Confidential]); Chelvapathi Chettiar's manuscript account cited by Veeraraghavan 1987; Chelvapathi's published account (Chettiar 1961, 3–4); Eamon Murphy's (1981) interview with Chelvapathi; Souvenir 1963; and Kalyanasundaram [1944] 2003.

10. Report 162-C, 4 Mar. 1918, TNA, GO 342, 18 Apr. 1918, Public (Confidential).

11. Interestingly, the police report makes no mention of this tension at the time, though notes among the officers in the Secretariat over the next month or so express pleasure at reports of dismay among SVGS members at their descent into politics.

12. Wadia's account of the meeting betrays a rather embarrassing, albeit wholly well-intentioned philanthropic liberalism utterly detached from the lives of the vast majority of people then living in Madras:

> How well I remember the forenoon when two men, unknown to me, whom I had never seen before, came and told me something about the "suffering labourers." They referred to the Buckingham and Carnatic Mills, of which I had vaguely heard, but of which I knew less than little. They referred to "a few minutes for food," "swallowing a few morsels," "running lest they be shut out." It was at New India office, where I was then working under my beloved and respected Chief, Mrs. Besant. She was not in office that day, and I was loath to leave it in her absence even for a couple of hours. But my Theosophical spirit got the better of my political duties. I immediately ordered my car, took the two strangers, and went to Perambur and watched outside the Mills where I saw the poor labourers at their noon-day meal. It was quick work. They came, they gobbled, they returned. (1921, xv)

13. No. 257-c, dt. 17 Apr. 1918, TNA, GO 342, 18 Apr. 1918, Public (Confidential).

14. Wadia and Thiru. Vi. Ka. both saw their positions as articulating the words of a single person, a point Wadia acknowledges in the dedication of his 1921 book of the speeches to Thiru. Vi. Ka.: "This is your book as much as mine. If the speeches delivered here achieved any good among our friends at Perambur it is due to your excellent translations of them. What could I have done in the Labour work in this city without you? You translated my speeches not my words merely but their very spirit" (1921, v).

15. Thiru. Vi. Ka. names V. Chakkarai Chetti, E. L. Iyer, N. Dandapani Pillai, Harisarvothama Rao, C. Rajagopalachari (Rajaji), Adhinarayana Chettiar, M. S. Subramania Iyer, V. O. Chidambaram Pillai, A. S. Ramulu, M. C. Raja, Dr. Natesa Mudaliar, S. Kasturiranga Ayangar, V. P. Pakkiriswami Pillai, M. S. Ramaswamy Iyengar in Coimbatore, and George Joseph in Madurai.

16. TNA, GO 566, 7 Sept. 1920, Public (Confidential).

17. Add to this list the union of motorcar drivers; the cutters of army clothing; government clerks; Public Works Department employees; workmen of the Madras Port; workmen of the Reliance Foundry; workmen of all the major oil companies such as the Burmah Oil Company, Asiatic Petroleum, and Standard Oil; and, of course, workmen of all the printing establishments that the administrative and political hub that was Madras could support.

18. For these reports, see the collection of CID Reports covering the period in TNA, GO 566, 7 Sept. 1920, Public (Confidential).

19. CID Report on a meeting of the Madras Labour Union (B&C Mills), Perambore, 18 Feb. 1920, TNA, GO 566, 7 Sept. 1920, Public (Confidential).

20. Yet, in contrast to descriptions of the public sphere, this public was perhaps less an empirical reality as such than an empirically consequential illusion (resulting in such expansions). Indeed, less a universal, homogeneous space of communicative rationality, the bourgeois public sphere was produced through the production and circulation of text-artifacts among a limited social network of men who represented themselves as the universal human subject. It was a utopia of homogeneity, a homogeneity of time, space, and social order built on a series of exclusions based on gender, race, and class (and caste, in the South Asian case). The notion of the universalization of the public sphere was never more than the universalization of a normative model based on particularistic positions within the society represented as neutral. All of these productions, however, were effects of new communicative modalities entering into and transforming fields of social praxis, as we have seen from the examples of vernacular oratorical models and their roles in the production of regional modernities in South India. In short, what we find actually unfolding in the Tamil world—and elsewhere—does not quite match up with such descriptions. To this day, the notion of the (monoglot) public remains somewhat difficult to pin down in (heteroglot) Madras. Given all this, one wonders if there has ever been anything that actually matches up to the notion of the public sphere at all. As we might say, to paraphrase Bruno Latour, "We have never been public." [Editorial note: This note was taken and redacted from the fragments "Bate_2011-11-28_we-have-never-been-public_nanterre-abstract.rtf"; and "Bate_2014-04-09_AAA_we-have-never-been-public.docx"; earlier drafts of the book's outline (titled *Speaking the Public Sphere: Protestant Textuality and the Tamil*

Modern; see "Bate_2010-11-16_Speaking the Public Sphere_OUTLINE.docx," 2) include plans for a conclusion that would provide a "speculative/theoretical piece on the nature of the public sphere, in theory and as we actually find it unfolding in the Tamil world. Wonders if there has ever been anything that actually matches up to the notion of the public sphere at all. A consequential illusion."]

Afterword

1. It is comforting to use the present tense; it registers the fact that Bate's ideas have presence.

2. Although there is no scope to discuss this theme in this afterword, we should note the sophistication of Bate's notion of modernity. It is not an overwhelming single process that flattens all diversity of the preexisting world but one that enters into particular histories to get modified and inflected. In South India, we should not simply describe the triumphal march of modernity but attend to the slow construction of the Indian and Tamil modern. See the main text for more discussion of how this modernity for Bate was truly Indic and Tamil.

3. Michael Walzer, *The Revolution of the Saints: A Study in the Origins of Radical Politics* (Cambridge, MA: Harvard University Press, 1965).

4. Walzer.

5. Jürgen Habermas, *The Structural Transformation of the Public Sphere* (1962; repr., Cambridge, MA: MIT Press, 1991).

6. Rabindranath Tagore, "Hing Ting Chat," in *Rabindra Rachanabali*, vol. 3 (Calcutta: Visvabharati, 1904).

7. E. Valentine Daniel, *Charred Lullabies: Chapters in an Anthropography of Violence* (Princeton, NJ: Princeton University Press, 1996).

8. Interestingly, the term *mahajana* is used in the Vanaparva of the *Mahabharata* in a famous *śloka*. Yudhisthira says in answer to a question by Dharma disguised as the stork:

> *Veda bibhinnah smrtayo bibhinnah*
> *Nasau muniryasya matam na bhinnam*
> *Dharmasya tattvam nihitam guhayam*
> *Mahajano yena gatah sa panthah.*

> The Vedas are different, the smritis are different, a man is not called a sage if his views are not different from all others. The truth of dharma is hidden in a cave. The path is the one taken by the *mahajana*.

Here, *mahajana* can mean great men or the great number of men.

9. Henry W. Nevinson, "On the Beach," in *The New Spirit in India*, by Henry W. Nevinson (London: Harper and Brothers, 1908), 125–33.

10. Nevinson, 125.

11. Nevinson, 128–29.

12. In Sanskrit there are analyses of speech perfection that indicate two types of values: sonic effects and semantic effects. The possessor of perfect speech is called a *vavaduka*. Sonic features are the selection of pleasing word combinations, their clear enunciation, in a voice that sounds sweet. The four semantic features are *upanyasa-paripati* (skilled at persuading those who hold a different view); *yukti-paripati* (skilled at using arguments that surmount objections); *yatharthtya-paripati* (skilled at marshaling incontrovertible evidence); and *pratibha-paripati* (skilled at presenting his side with a winning combination of tropes.) See Goswami Rupa, *Bhakti-Rasamrta-Sindhu* [Ocean of the nectar of rasa], ed. Haridas Das (Haribol Kutir: Nabadwip, 1946).

13. Krishna famously says to Arjuna in the *Bhagavad Gita* before the apocalyptic battle: "*yada yada hi dhramasya glanir bhabati bharata / abhyutthanam adharmasya tadatmanam srjamyaham / paritranay sadhunam vinasaya ca duskrtam / dharmasamsthapanarthaya sambhavami yuge yuge*" (Whenever there is a decay of religion, O Bharata, and there is a rise of irreligion, then I manifest Myself).

14. A large number of modern Indian thinkers invoke the message of the *Bhagavad Gita*, though interpreted in very divergent ways.

15. Sudipta Kaviraj, *The Unhappy Consciousness: Bankimchandra Chattopadhyay and the Formation of Indian Nationalist Discourse* (Delhi: Oxford University Press, 1995).

16. Benedict Anderson recognized this fact in his *Imagined Communities* (1983; London: Verso, 2006); and it has been widely chronicled in the history of Indian nationalism.

17. Sudipta Kaviraj, "Writing, Speaking, Being: Language and the Historical Formation of Identities in India," in *Nationalstaat und Sprachkonflickt in Sud—und Sudostasien*, ed. Dagmar Hellmann-Rajanayagam and Dietmar Rothermund (Stuttgart: Steiner, 1992), 25–65.

18. Bernard Bate, *Tamil Oratory and the Dravidian Aesthetic* (New York: Columbia University Press, 2009).

REFERENCES

Drafts Cited in Editorial Notes

Bate_2008-2009_Misc Writing 2008-09.doc
Bate_2009-05-29_Notes on Speaking_RMRL.doc
Bate_2009-06-04_A Vellala Woman in Madurai.doc
Bate_2009-11-01_SpeakingSwadeshi_WORKING.doc
Bate_2010-09-27_Political Tamil and the Tamil Political_WORKING.doc
Bate_2010-11-16_Speaking the Public Sphere_OUTLINE.docx
Bate_2011-11-28_we-have-never-been-public_nanterre-abstract.rtf
Bate_2013-05-02_Tutukudi-oratorical-incandescence.docx
Bate_2013-11-01_Tutukudi-oratorical-incandescence.docx
Bate_2013-11-03_Swadeshi-Bharati_NMML.pdf
Bate_2014-04-09_AAA_we-have-never-been-public.docx
Bate_2014-05-29_Elocutionary-incandescence_Chicago.docx
Bate_2015-06-15_Swadeshi-Bharati_WRKG.docx
Bate_2016-03-01_Swadeshi-Bharati_Berkeley_FINAL.docx
Bate_2016-03-03_Swadeshi-Bharati_WRKG.docx
SPS-Ch03_2011-10-28_SpeakingSwadeshi_Stanford.pdf
SPS-Ch03_2014-06-21_SpeakingSwadeshi_WRKG.docx
SPS-Ch05_Bharati-and-the-Tamil-Modern_2011-01-12.pdf
SPS_Four Moments.docx (dated 22 January 2011)
SPS_Fragment_events of 9 March throughout the Presidency.docx (dated 20 May 2014)
SPS_Fragment_the-press-and-the-platform.docx (dated 10 May 2009)

References Cited

ACM TR. 1830. *The Second Triennial Report of the American Mission Seminary, Jaffna, Ceylon*. Nellore: Church Mission Press. Signed by B. C. Meigs, D. Poor, M. Winslow, L. Spaulding, H. Woodward, J. Scudder.

ACM TR. 1839. *The Fifth Triennial Report of the American Mission Seminary, Jaffna, Ceylon*. With an Appendix. Jaffna: Press of the American Mission.

Ali, Daud. 2004. *Courtly Culture and Political Life in Early Medieval India*. Cambridge: University of Cambridge Press.

Amin, Shahid. 1988. "Gandhi as Mahatma: Gorakhpur District, Eastern UP, 1921–2." In *Selected Subaltern Studies*, edited by Ranajit Guha and Gayatri Chakravorty Spivak, 288–348. New York: Oxford University Press.

Anderson, Benedict. (1983) 2006. *Imagined Communities: Reflections on the Origin and Spread of Nationalism*. London: Verso.

Arendt, Hannah. 1958. *The Human Condition*. Chicago: University of Chicago Press.

Arnold, David. 1986. *Police Power and Colonial Rule: Madras 1859–1947*. New Delhi: Oxford University Press.

Asad, Talal. 1993. *Genealogies of Religion: Discipline and Reasons of Power in Christianity and Islam*. Baltimore: Johns Hopkins University Press.

Asha, C. 2009. "A Critical Phase in the History of Freedom Movement in Madras Presidency 1885–1914." PhD diss., Department of History, Manonmaniam Sundaranar University.

Bakhtin, Mikhail M. 1981. "Discourse in the Novel." In *The Dialogical Imagination*, translated by Michael Holquist, 259–300. Austin: University of Texas Press.

Balagangadhara, S. N. 1994. *The Heathen in His Blindness . . . : Asia, the West, and the Dynamic of Religion*. Leiden, Netherlands: E. J. Brill.

Banerjee, Sumanta. 2002. *Logic in a Popular Form: Essays on Popular Religion in Bengal*. Chicago: University of Chicago Press.

Bannerjee, Sumanta. 1990. "Marginalization of Women's Popular Culture in Nineteenth Century Bengal." In *Recasting Women: Essays in Indian Colonial History*, edited by Kumkum Sangari and Sudesh Vaid, 127–79. New Brunswick, NJ: Rutgers University Press.

Bate, Bernard. 2005. "Arumuga Navalar, Saivite Sermons and the Delimitation of Religion." *Indian Economic and Social History Review* 42 (4): 469–84.

Bate, Bernard. 2009a. "Nāṟpatu Vayatu Matikkattakka Vēḷālap Peṇ—Tamiḻaga Cutēci Iyakkac Coṟpoḻivāḷarkaḷ Kuṟitta Kuṟippukaḷ" [A Vellala woman about forty years old—notes on orators in the Swadeshi movement in Tamilagam]. *Matruveli* (Tamil Nadu) 2:49–53. http://www.keetru.com/index.php?option=com_content&view=article&id=457:2009-09-13-15-38-47&catid=918:09&Itemid=166.

Bate, Bernard. 2009b. *Tamil Oratory and the Dravidian Aesthetic: Democratic Practice in South India*. New York: Columbia University Press.

Bate, Bernard. 2010. "The Ethics of Textuality: The Protestant Sermon and the Tamil Public Sphere." In *Genealogies of Virtue: Ethical Practice in South Asia*, edited by Daud Ali and Anand Pandian, 101–15. Bloomington: Indiana University Press.

Bate, Bernard. 2012a. "Bharati Style and the Tamil National Popular." *Almost Island* 7 (Winter). http://almostisland.com/winter_2012/.

Bate, Bernard. 2012b. "Swadeshi Oratory and the Development of Tamil Shorthand." In "Swadeshi in the Time of Nations: Reflections on Sumit Sarkar's *The Swadeshi Movement in Bengal, India and Elsewhere*," edited by B. Bate and Dilip Menon, special section of *Economic and Political Weekly* 47 (42): 70–75.

Bate, Bernard. 2013. "'To Persuade Them into Speech and Action': Oratory and the Tamil Political, Madras, 1905–1919." *Comparative Studies of Society and History* 55 (1): 142–66.

Bate, Bernard. 2014. "Oratory, Rhetoric, Politics." In *Cambridge Handbook of Linguistic Anthropology*, edited by N. J. Enfield, Paul Kockelman, and Jack Sidnell, 517–38. Cambridge: Cambridge University Press.

Bate, John Bernard. 2000. "Mēṭaittamiḻ: Oratory and Political Practice in Tamilnadu." PhD diss., Department of Anthropology, University of Chicago.

Bauman, Richard, and Charles Briggs. 2003. *Voices of Modernity: Language Ideologies and the Politics of Inequality*. Cambridge: Cambridge University Press.

Bayly, Christopher. 1993. "Knowing the Country: Empire and Information in India." *Modern Asian Studies* 27 (1): 3–43.

Bayly, Christopher. 1996. *Empire and Information: Intelligence Gathering and Social Information in India, 1780–1870*. Cambridge: Cambridge University Press.

Bharathi, Lalitha. 1986. *Makākavi Suppiramaṇiya Bāratiyārin Pāḍalkaḷ* [The songs of the great poet Subramania Bharathi]. Chennai: Isaitturai Chennai Palkalaik Kalakam.

Blackburn, Stuart. 1988. *Singing of Birth and Death: Texts in Performance*. Philadelphia: University of Pennsylvania Press.

Blackburn, Stuart. 2003. *Print, Folklore, and Nationalism in Colonial South India*. Delhi: Permanent Black.

Bloch, Maurice, ed. 1975. *Political Language and Oratory in Traditional Society*. London: Academic Press.

Chakrabarty, Dipesh. 1989. *Rethinking Working Class History: Bengal 1890–1940*. Princeton, NJ: Princeton University Press.

Chakrabarty, Dipesh. 1991. "Open Space/Public Place: Garbage, Modernity, and India." *South Asia* 14 (1): 15–31.

Chatterjee, Partha. 1993. *The Nation and Its Fragments: Colonial and Postcolonial Histories*. Princeton, NJ: Princeton University Press.

Chatterjee, Partha. 2004. *The Politics of the Governed: Reflections on Popular Politics in Most of the World*. Delhi: Permanent Black.

Chettiar, G. Chelvapathi. 1961. *Intiyā Toḻiliyakkam Tonṟiya Varalāṟu* [History of India's labor movement]. Singai: Babanasam Press.

Clark-Decès, Isabelle. 2005. *No One Cries for the Dead: Tamil Dirges, Rowdy Songs, and Graveyard Petitions*. Berkeley: University of California Press.

Cody, Francis. 2009. "Daily Wires and Daily Blossoms: Cultivating Regimes of Circulation in Tamil India's Newspaper Revolution." *Journal of Linguistic Anthropology* 19 (2): 286–309.

Cody, Francis. 2011a. "Echoes of the Teashop in a Tamil Newspaper." *Language and Communication* 31:243–54.

Cody, Francis. 2011b. "Publics and Politics." *Annual Review of Anthropology* 40:37–52.

Cohn, Bernard. 1987. "The Census, Social Structure, and Objectification in South Asia." In *An Anthropologist among the Historians and Other Essays*, by Bernard Cohn, 224–54. New Delhi: Oxford University Press.

Cohn, Bernard. 1996. *Colonialism and Its Forms of Knowledge*. Princeton, NJ: Princeton University Press.

Daniel, E. Valentine. 1996. *Charred Lullabies: Chapters in an Anthropography of Violence*. Princeton, NJ: Princeton University Press.

Daniel, E. Valentine. 2002. "The Arrogation of Being and the Blindspot of Religion." In *Discrimination and Toleration*, edited by K. Hastrup and G. Ulrich, 31–53. London: Kluwer Law International.

Davis, Richard. 2015. *The* Bhagavad Gita*: A Biography*. Princeton, NJ: Princeton University Press.

Divan, Che. 2008. "Tirunelveli Eḻucci—Naḍantatu Enna?" [The Tirunelveli uprising—what happened?] *Dinamalar* 4:9.

Durkheim, Émile. (1912) 1995. *The Elementary Forms of Religious Life*. Translated by Karen E. Fields. Reprint, New York: Free Press.

Duthie, James. 1885. *Homiletics*. Translated by M. Lazarus. Madras: Madras Religious Tract Society.

Fernandez, James. 1986. *Persuasions and Performances: The Play of Tropes in Culture*. Bloomington: Indiana University Press.

Fernandez, James. 1991. "Introduction." In *Beyond Metaphor: The Theory of Tropes in Anthropology*, edited by James Fernandez, 1–13. Stanford, CA: Stanford University Press.

Fisher, Elaine. 2017. *Hindu Pluralism: Religion and the Public Sphere in Early Modern South India*. Berkeley: University of California Press.

Friedrich, Paul. 1979. *Language, Context, and the Imagination: Essays by Paul Friedrich*. Edited by Anwar S. Dil. Stanford, CA: Stanford University Press.

Friedrich, Paul. 1986. *The Language Parallax: Linguistic Relativism and Poetic Indeterminacy*. Austin: University of Texas Press.

Friedrich, Paul. 1991. "Polytropy." In *Beyond Metaphor: The Theory of Tropes in Anthropology*, edited by James Fernandez, 17–55. Stanford, CA: Stanford University Press.

Friedrich, Paul. 2006. "Maximizing Ethnopoetics: Fine-Tuning Anthropological Experience." In *Language, Culture, and Society*, edited by Christine Jourdan and Kevin Tuite, 207–28. Cambridge: Cambridge University Press.

Frykenberg, Robert Eric. 1999. "The Halle Legacy in Modern India: Information and the Spread of Education, Enlightenment, and Evangelization." In *Missionsberichet aus Indien im 18. Jahrhundert*, edited by Michael Bergunder, 6–29. Halle: Verlag der Franckeschen Stiftungen zu Halle.

Geetha, V., and S. V. Rajadurai. (1998) 2008. *Towards a Non-Brahmin Millennium: From Iyothee Thass to Periyar*. Reprint, Kolkata: Samya.

Goffman, Erving. 1974. *Frame Analysis: An Essay on the Organization of Experience*. Cambridge, MA: Harvard University Press.

Goffman, Erving. 1981. *Forms of Talk*. Philadelphia: University of Pennsylvania Press.

Government of Tamil Nadu. 1982. "Tinnevelly Riots Conspiracy and Ashe Murder, Part II." Select Document Series 1900–1947. Commissioner of Archives and Historical Research, Tamil Nadu Archives.

Grafe, Hugald. (1982) 1992. *History of Christianity in India*. Vol. 3, *South India*. Reprint, Bangalore: Church History Association of India/Theological Publications in India.

Grafe, Hugald. 1999. "Hindu Apologetics at the Beginning of the Protestant Mission Era in India." In *Missionsberichet aus Indien im 18. Jahrhundert*, edited by Michael Bergunder, 69–93. Halle: Verlag der Franckeschen Stiftungen zu Halle.

Guha, Ranajit. 1973. "The Mahatma and the Mob." Review of *Essays on Gandhian Politics: The Rowlatt Satyagraha of 1919*, edited by R. Kumar. *South Asia* 3 (1): 107–11.

Guha, Ranajit. 1997. *Dominance without Hegemony: History and Power in Colonial India*. Cambridge, MA: Harvard University Press.

Guha, Ranajit. 1998. "Discipline and Mobilize: Hegemony and Elite Control in Nationalist Campaigns." In *Dominance without Hegemony: History and Power in Colonial India*, by Ranajit Guha, 100–151. Delhi: Oxford University Press.

Habermas, Jürgen. (1962) 1991. *The Structural Transformation of the Public Sphere*. Reprint, Cambridge, MA: MIT Press.

Hacking, Ian. 1982. "Biopower and the Avalanche of Printed Numbers." *Humanities in Society* 5 (3–4): 279–95.

Hall, David D. 1996. *Cultures of Print: Essays in the History of the Book*. Amherst: University of Massachusetts Press.

Hallisey, Charles, and Anne Hansen. 1996. "Narrative, Sub-ethics and Moral Life: Some Evidence from Theravada Buddhism." *Journal of Religious Ethics* 24 (2): 305–27.

Hansen, Thomas Blom. 1996. "Recuperating Masculinity: Hindu Nationalism, Violence and the Exorcism of the Muslim 'Other.'" *Critique of Anthropology* 16 (2): 137–72.

Hardiman, David. 1982. "The Indian 'Faction': A Political Theory Examined." In *Subaltern Studies I*, edited by Ranajit Guha, 198–231. New Delhi: Oxford University Press.

Hudson, Dennis. 1992a. "Arumuga Navalar and the Hindu Renaissance among Tamils." In *Religious Controversy in British India: Dialogues in Asian Languages*, edited by Kenneth W. Jones, 27–51. Albany: SUNY Press.

Hudson, Dennis. 1992b. "Winning Souls for Siva: Arumuga Navalar's Transmission of Saiva Religion." In *A Sacred Thread: Transmission of Hindu Traditions in Times of Rapid Change*, edited by Raymond B. Williams and John B. Carmen, 23–51. Chambersburg, PA: Anima Press.

Hudson, Dennis. 1994. "Tamil Hindu Responses to Protestants: Nineteenth-Century Literati in Jaffna and Tinnevelly." In *Indigenous Responses to Western Christianity*, edited by Steven Kaplan, 95–123. New York: New York University Press.

Irvine, Judy. 1989. "When Talk Isn't Cheap: Language and Political Economy." *American Ethnologist* 16 (2): 248–67.

Jackson, Jennifer. 2006. "To Be a Developed Nation Is to Speak as a Developed Nation: Constructing Tropes of Transparency and Development through Syntax, Register, and Context in the Political Oratory of Imerina, Madagascar." *Texas Linguistic Forum* 49:72–83.

Jackson, Jennifer. 2008. "Building Publics, Shaping Public Opinion: Interanimating Registers in Malagasy Kabary Oratory and Political Cartooning." *Journal of Linguistic Anthropology* 18 (2): 214–35.

Jackson, Jennifer. 2009. "To Tell It Directly or Not: Coding Transparency and Corruption in Malagasy Political Oratory." *Language in Society* 38 (1): 47–69.

Jackson, Jennifer. 2013. *Political Oratory and Cartooning: An Ethnography of Democratic Processes in Madagascar*. Chichester, UK: Wiley-Blackwell.

Jakobson, Roman. 1960. "Closing Statement: Linguistics and Poetics." In *Style in Language*, edited by T. Sebeok, 350–77. Cambridge, MA: MIT Press.

Jakobson, Roman. 1987. "What Is Poetry?" In *Language in Literature*, edited by K. Pomorska and S. Rudy, 369–78. Cambridge, MA: Harvard University Press.

Johns, Adrian. 1998. *The Nature of the Book: Print and Knowledge in the Making*. Chicago: University of Chicago Press.

Kailasapathy, K., ed. 1979. *Nāvalar Nūrrāṇḍu Malar, 1979* [Navalar centenary edition, 1979]. Colombo: n.p.

Kailasapathy, K. 1986. *On Art and Literature*. Madras: New Century Book House.

Kailasapillai, T. (1918) 1955. *Ārumuga Nāvalar Carittiram* [The life of Arumuga Navalar]. Reprint, Madras: Vittiyānupālanayantiracālai.

Kalyanasundaram, Thiru. Vi. (1944) 2003. *Vāḻkkai Kuṟippukaḷ* [Reflections on my life]. Reprint, Chennai: Pumpuhar Pathipagam.

Kaviraj, Sudipta. 1992. "Writing, Speaking, Being: Language and the Historical Formation of Identities in India." In *Nationalstaat und Sprachkonflickt in Sud—und Sudostasien*, edited by Dagmar Hellmann-Rajanayagam and Dietmar Rothermund, 25–65. Stuttgart: Steiner.

Kaviraj, Sudipta. 1997. "Filth and the Public Sphere: Concepts and Practices about Space in Calcutta." *Public Culture* 10 (1): 83–113.

Kaviraj, Sudipta. 2005a. "On the Enchantment of the State: Indian Thought on the Role of the State in the Narrative of Modernity." *European Journal of Sociology* 46 (2): 263–96.

Kaviraj, Sudipta. 2005b. "An Outline of a Revisionist Theory of Modernity." *European Journal of Sociology* 46 (3): 497–526.

Kaviraj, Sudipta. 2010. *The Imaginary Institution of India: Politics and Ideas.* New York: Columbia University Press.

Keane, Webb. 2007. *Christian Moderns: Freedom and Fetish in the Mission Encounter.* Berkeley: University of California Press.

Keenan, Elinor O. 1973. "A Sliding Sense of Obligatoriness: The Poly-Structure of Malagasy Oratory." *Language in Society* 2 (2): 225–43.

Kersenboom, Saskia. 1995. *Word, Sound, Image: The Life of the Tamil Text.* Oxford: Berg.

Kesavan, Go. 1991. *Bharatiyum Arasiyalum.* Chennai: Alaigal Veliyeettagam.

King, Richard. 1999. *Orientalism and Religion: Postcolonial Theory, India, and Mythic East.* London: Routledge.

Kulendran, Sababathy. 1958. "The Tentative Version of the Bible or 'The Navalar Version.'" *Tamil Culture* 7 (3): 239–50.

Kulendran, Sababathy. 1967. *Kiṟistava Tamiḻ Vētāgamattin Varalāṟu* [History of the Tamil Bible]. Bangalore: Bible Society of India.

Kulick, Don. 1992. *Language Shift and Cultural Reproduction: Socialization, Self and Syncretism in a Papua New Guinean Village.* Cambridge: Cambridge University Press.

Kulick, Don. 1993. "Structure and Gender in Domestic Arguments in a New Guinea Village." *Cultural Anthropology* 8 (4): 510–41.

Kulick, Don. 1998. "Anger, Gender, Language Shift, and the Politics of Revelation in a Papua New Guinean Village." In *Language Ideologies: Practice and Theory*, edited by Bambi Schieffelin, Kathryn Woolard, and Paul Kroskrity, 87–102. New York: Oxford University Press.

Larkin, Brian. 2008. "Ahmed Deedat and the Form of Islamic Evangelism." *Social Text* 26 (3): 101–21.

Mahadevan, P. 1957. *Subramania Bharati Patriot and Poet: A Memoir*. Madras: Atri Publishers.

Makihara, Mimi, and Bambi Scheiffelin, eds. 2007. *Consequences of Contact: Language Ideologies and Sociocultural Transformations in Pacific Societies*. Oxford: Oxford University Press.

Mani, Pe. Cu. 2004. *Vīra Murasu Suppiramaṇiya Sivā* [Victory drum Subramania Siva]. Chennai: Pūṅkoṭi Patippakam.

Mani, Pe. Cu. 2005. *Kaṭṭuraik Kottu* [Collected essays]. Chennai: Pūṅkoṭi Patippakam.

Manjapra, Kris. 2010. *M. N. Roy: Marxism and Colonial Cosmopolitanism*. Delhi: Routledge.

Manjapra, Kris. 2012. "Knowledgeable Internationalism and the Swadeshi Movement, 1903–1921." In "Swadeshi in the Time of Nations: Reflections on Sumit Sarkar's *The Swadeshi Movement in Bengal, India and Elsewhere*," edited by Bernard Bate and Dilip Menon, special section of *Economic and Political Weekly* 47 (42): 53–62.

Marchart, Oliver. 2007. *Post-foundational Political Thought: Political Difference in Nancy, Lefort, Badiou and Laclau*. Edinburgh: Edinburgh University Press.

Maturai Jillā Tiyākikaḷ Malar [Madurai District's martyrs' edition]. 1948, March.

Meenakshisundaran, T. P. (1954) 1978. *Nīṅkaḷum Cuvaiyuṅkaḷ* [You too enjoy]. Collected Works of Prof. T. P. Meenakshisundaran, vol. 6. Madurai: Sarvodaya Ilakkiya Pannai.

Menon, Dilip. 2012. "The Many Spaces and Times of Swadeshi." In "Swadeshi in the Time of Nations: Reflections on Sumit Sarkar's *The Swadeshi Movement in Bengal, India and Elsewhere*," edited by Bernard Bate and Dilip Menon, special section of *Economic and Political Weekly* 47 (42): 44–52.

Mitchell, Lisa. 2009. *Language, Emotion, and Politics in South India: The Making of a Mother Tongue*. Bloomington: Indiana University Press.

Murphy, Eamon. 1981. "Labour Leadership and Politics in India: Profiles of Three South Indian Unionists." *South Asia: Journal of South Asian Studies* 4 (2): 79–93.

Muttucumaraswamy, V. 1965. *Sri La Sri Arumuga Navalar, the Champion Reformer of the Hindus 1822–1879: A Biographical Study*. Colombo: Ranjana Printers.

Narayana Rao, Velcheru, David Shulman, and Sanjay Subrahmanyam. 1992. *Symbols of Substance: Court and State in Nayaka Period Tamilnadu*. New York: Oxford University Press.

Nevinson, Henry W. 1908. "On the Beach." In *The New Spirit in India*, by Henry W. Nevinson, 125–33. London: Harper and Brothers.

Pandian, Anand. 2009. *Crooked Stalks: Cultivating Virtue in South India*. Durham, NC: Duke University Press.

Pandian, M. S. S. 1996. "Towards National-Popular: Notes on Self-Respecters' Tamil." *Economic and Political Weekly* 31 (51): 3323–29.

Pandian, M. S. S. 2007. *Brahmin and Non-Brahmin: Genealogies of the Tamil Political Present.* New Delhi: Permanent Black.

Peterson, Indira. 1982. "Singing of a Place: Pilgrimage as Metaphor and Motif in the Tēvāram Songs of the Tamil Śaivite Saints." *Journal of the American Oriental Society* 102 (1): 69–90.

Peterson, Indira. 1991. *Poems to Siva: The Hymns of the Tamil Saints.* New Delhi: Motilal Barnasidas.

Peterson, Indira. 1999. "Science in the Tranquebar Mission Curriculum: Natural Theology and Indian Responses." In *Missionsberichet aus Indien im 18. Jahrhundert*, edited by Michael Bergunder, 175–219. Halle: Verlag der Franckeschen Stiftungen zu Halle.

Peterson, Indira. 2002. "*Bethlehem Kuravanci* of Vedanayaka Sastri of Tanjore: The Cultural Discourse of an Early-Nineteenth Century Tamil Christian Poem." In *Christians, Cultural Interactions, and India's Religious Traditions*, edited by Judith Brown and Robert Eric Frykenberg, 9–36. Grand Rapids, MI: Eerdmans.

Peterson, Indira. 2004. "Between Print and Performance: The Tamil Christian Poems of Vedanayaka Sastri and the Literary Cultures of Nineteenth-Century South India." In *India's Literary History: Essays on the Nineteenth Century*, edited by Stuart Blackburn and Vasudha Dalmia, 25–59. Delhi: Permanent Black.

Peterson, Indira. 2011. "Multilingual Dramas at the Tanjavur Maratha Court and Literary Cultures in Early Modern South India." *Medieval History Journal* 14 (2): 285–321.

Pope, G. U., ed. 1893. *The Nālaḍiyār or Four Hundred Quatrains in Tamil.* Oxford: Clarendon Press.

Raheja, Gloria, and Anne Gold. 1994. *Listen to the Heron's Words: Reimagining Gender and Kinship in North India.* Berkeley: University of California Press.

Ramalingam Pillai, V. (Nammakkal Kaviñar). (1944) 1955. *En Katai* [My story]. Reprint, Chennai: Palaniappa Brothers.

Raman, Bhavani. 2012. *Document Raj: Writing and Scribes in Early Colonial South India.* Chicago: University of Chicago Press.

Ramaswami Iyengar, V. (Va. Ra.). 1944. *Makākavi Bāratiyār* [The great poet Bharatiyar]. Chennai: Cakti Kāriyālayam.

Ramaswamy, Sumathi. 1997. *Passions of the Tongue.* Berkeley: University of California Press.

Ricoeur, Paul. 1965. "The Political Paradox." In *History and Truth*, by Paul Ricoeur, 247–70. Evanston, IL: Northwestern University Press.

Robbins, Joel. 2001. "God Is Nothing but Talk: Modernity, Language, and Prayer in a Papua New Guinea Society." *American Anthropologist* 103 (4): 901–12.

Robinson, Edward Jewitt. 1867. *Hindu Pastors: A Memorial.* London: Wesleyan Conference Office.

Rosaldo, Michele. 1984. "Words That Are Moving: The Social Meanings of Ilongot Verbal Art." In *Dangerous Words: Language and Politics in the Pacific*, edited by D. Brenneis and F. Myers, 131–60. Prospect Heights, IL: Waveland Press.

Sahlins, Marshall. 1991. "The Return of the Event, Again: With Reflections on the Beginnings of the Great Fijian War of 1843 to 1845 between the Kingdoms of Bau and Rewa." In *Clio in Oceania*, edited by Aletta Biersack, 37–100. Washington, DC: Smithsonian Institution Press.

Sahlins, Marshall. 2004. *Apologies to Thucydides: Understanding History as Culture, and Vice Versa.* Chicago: University of Chicago Press.

Sakai, Naoki. 1997. *Translation and Subjectivity: On "Japan" and Cultural Nationalism.* Minneapolis: University of Minnesota Press.

Sarkar, Sumit. 1970. "Imperialism and Nationalist Thought (A Case Study of Swadeshi Bengal)." *Proceedings of the Indian History Congress* 32 (2): 111–19.

Sarkar, Sumit. (1973) 2010. *The Swadeshi Movement in Bengal, 1903–1908.* New ed. Ranikhet: Permanent Black.

Scudder, H. M. 1865. *The Bazaar Book, or, Vernacular Preacher's Companion. Kiraṇamālikai.* Madras: American Mission Press for the American Arcot Mission.

Scudder, H. M. 1869. *The Bazaar Book, or, Vernacular Preacher's Companion.* Originally prepared in Tamil by Rev. H. M. Scudder, D.D., American Arcot Mission. Translated by Rev. J. W. Scudder, M.D. Madras: Graves, Cookson.

Seneviratne, H. L. 2000. *The Work of Kings: The New Buddhism in Sri Lanka.* Chicago: University of Chicago Press.

Sherinian, Zoe. 2014. *Tamil Folk Music as Dalit Liberation Theology.* Bloomington: Indiana University Press.

Silverstein, Michael. 1976. "Shifters, Linguistic Categories, and Cultural Description." In *Meaning in Anthropology*, edited by Keith H. Basso and Henry A. Selby, 11–55. Albuquerque: School of American Research, University of New Mexico Press.

Silverstein, Michael. 1993. "Metapragmatic Discourse, Metapragmatic Function." In *Reflexive Language: Reported Speech and Metapragmatics*, edited by J. Lucy, 33–58. Cambridge: Cambridge University Press.

Silverstein, Michael. 2000. "Whorfianism and the Linguistic Imagination of Nationality." In *Regimes of Language*, edited by Paul Kroskrity, 85–138. Santa Fe, NM: School of American Research Press.

Silverstein, Michael. 2004. "'Cultural' Concepts and the Language-Culture Nexus." *Current Anthropology* 45 (5): 621–52.
Silverstein, Michael, and Greg Urban, eds. 1996. *Natural Histories of Discourse*. Chicago: University of Chicago Press.
Singer, Milton. 1968. "The Indian Joint Family in Modern Industry." In *Structure and Change in Indian Society*, edited by M. Singer and B. Cohn, 423–52. Chicago: Aldine.
Singer, Milton. 1972. *When a Great Tradition Modernizes: An Anthropological Approach to Indian Civilization*. New York: Praeger Publishers.
Sivasubramanian, A. 1986. *Va. U. Ci.yum Mutal Toḻilāḷar Vēlai Niṟuttamum (1908)* [V.O.C. and the first labor work stoppage (1908)]. Chennai: Makkal Veliyeedu.
Sivathamby, Karthigesu. 1978. "Politics of a Literary Style." *Social Scientist* 6 (8): 16–33.
Sivathamby, Karthigesu. 1979. "Hindu Reaction to Christian Proselytization and Westernization in the Nineteenth Century Sri Lanka." *Social Science Review* 1 (1): 41–75.
Smith, Cantwell. 1962. *The Meaning and End of Religion*. New York: Macmillan.
Soneji, Davesh. 2012. *Unfinished Gestures: Devadāsīs, Memory, and Modernity in South India*. Chicago: University of Chicago Press.
Soneji, Davesh. 2013. "The Powers of Polyglossia: Marathi Kīrtan, Multilingualism, and the Making of a South Indian Devotional Tradition." *International Journal of Hindu Studies* 17 (3): 339–69.
Souvenir. 1963. *G. Chelvapathi Chettiar 75th Birthday Souvenir*. Madras: Anbu Press.
Strecker, Ivo, and Stephen Tyler, eds. 2009. *Culture and Rhetoric*. Vol. 1. New York: Berghahn Books.
Sundarama Iyer, K. 1902. "Religious Education in Indian Schools." *Indian Review* 3 (4): 174–79.
Suntharalingam, R. 1974. *Politics and Nationalist Awakening in South India, 1852–1891*. Tucson: Association for Asian Studies and University of Arizona Press.
Swaminatha Sharma, Ve. 1959. *Nan Kaṇḍa Nālvar* [The four men I knew]. Chennai: Prapanjajothi Prachuralayam.
Taylor, Charles. 2003. *Modern Social Imaginaries*. Durham, NC: Duke University Press.
Taylor, Charles. 2007. *A Secular Age*. Cambridge, MA: Harvard University Press.
Trautmann, Thomas. 2006. *Languages and Nations: The Dravidian Proof in Colonial Madras*. Berkeley: University of California Press.
Tyler, Stephen. 1978. *The Said and the Unsaid: Mind, Meaning, and Culture*. New York: Academic Press.

Van der Veer, Peter. 2001. *Imperial Encounters: Religion and Modernity in India and Britain*. Princeton, NJ: Princeton University Press.

Veeraraghavan, Dilip. 1987. "The Rise and Growth of the Labour Movement in the City of Madras and Its Environs, AD 1918–1939." PhD diss., Department of Humanities and Social Sciences, Indian Institute of Technology, Madras.

Veeraraghavan, Dilip. 2013. *The Making of the Madras Working Class*. New Delhi: Left Word.

Venkatachalapathy, A. R. 1987. *V. O. C.yum Tirunelveli Eḻucciyum* [V.O.C. and the Tirunelveli riots]. Madras: Makkal Veliyeedu.

Venkatachalapathy, A. R. 1994. "Reading Practices and Modes of Reading in Colonial Tamil Nadu." *Studies in History* 10 (2): 273–90.

Venkatachalapathy, A. R., ed. 2008. *Bharathi Karuvūlam* [Bharathi's letters]. Chennai: Kalachuvadu Publications.

Venkatachalapathy, A. R. 2010. "In Search of Ashe." *Economic and Political Weekly* 45 (2): 37–44.

Venkatachalapathy, A. R. 2012. *The Province of the Book: Scholars, Scribes, and Scribblers in Colonial Tamilnadu*. Ranikhet: Permanent Black.

Viswanathan, Seeni. 1998–2010. *Kālavaricaip Paḍuttappaṭṭa Bārati Paḍaippukaḷ* [Chronological edition of Bharati's works]. Vols. 1–23. Chennai: Seeni. Viswanathan.

Vološinov, Valentin N. 1977. *Marxism and the Philosophy of Language*. Cambridge, MA: Harvard University Press.

Wadia, B. P. 1921. *Labour in Madras*. Triplicane, Madras: S. Ganesan.

Walzer, Michael. 1965. *The Revolution of the Saints: A Study in the Origins of Radical Politics*. Cambridge, MA: Harvard University Press.

Warner, Michael. 1990. *The Letters of the Republic: Publication and the Public Sphere in Eighteenth-Century America*. Cambridge, MA: Harvard University Press.

Warner, Michael. 2002. *Publics and Counterpublics*. New York: Zone Books.

Washbrook, David. 1976. *The Emergence of Provincial Politics: The Madras Presidency 1870–1920*. Cambridge: Cambridge University Press.

Washbrook, David, and Christopher Baker. 1975. *South India: Political Institutions and Political Change 1880–1940*. Delhi: Macmillan India.

Weber, Max. (1904–5) 1958. *The Protestant Ethic and the Spirit of Capitalism*. Translated by T. Parsons. New York: Scribner.

Weber, Max. (1915) 1946. "The Social Psychology of World Religions." In *From Max Weber: Essays in Sociology*, translated and edited by H. H. Gerth and C. Wright Mills, 267–301. New York: Oxford University Press.

Weber, Max. (1922) 1946. "The Sociology of Charismatic Authority." In *From Max*

Weber: Essays in Sociology, translated and edited by H. H. Gerth and C. Wright Mills, 245–52. New York: Oxford University Press.

Wentworth, Blake. 2009. "Yearning for a Dreamed Real: The Procession of the Lord in the Tamil Ulās." PhD diss., Faculty of the Divinity School, University of Chicago.

Woolard, Kathryn. 1998. "Introduction: Language Ideology as a Field of Inquiry." In *Language Ideologies: Practice and Theory*, edited by Bambi Schieffelin, Kathryn Woolard, and Paul Kroskrity, 3–50. New York: Oxford University Press.

Yankah, Kwesi. 1995. *Speaking for the Chief: Okyeame and the Politics of Akan Royal Oratory.* Bloomington: Indiana University Press.

Yelle, Robert. 2003. *Explaining Mantras: Ritual, Rhetoric, and the Dream of a Natural Language in Hindu Tantra.* New York: Routledge.

Young, Richard F., and S. Jebanesan. 1995. *The Bible Trembled: The Hindu-Christian Controversies of Nineteenth-Century Ceylon.* Vienna: Publications of the De Nobili Research Library.

Zvelebil, Kamal. 1992. *Companion Studies to the History of Tamil Literature.* Leiden, Netherlands: E. J. Brill.

INDEX

Note: page numbers in italics refer to figures. Those followed by n refer to notes, with note number.

Lightning Source UK Ltd.
Milton Keynes UK
UKHW012142140721
387169UK00002B/77

9 781503 628656